WHAT IS A REFUGEE?

WILLIAM MALEY

What is a Refugee?

HURST & COMPANY, LONDON

First published in the United Kingdom in 2016 by
C. Hurst & Co. (Publishers) Ltd.,
41 Great Russell Street, London, WC1B 3PL
© William Maley, 2016
All rights reserved.
Printed in the United Kingdom by Bell & Bain Ltd, Glasgow

The right of William Maley to be identified as the author of
this publication is asserted by him in accordance with the
Copyright, Designs and Patents Act, 1988.

A Cataloguing-in-Publication data record for this book
is available from the British Library.

ISBN: 9781849046794 *paperback*

This book is printed using paper from registered sustainable
and managed sources.

www.hurstpublishers.com

In affectionate memory of
William Alexander Higgie, OAM

7 November 1923—7 September 2015

CONTENTS

CONTENTS

PREFACE AND ACKNOWLEDGEMENTS

The genesis of this book was a suggestion from Michael Dwyer of Hurst Publishers that in light of mounting refugee flows into Europe, it would be timely to have a short book on refugees that could give to the general reader a sense of some of the complexities surrounding the issue of refugees. I am extremely grateful to Michael and his team for prompting me to produce such a study, and for all their help along the way. Any errors are my own.

My colleagues at the Asia-Pacific College of Diplomacy at The Australian National University have been extremely helpful and supportive, and I would like to thank the Director of the College, Dr Jochen Prantl, together with Dr Pauline Kerr, Dr Jeremy Farrall, Mrs Andrea Haese and Mr Craig Hanks for assisting or obliging me in numerous ways. The Asia-Pacific College of Diplomacy also had the good fortune to undertake, with support from an Australian Research Council Linkage Grant, a joint project with AUSTCARE and Griffith University on protracted refugee situations in Asia. During the course of the project, I benefited greatly from interactions with Major-General Michael Smith, Dr Susanne Schmeidl, and Professor Howard Adelman. I have also profited from discussing refugee issues with research scholars at the College, particularly Mr Niamatullah Ibrahimi and Ms Akiko Okudaira.

PREFACE AND ACKNOWLEDGEMENTS

This book reflects a large number of intellectual debts accumulated over the years to various scholars and practitioners whose own thoughts about refugees, or actions in defence of refugees, have shaped my own understanding of the issue. Here I wish to thank the very remarkable Mrs Marion Le, Dr Nasir Andisha, Professor Pierre Centlivres and Dr Micheline Centlivres-Demont, Mrs Nancy Hatch Dupree, Mr David Manne, Professor Pene Mathew, Dr Susan Harris Rimmer, Mr Barry Smith, Dr Astri Suhrke, Dr Savitri Taylor, Dr Fiona Terry, Mr Richard J. Towle, Professor Anna Wierzbicka, and especially Dr Liza Schuster and Professor Chandran Kukathas. I would also like to thank a large number of refugee friends and acquaintances who have shared their experiences with me over the years. I hope the book is stronger for their courage in re-living experiences that many of them would doubtless prefer to forget.

I owe a particular debt of gratitude to the staff and board of the Refugee Council of Australia, of which I was Chair from 1998 to 2003, and on the Executive of which I continue to serve. Under the leadership of Mr Phil Glendenning as President, Mr Paul Power as Chief Executive Officer, and Ms Sonia Caton as Chair, the Council staff produce analyses of the highest quality, which I have found extremely useful.

My interest in politics was initially stimulated by an acquaintance with Sir Robert Menzies, who served as Australian Prime Minister from 1939 to 1941 and 1949 to 1966, and for whom my late father worked as Press Secretary from 1961 to 1964. Sir Robert in 1968 gave me a copy of his book *Central Power in the Australian Commonwealth*, which appeared just over fifty years after his first publication, a 1917 study entitled *The Rule of Law During the War*. His interest in the rule of law informed his views on refugee policy, which are not widely known, but worth recalling. Policy with respect to refugees, he argued in a speech in 1949, 'must be applied by a sensible administration, neither rigid nor peremptory but wise, exercising judgment on individual cases, always remembering the basic principle but always understanding that harsh administration never yet improved any law but only impaired it, and that notoriously harsh administration raises up to any law hostilities that may some day destroy it'. The approach in this book is very much informed by these thoughts.

My interest in refugees was triggered forty years ago when I stayed in Belgrade at the home of William Alexander Higgie, who at that time was Counsellor in the Australian Embassy to Yugoslavia. Bill Higgie, a warm, generous and immensely kind-hearted man, was a longtime officer of the Australian Department of Immigration, and during the course of a career that lasted from 1949 to 1989, also served in The Hague, Vienna, Paris and Rome, and worked closely with the Office of the United Nations High Commissioner for Refugees in Geneva. He devoted a great deal of his life to finding ways to assist refugees, and never lost sight of the vital human dimension of the refugee issue. He remained deeply interested in refugees until the onset of his final illness in August 2015, and was a perpetual source of wisdom and good judgment, always conveyed with the benefit of a wonderful sense of humour. It is an honour and a privilege to be able to dedicate this book to his memory.

William Maley   Canberra, August 2016

INTRODUCTION

In early January 2016, the Office of the United Nations High Commissioner for Refugees estimated that 1,008,616 refugees and migrants had sought to cross into Europe by sea in 2015, with a further 3771 dead or missing in the attempt. Of those who arrived, 49% were from Syria, 21% from Afghanistan, and 9% from Iraq. Some 58% were men, 17% woman, and 25% children. While the countries of the European Union have a population totaling 506 million, the initial burden of arrivals fell disproportionately on just two, Greece and Italy, which received 851,319 and 153,600 persons respectively.[1] As refugees sought to move on to other European destinations, a palpable air of crisis began to emerge, with high-level meetings of officials and political leaders, strident demands from the right of the political spectrum for intensified border control and the expropriation of refugees' meagre assets,[2] and depictions of refugees as either not really refugees at all,[3] or as potential fifth columnists disposed to harm the West in the name of religious extremism.[4] Complaints from the far right intensified greatly after robberies and attacks on women near Cologne railway station on New Year's Eve of 2015, although it subsequently emerged that virtually none of the alleged offenders were from Syria, Afghanistan or Iraq, the main countries that supplied the 2015 influx.[5] Amidst this cacophony, the humanity of the refugees was easily overlooked, although in many countries, ordinary people reacted to their plight with balance and compassion. The question of what exactly is a refugee sat uneasily in the background of much of the debate.

> One day Larissa Fedorovna left the house and did not come back. Evidently she was arrested in the street, as happened in those days, and she died or vanished somewhere, forgotten as a nameless number on a list which was afterwards mislaid, in one of the countless general or women's concentration camps in the north.[6]

Thus wrote Boris Pasternak towards the end of *Doctor Zhivago*. The idea of the nameless number provides a sobering reminder that most victims of oppression go unremarked by the wider world. It is all too easy when confronted with substantial refugee flows, such as Europe witnessed from 2015, to lose sight of the individuality of refugees, of the specific experiences of suffering, separation and dislocation that so often have come to dominate their lives. For this reason, it is useful to commence our own journey in this book with some brief stories from both ancient and modern times of people who have had to seek refuge in the face of perils that others have been mercifully spared. Through such stories we can begin to glimpse in outline what is a refugee.

For Christians, the story of Moses, told in the Book of Exodus, is quintessentially one of flight from persecution:

> And Moses said unto the people, Remember this day, in which ye came out from Egypt, out of the house of bondage; for by strength of hand the LORD brought you out from this *place*.[7]

The story of Jesus is equally instructive. The New Testament, in the Gospel According to Saint Matthew, records that

> the angel of the Lord appeareth to Joseph in a dream, saying, Arise, and take the young child and his mother, and flee into Egypt, and be thou

there until I bring thee word: for Herod will seek the young child to destroy him. When he arose, he took the young child and his mother by night, and departed into Egypt: and was there until the death of Herod.[8]

For Muslims, a similar story can be found in the life of the Prophet Muhammad. In 622 AD, the Prophet travelled from Mecca to Medina, an event that is described with the Arabic word *hijra*,[9] in order to escape from the oppression of Muslims by the ruling authorities.[10] In each of these cases, a perceived threat to prevailing power generated a threat of repression, to which flight was a rational response.

In a cemetery in Zürich, there is a tombstone headed with the words '*Ein Stern Fällt*'. The grave is that of the lyric tenor Joseph Schmidt, one of the finest singers of the twentieth century, and also one of the most tragic. The epitaph comes from the chorus of his 1934 song 'A Star Falls from Heaven'. Schmidt was a dwarf, and he was also Jewish. With the rise of Nazism, much of Europe was too dangerous for him. Interned as an illegal immigrant in a Swiss refugee camp in October 1942,[11] he died of a heart attack the following month at the age of only 38. Being a great artist was no guarantee of safety when the darkness approached. Another to learn this was Kurt Gerron, the Jewish entertainer who introduced 'The Ballad of Mack the Knife' in the 1928 Berlin première of *The Threepenny Opera* by Bertolt Brecht and Kurt Weill. Gerron had a distinguished record of military service as a German soldier in the First World War, and believed that it offered him some protection. It did not. He was detained at the 'show camp' at Theresienstadt, and in late 1944, transported to Auschwitz where he was murdered in the gas chambers.[12] For him there was to be no tombstone.

For some, the loss of one's roots can prove intolerable. Such a figure was the Austrian writer Stefan Zweig, who took his own life with an overdose of barbiturates in Brazil in February 1942.[13] Zweig was not someone who had fled with the Gestapo at his heels, and nor was he facing destitution: his works continued to be published, and indeed, he completed his autobiography the day before his death. But as a lifelong pacifist, he was overwhelmed by the threat to European culture posed by the war, and he was also of Jewish descent. Furthermore, his wife, who died with him, was incurably ill. It is hardly surprising that at a certain point, life became for him too much of a burden. Yet Zweig's sense of despair was by no means a universal response to the trials of exile in those times. The great German novelist Thomas Mann, who had won the Nobel Prize for Literature in 1929, was critical of the politics of Zweig's suicide, which he saw as handing a triumph to the Nazi archenemy.[14] An exile from Germany since 1933, and living in Pacific Palisades in California, Mann was a resolute and committed opponent of Nazism, as was his extended family. His eminence was such that the rise of Hitler, and the war, had little effect on the volume or quality of his own writings.[15] Nonetheless, exile took its toll on the Mann family: the wife of his brother Heinrich Mann, struggling with the burdens of exile, took her own life in December 1944, as did Thomas Mann's fervently anti-Nazi, but troubled, son Klaus Mann in May 1949.[16] The effects of exile can be insidious and long-lasting.

In that respect, the twenty-first century has brought no obvious improvement. In downtown Melbourne lives a young Australian named Ali Mullaie, who works as an information technology consultant for an international company. He was born in Afghanistan in 1983 in the district of Jaghori in the province of Ghazni, and his ancestors were members of the Hazara ethnic group. In contrast to most other Afghans, Hazaras have a distinctively East Asian appearance, and for the most part are Shiite rather than Sunni Muslims. The rise of the Taliban from 1994 was a disaster for the Hazaras: in just three days, from 8–11 August 1998, several thousand Hazaras were massacred in

the northern city of Mazar-e Sharif in a pogrom that one journalist described as 'genocidal in its ferocity'.[17] As the Taliban's
control spread, panic swept through Hazara communities, and
many Hazaras sought to leave. Following threats to his family,
Ali Mullaie was one of them. Assisted by a people smuggler, he
boarded a fishing boat from Indonesia to Australia. The over-
crowded boat sank on 8 November 2001, and Ali survived by
clinging for two hours to a piece of decking.[18] He was rescued by
the Royal Australian Navy, but was then despatched to a camp
on the impoverished Pacific island of Nauru, spending years in
limbo before finally being accepted into Australia as a refugee on
8 June 2005.[19] Articulate and good-humoured, Ali Mullaie has
adapted to his new life, but has borne costs as well, notably
through losing information about the whereabouts of most of
his family. In 2011, as an Australian, he returned to Afghanistan
in the hope of finding his parents, but was unable to reach
Jaghori; instead, he found himself caught in a firefight between
the Taliban and government forces, and he was robbed of the
money he had saved to give to his parents in the event that he
found them.[20]

Young men are often at gravest risk in theatres of conflict, but
women and children figure very prominently in exile as well. In
2014, the Nobel Peace Prize was awarded to its youngest-ever
recipient, the 17-year old Malala Yousafzai of Pakistan.[21] Reared
as an enthusiast for female education, she was the central figure
in a powerful 2009 *New York Times* documentary, *Class Dismissed*,
in which she detailed the repression she had experienced when
Taliban extremists moved into her home valley of Swat. On
9 October 2012, she was shot by Taliban extremists, provoking
global outrage. Evacuated to the United Kingdom, she made a
remarkable recovery and resumed her advocacy, but faced with
ongoing threats from the Taliban, she and her family were unable
to return to Pakistan.

The last story to set the scene for our journey is short and anguishing. In early September 2015, a single photograph produced what may become one of the iconic images of our time. Its roots lay in the maelstrom that is contemporary Syria. Alan Kurdi, of Syrian Kurdish background, was only three years old when he drowned as an inflatable boat in which he and his family were attempting to cross from Turkey to Greece capsized. His mother and brother perished at the same time. A picture of his tiny body, lying face down on the sandy beach, flashed around the world, serving as a terrible reminder of the dangers that face people who are seeking to flee danger.[22] But as reports surfaced that relatives in Canada had struggled without success to sponsor the Kurdi family for resettlement, a sharp light also fell on the adequacy of Western responses to refugee crises,[23] and at the 19 October 2015 Canadian election, Immigration Minister Chris Alexander lost his seat.

Some categories and distinctions

From these diverse stories, a number of complexities associated with the refugee experience begin to appear. The circumstances that lead people to become refugees are extremely diverse. Some refugee movements are the product of what the scholar E.F. Kunz called 'great political changes or movements of armies'.[24] Those who move in such circumstances he called 'acute' refugees, and the vast majority of refugees in the contemporary world fall into that category, for it is only events on a grand scale that are likely to generate population movements on a grand scale. Sometimes the great political changes in point have taken place in the refugees' country of origin, but on occasion those who have already sought asylum in one place may be obliged by a deterioration of circumstances there to seek protection in yet another country. Russian Jews who fled to Weimar Germany only to experience the Nazi takeover in 1933 are a case in point.[25] Ali Mullaie and Alan Kurdi provide good examples of acute refugees, but their experiences also highlight another distinction worth noting. Some in refugee populations, like Ali Mullaie, are old enough to be active agents, making decisions about how themselves to proceed; but not all are. Alan Kurdi was part of wider group of people seeking protection, and like many infant refugees had no involvement in deciding how that protection might be sought.

The acute refugee probably most closely matches popular understandings of the term. Kunz, however, highlighted another sense of the term, just as important, when he discussed the phenomenon of the anticipatory refugee, who 'leaves his home country before the deterioration of the military or political situation prevents his orderly departure'.[26] Refugees are not simply people who have experienced persecution; they can also be people who see what is coming and get out before it is too late. When Joseph took Jesus and Mary to Egypt, he acted as a classic anticipatory refugee. The dangers of *not* anticipating the worst are poignantly illustrated by the case of Gerron. After Hitler took power, Gerron left Germany but remained in Europe, and finally was caught up in the German invasion of the Low Countries in 1940. Various emigré friends had sought to bring Gerron to America, but until it was too late, he seemed not to grasp the urgency of the situation. And in a way this is understandable. Not everyone is acutely attuned to political currents around them, and even the worst regimes often build up over time to a crescendo of persecution.

It is tempting to think of refugees as people in flight, but in some circumstances this image can be misleading, as is illustrated by the phenomenon of the refugee *sur place*. Thomas Mann provides an obvious example. While he was travelling outside Germany following the appointment of Hitler as Chancellor in 1933, he received a warning from two of his children that it would be unwise to return, and it was not until after the Second World War that he was again able to set foot in his homeland. He was well placed to re-establish himself and his family elsewhere, which indeed he did; but he was no less a refugee by virtue of being well off. Refugees *sur place* tend to be much smaller in number than acute or even anticipatory refugees, but often they are figures of considerable note, whose experiences symbolise the dislocation that the refugee experience involves.

The Nazis routinely used the label *Wirtschaftsemigranten* ('economic migrants') to refer to refugees who had fled Germany, especially if they were Jewish.[27] The Nazi origins of the expression should serve as warning to those who blithely apply the term to refugees in the twenty-first century. Most people want a better life; this does not mean that they cannot be refugees. Nor are refugees necessarily 'tired, poor, huddled masses' with their hands stretched out for assistance. On the contrary, many are resourceful and energetic, not something for which they should be scorned. Indeed, the willingness of people to part with their life savings may serve to establish just how severe is the threat that those who are in flight actually face. Winston Churchill captured this brilliantly in 1944 in a minute he sent to Foreign Secretary Anthony Eden entitled 'Escape of Jews from Greece': 'It is quite possible that rich Jews will pay large sums of money to escape being murdered by the Huns ... We should take a great responsibility if we prevented the escape of Jews, even if they should be rich Jews. I know it is the modern view that all rich people should be put to death wherever found, but it is a pity that we should take up that attitude at the present time. After all, they have no doubt paid for their liberation so high that in future they will only be poor Jews, and therefore have the ordinary rights of human beings.'[28]

In twenty-first century usage, the term 'asylum seeker' is encountered nearly as frequently as 'refugee'. The two are not, however, mutually exclusive. An asylum seeker is someone seeking to be *recognised* as a refugee. A person can be both a refugee (on the basis of the circumstances surrounding his or her flight or exile) *and* an asylum seeker (seeking the protection of the authorities in a state of which he or she is not a citizen). One of the paradoxes of the refugee experience is that a person can be a refugee without being stamped as such by a state, but that the *system* of states plays a central role in giving rise to the phenomenon of the refugee in the first place.

Some recurring themes

Throughout this book, various themes recur, and it may be helpful for the reader to identify some of these at the outset. First of all, as the previous section shows, the ideas of exile and refuge are complex, and simplistic images of what is a refugee should be set aside. All too often, those who speak of 'real' or 'genuine' refugees prove to have rather poor understandings of what is a refugee, and instead substitute their own ideas of what a refugee should be like. The disposition to favour refugees who seem to be 'like us' is a common and dangerous one, currently on display in the suggestion in some Western countries that Christians from Syria should be prioritised for resettlement over Muslims, even though there is compelling evidence of extremist groups viciously targeting those Muslims they regard as heretics.[29] Ultimately, whether someone is a refugee is properly determined by their individual circumstances. In some cases (for example Jews fleeing an avowedly anti-Semitic regime) it will be quite straightforward to conclude that someone is a refugee, but in other cases it will require careful exploration of an individual's subjective fears and personal circumstances.

Furthermore, the assumption that most people want to make their way to a Western country, which underpins fears of floodgates about to open, also needs to be treated with caution. The ties of the familiar tend to discourage flight, as Kurt Gerron's experience showed. Even in the most urgent of situations, creating acute refugee movements, a majority of those at risk tend not to move, or at most opt for internal displacement within their own countries. To leave one country for another is a traumatic decision to take. It can involve separation from family and other loved ones, the need to learn a completely new language in order to be able to function in a new society, and a loss of social status if one's achievements and qualifications are not recognised in a country of asylum. If one is caught in an environment in which there is no opportunity to put down new roots, but equally no hope of returning home, the burdens of depression can prove unbearable. Afghanistan since the late 1970s has been one of the largest sources of refugees worldwide, but a 2015 survey conducted in Afghanistan by The Asia Foundation found that 57.9 per cent of respondents would not leave Afghanistan and live somewhere else even if given the opportunity.[30]

An additional theme is that real people in the real world almost always have a range of motivations for how they behave, which makes it dangerous to draw hasty conclusions about how they should be viewed if they seek to be recognised as refugees. One of the least informative questions one can ask of such a person is whether he or she wants a better life. Except for religious ascetics, most people would probably answer yes. Such an answer, however, can have many different bases. Some people might see a better life as one free of coercion or harassment. Some might see it as more prosperous. (As the singer Sophie Tucker reputedly put it, 'I've been rich and I've been poor. Rich is better'.) But for many, a more prosperous life *and* a life free of persecution would *both* be desirable ends; and very often those who seek a more prosperous life are not driven by greed, but by the hope that their children can enjoy safer or more meaningful lives than would be possible in an environment marked by pervasive fear and repression. In other words, it should be taken for granted that people in general want better lives, and refugees who voice such a hope should not be spurned on that basis.

Just as individuals have complex motivations, so also do states. Governments, whether totalitarian, autocratic or democratic, are typically made up of politicians with a range of ambitions. Some may have a strong sense of public duty, but others may be driven more by a taste for power, and for the latter in democratic states, vulnerable refugees may figure less prominently on their list of those to be respected than swinging voters with rabid views. It is rare for cynical leaders to confess their cynicism, but occasionally evidence surfaces. In 2001, facing a threat from the far-right 'One Nation' party, Australian Prime Minister John Howard decided that the MV Tampa, a Norwegian vessel which had rescued asylum seekers from a sinking boat in the Indian Ocean, would not be allowed to enter Australian waters. His biographers reported Howard's announcement as follows:[31]

> Monday 27 August was John Howard's turning point. As he walked towards the House of Representatives for Question Time, the minister for Sport and Tourism, Jackie Kelly, approached him. Kelly's seat of Lindsay took in the far western fringes of Sydney. It was 'Howard battler' territory and Kelly was worried that the boat people issue was re-igniting support for One Nation. She had continued to be a Howard favourite, enjoying a self-described father/daughter relationship with the Prime Minister. 'One Nation is just chewing us up,' Kelly told Howard. 'I've lost two branches to them; one of them is my best fundraising branch. We need to do something or I'm a goner.' Howard waved his speaking notes at her. 'Don't worry, Jackie,' he responded. 'That's all about to change'.

There is a sobering message here: those in dire peril should be wary of assuming that governments will hasten to their rescue.

A final theme that runs through this book is that refugees are *products* of the system of states, rather than threats to it.[32]

Scholars usually trace the origin of the modern system of states to the Peace of Westphalia of 1648. The 'Westphalian Settlement' consisted primarily of two treaties, the Treaty of Münster and the Treaty of Osnabrück, which brought to an end the Thirty Years War by recognising the right of European sovereigns to determine the form of Christian religious practice that would prevail on the territories they controlled, a principle initially canvassed in the Peace of Augsburg of 1555. Neither the 'Westphalian Settlement' nor the idea of sovereignty was anything like as simple as statesmen were inclined to suggest, but in combination they created a novel form of Continental order. An underlying implication of the Westphalian Settlement, which was complemented by subsequent Enlightenment thinking and ideas of human rights,[33] was that states would carry responsibility for the wellbeing of subjects or citizens. Indeed, the argument has been mounted that the principal moral justification for a system of states should be framed in terms of such 'assigned responsibility'.[34] Yet it is a matter of common knowledge that some states fail—sometimes egregiously—to discharge such responsibilities, either because they lack the capacity to do so, or because they have taken a murderous or genocidal turn, directing the powers of the state against particular elements of their populations.[35] When a particular state fails to protect its own people, they may look for protection to other parts of the system of states. Refugees are symptoms of a system of states that has failed properly to live up to its responsibilities.

The objectives and structure of this book

The plight of refugees has been discussed very extensively, and ever since Sir Norman Angell and Dorothy Frances Buxton published *You and the Refugee* in 1939,[36] there has been no shortage of serious works on refugee policy for the general reader. Nonetheless,

INTRODUCTION

while the plight of refugees is an enduring one, the circumstances
generating specific refugee flows, and the frameworks within
which refugee flows are managed, have a tendency to change over
time, not only because of shifts in the political environment in
potential recipient states, but also because the legal processes for
assessing protection claims are subject to frequent amendment as
lessons are learned (or not learned) about how the protection of
refugees should best be accomplished. This book provides for the
lay reader an account of how some of the key challenges of refugee
protection are being managed in the twenty-first century. There
is, of course, a vast technical literature dealing with diverse aspects
of refugee policy, with academic centres such as the Refugee
Studies Centre at Oxford University and the Andrew and Renata
Kaldor Centre for International Refugee Law at the University of
New South Wales nurturing scholarship of the highest quality,
and venues such as the *Journal of Refugee Studies* and the
International Journal of Refugee Law providing outlets for the publication of original research. This book does not seek to add to this
technical literature, but it does refer in the footnotes to some of
this material, in case readers are interested in exploring complex
issues in more detail.

The book is divided into eight chapters. Chapter Two explores
the definition of 'refugee', both as a matter of international law,
and in philosophical and 'ordinary language' discussions. It also
looks briefly at processes that states have used to attempt to
determine whether people should be recognised as refugees.
Chapter Three surveys the history of exile and displacement,
noting how diverse the experiences of both individual and mass
displacement have proved to be. Chapter Four examines in some
detail how it is that refugees are created by the system of states,
and how 'people smuggling' represents a market response to protection needs that states are not willing or able to meet. Chapter
Five discusses the dynamics of refugee crises in a globalised

world, and examines a number of factors that make twenty-first century movements somewhat distinctive. Chapter Six investigates the ways in which the tools of modern diplomacy are used to try to manage refugee flows, and identifies some of the obstacles that need to be overcome for diplomacy to be effective in meeting refugees' needs. Chapter Seven takes up the argument that military intervention, perhaps justified by reference to a global 'responsibility to protect', may offer a durable solution to refugees' problems. Chapter Eight concludes the book by taking up the issue of freer movements of people, and highlights the ways in which border controls impose substantial moral and material costs on societies and peoples in ways that are often overlooked or discounted.

2

DEFINING 'REFUGEES'

Terms such as 'refugee' can be defined lexically (through reference to how the word is used in actual discourse) or stipulatively (via a statement setting out what the word should be taken to mean when it is used).[1] The most commonly-used stipulative definitions come from law, in particular international law, and it is on those that I initially focus. In order, however, to set these in proper context, it is important at the outset to say a little bit about the nature of international law and its importance, not least because in recent times there has been a tendency on the part of conservative commentators, especially in the USA, to decry international law and the obligations that flow from it.[2] International law provides some of the key norms of behaviour in international relations that ameliorate the effects of what might otherwise be an anarchical system governed by power alone. The observation of Shakespeare's Isabella that 'it is excellent To have a giant's strength; but it is tyrannous To use it like a giant'[3] is one which smaller players in a world of asymmetrical power tend to understand only too well.

WHAT IS A REFUGEE?

International refugee law: origins

The two main sources of international law are on the one hand custom, and on the other hand treaties and conventions.[4] A treaty, as defined in Article 2.1(a) of the *Vienna Convention on the Law of Treaties*, is 'an international agreement concluded between States in written form and governed by international law, whether embodied in a single instrument or in two or more related instruments and whatever its particular designation'.[5] The term 'convention' is typically reserved for multilateral treaties with more than two parties. Article 31.1 of the *Vienna Convention* additionally provides that 'A treaty shall be interpreted in good faith in accordance with the ordinary meaning to be given to the terms of the treaty in their context and in the light of its object and purpose'. The most widely-accepted explanation for the legal force of international law is that it is grounded in the *consent* of states to be bound by particular rules, and ratification of, or accession to, a treaty is one of the obvious forms of consent.

But that said, fidelity to the requirements of international law is important not just for legal but also for political reasons. Here, the most important consideration is that of reciprocity.[6] From time to time, states and their rulers or leaders have undoubtedly found some of the requirements of international law to be quite burdensome, and international refugee law especially so. Yet for every provision of international law that a state would like to see disappear, there is likely to be some other provision that it would wish all other states to respect. Thus, a state seeking to evade responsibilities under the 1951 *Convention Relating to the Status of Refugees* needs to reflect on how it would feel if its own nationals were to be denied the protections of the 1949 *Third Geneva Convention Relative to the Treatment of Prisoners of War* or the 1963 *Vienna Convention on Consular Relations*. Considerations of reciprocity go a long way to explaining why international law continues to be broadly respected even in the absence of robust enforcement mechanisms.

On the question of refugees, customary international law has had relatively little to say,[7] if only because until relatively recently, people who were disposed to move from one country to another could do so without much difficulty if they had the means. Until the First World War, it was possible to travel to many countries without even possessing a passport. In the aftermath of that war however, a range of instruments were developed to try to deal with the needs of those who had been forcibly displaced. One study has divided the period between the end of the First World War and the adoption of the 1951 *Convention* into three phases, depending upon how the refugee experience was framed: the juridical (1920–1935); the social (1935–1938); and the individualist (1938–1950).[8] The first phase witnessed the adoption of the 1933 *Convention Relating to the International Status of Refugees*, which, drawing on earlier definitions, essentially defined being a refugee in terms of (a) not enjoying the protection of the government in one's country of origin; and (b) not having acquired any other nationality.[9] The second phase saw the adoption of the 1938 *Convention Concerning the Status of Refugees coming from Germany*, which also covered 'Stateless persons not covered by previous conventions or agreements who have left the territory of the Reich after being established therein'. It is notable that none of these definitions focused explicitly on fear of persecution, but there is evidence that it was implicitly understood to be a key factor at work in the displacement of refugees.[10] The third phase was marked by vast acute displacements as a result of the Second World War and this led the focus of international attention to shift, for a while at least, from the definition of 'refugee' to the management of displaced people. One product was a key actor in twenty-first century refugee affairs, namely UNHCR.

WHAT IS A REFUGEE?

The Office of the United Nations High Commissioner for Refugees (UNHCR)

The first major organisation set up to deal with wartime displacement was the International Refugee Organization, which operated from 20 August 1948 to 1 March 1952.[11] Its main focus was resettlement: between 1 July 1947 (when its Preparatory Commission commenced work) and 31 December 1951, it resettled 1,038,750 refugees, of whom 328,851 went to the US, 182,159 to Australia, and 132,109 to Israel.[12] Always seen as having a finite task, it was replaced by the Office of the United Nations High Commissioner for Refugees, or UNHCR, established on 14 December 1950 by Resolution 428 (V) of the United Nations General Assembly.[13] Since its establishment, eleven High Commissioners have led the organisation; the incumbent High Commissioner, Filippo Grandi of Italy, took up the position on 1 January 2016. UNHCR has a staff of over 9300 located in 123 different countries. In November 1957, the General Assembly established the UNHCR Executive Committee as the organisation's governing body. The 'ExCom' meets annually in Geneva and adopts 'Conclusions' on a wide range of issues. These are not formally binding, but are widely regarded as a form of 'soft law'. In 2015, it had ninety-eight members.

UNHCR's responsibilities are primarily defined by its Statute, which was annexed to the December 1950 resolution that established the office.[14] Article 1 provides that the High Commissioner 'shall assume the function of providing international protection, under the auspices of the United Nations, to refugees who fall within the scope of the present Statute and of seeking permanent solutions for the problem of refugees by assisting Governments and, subject to the approval of the Governments concerned, private organizations to facilitate the voluntary repatriation of such refugees, or their assimilation within new national communities'.

Article 2 provides that 'The work of the High Commissioner shall be of an entirely non-political character; it shall be humanitarian and social and shall relate, as a rule, to groups and categories of refugees'. Article 8 elaborates ways in which the High Commissioner can provide for the protection of refugees: these include 'Promoting the conclusion and ratification of international conventions for the protection of refugees, supervising their application and proposing amendments thereto'; 'Promoting through special agreements with Governments the execution of any measures calculated to improve the situation of refugees and to reduce the number requiring protection'; and 'Promoting the admission of refugees, not excluding those in the most destitute categories, to the territories of States'.

To focus simply on provisions such as these, however, would give an unduly static impression of what the work of UNHCR involves. Like any complex organisation with a long history, its activities have evolved considerably over time, in part in response to the initiatives of particular High Commissioners, but in part because the environment within which UNHCR operates has itself changed very considerably.[15] From a Eurocentric organisation, it morphed into one with a focus on Africa and then on the wider world, and it increasingly became involved in mass relief operations. It proved active in trying to promote burden-sharing in response to mass outflows such as those which followed the fall of South Vietnam in April 1975. But it also was beset with management and administrative problems, compounded by poor leadership at the end of the 1980s, and early in the twenty-first century, with two High Commissioners being forced from office.

The history of the organisation highlights two features of UNHCR that make its work for refugees rather challenging. On the one hand, it is a conflicted organisation.[16] It is charged by its Statute to pursue the protection of refugees, but it increasingly has been mandated to assist a range of vulnerable people, including internally-displaced persons requiring not so much protection as emergency relief in the form of food, shelter, and sanitation. This was spectacularly the case during the Bosnian conflict in the first half of the 1990s.[17] In 1999, it was even reported that a spokesman for the UNHCR office in Pakistan had urged Afghan refugees 'not to approach its offices' with a view to resettlement, on the basis that 'UNHCR simply does not have the capacity to handle the increased volume of people demanding to be sent to the Western countries', adding that 'we cannot cope with it, and our daily work on behalf of refugees has been seriously disrupted by this outpouring'.[18] On the other hand, UNHCR is a vulnerable organisation. While it has a strong reputation and has done an enormous amount to assist people in desperate need, its funding comes largely from voluntary contributions by governments and the European Union,[19] which can easily be withheld as a way of bringing pressure to bear on UNHCR. In 2014, UNHCR received contributions totalling US\$3.338 billion; of this total, less than US\$120 million came from the UN regular budget and other UN funds.[20]

The 1951 Convention relating to the Status of Refugees

In a resolution immediately following the resolution that adopted the Statute of UNHCR, the United Nations General Assembly called for a Conference of Plenipotentiaries to draft a new Convention relating to the status of refugees. The 'United Nations Conference on the Status of Refugees and Stateless Persons' was held in Geneva from 2–25 July 1951; the *Convention Relating to the Status of Refugees* was adopted on 28 July 1951; and it finally came into force on 22 April 1954.[21] The definition of refugee contained in Article 1.A (2) remains the most widely used in modern discussion of what is a refugee.[22] It provides that the term 'refugee' shall apply to any person who:

As a result of events occurring before 1 January 1951 and owing to well-founded fear of being persecuted for reasons of race, religion, nationality, membership of a particular social group or political opinion, is outside the country of his nationality and is unable or, owing to such fear, is unwilling to avail himself of the protection of that country; or who, not having a nationality and being outside the country of his former habitual residence as a result of such events, is unable or, owing to such fear, is unwilling to return to it.

In the case of a person who has more than one nationality, the term 'the country of his nationality' shall mean each of the countries of which he is a national, and a person shall not be deemed to be lacking the protection of the country of his nationality if, without any valid reason based on well-founded fear, he has not availed himself of the protection of one of the countries of which he is a national.

Several features of this definition stand out. First, in accordance with the gendered drafting conventions of the time, there is an apparent assumption that refugees are all male, although as a practical matter this is never the case. Second, the word 'persecuted' plays a central role in the definition of refugee, even though it is nowhere defined in the text of the *Convention*. Third, the word 'persecuted' is introduced in a 'passive voice' construction: 'persecution' is not limited to persecution carried out by states. Fourth, not all persecution gives rise to refugee claims: it must be persecution for particular reasons. Fifth, gender and sexual preference do not explicitly figure as such reasons. Sixth it is not subjective fear alone that can make one a refugee; the fear must be 'well-founded'. Seventh, there is an absolute requirement that to be a refugee, a person must be outside the country of his or her nationality; the definition has no direct relevance to internally-displaced persons. The import of all this is that the definition of refugee is actually quite narrow, and that it may be no easy matter for a refugee to persuade others that he or she should be recognised as a refugee.

The complexity of the idea of persecution is one of the factors that complicates determining what is a refugee. In the absence of a specific Convention definition, various approaches have been defended for determining what persecution might involve.[23] In the United States, which is not a party to the 1951 *Convention*, the *Refugee Act of 1980* (Public Law 96–212) in sec.201 (a) followed, although not word for word, the definition of refugee in the 1951 *Convention*, and offered no specific definition of persecution. This in effect left it to the executive, under the supervision of the judiciary, to determine the meaning of persecution. By contrast, in Australia, which *is* a party to the *Convention*, section 5J(4) of the *Migration Act* 1958 provides that persecution must involve 'serious harm to the person' and 'systematic and discriminatory conduct'. Furthermore, under section 5J(1)(c), there must be a 'real chance' of persecution that 'relates to all areas of a receiving country'. These provisions arguably import significant limitations that the *Convention* did not provide.[24] In addition, there has been much discussion of whether 'persecution' requires that a person be individually singled out for attention. Here, the better view is surely that one 'can be persecuted by a blind and uncaring tyrant just as much as by a government waging a particularized campaign of oppression against an individual or a small group'.[25] But that said, there are significant forms of human suffering that are typically viewed as not making one *per se* a refugee under the *Convention*, of which generalised armed conflict is the most notable example.[26]

The 1951 *Convention* does not simply define a refugee. It also establishes refugee rights, of which the most important is the non-*refoulement* right under Article 33.1:

> No Contracting State shall expel or return ('refouler') a refugee in any manner whatsoever to the frontiers of territories where his life or freedom would be threatened on account of his race, religion, nationality, membership of a particular social group or political opinion.

Article 33.2 qualifies this with the provision that:

The benefit of the present provision may not, however, be claimed by a refugee whom there are reasonable grounds for regarding as a danger to the security of the country in which he is, or who, having been convicted by a final judgment of a particularly serious crime, constitutes a danger to the community of that country.

On occasion the provision in Article 33.1 has been subject to eccentric interpretation. For example, the United States Supreme Court in *Sale v. Haitian Centers Council, Inc.* 509 U.S. 155 (1993) upheld by an 8–1 majority the policy of the Clinton Administration to force Haitians intercepted on the high seas back to Haiti without any assessment of their needs for protection as refugees. However, the decision was 'severely criticized by scholars, UNHCR and the Inter-American Commission on Human Rights';[27] and most states that are parties to the *Convention* (and the US in respect of people within its territory) treat the non-*refoulement* provision with the respect it deserves. In addition to the right of non-*refoulement*, the Convention outlines a range of other refugee rights, mainly concerned with access to the courts, welfare and education, and the capacity to travel.[28]

Not everyone who might initially seem to be a refugee will be able to secure the protections of the *Convention*. In particular, Article 1.F provides that:

The provisions of this Convention shall not apply to any person with respect to whom there are serious reasons for considering that:

(a) he has committed a crime against peace, a war crime, or a crime against humanity, as defined in the international instruments drawn up to make provision in respect of such crimes;

(b) he has committed a serious non-political crime outside the country of refuge prior to his admission to that country as a refugee;

(c) he has been guilty of acts contrary to the purposes and principles of the United Nations.

Furthermore, Article 1.C provides that the Convention shall cease to apply to a refugee in a number of circumstances, most importantly where 'He can no longer, because the circumstances in connexion with which he has been recognized as a refugee have ceased to exist, continue to refuse to avail himself of the protection of the country of his nationality'. This so-called 'cessation clause' is potentially of great significance if refugees have only been provided temporary asylum rather than permanent residence or citizenship in another country. In 1992, the UNHCR Executive Committee adopted Conclusion no. 69 (XLIII) on Cessation of Status, which stressed that 'in taking any decision on application of the cessation clauses based on "ceased circumstances", States must carefully assess the fundamental character of the changes in the country of nationality or origin, including the general human rights situation, as well as the particular cause of fear of persecution, in order to make sure in an objective and verifiable way that the situation which justified the granting of refugee status has ceased to exist', and went on that 'an essential element in such assessment by States is the fundamental, stable and durable character of the changes, making use of appropriate information available in this respect, *inter alia*, from relevant specialized bodies, including particularly UNHCR'. These qualifications are both sensible and practical, but they do not form binding law, and there is a danger that states wishing to be rid of refugees will rush to the conclusion that Article 1C applies when a regime changes, without pausing to question whether the new dispensation might not be equally threatening.[29]

Broader legal definitions

While the 1951 *Convention* is undoubtedly the most widely-cited source of a definition of refugee, other instruments have also come to play a role in shaping our understanding of what a refugee might be. First of all, from 1967, the 1951 *Convention* was augmented by a Protocol that eliminated the reference to 'events occurring before 1 January 1951'. This ensured that the *Convention* could apply as a source of universal guidance without either geographical or temporal limitations. The Protocol has now been widely accepted; one notable oddity is that the United States acceded to the Protocol on 1 November 1968 even though it was not then and is not now a party to the 1951 *Convention*. In the absence of the Protocol, the passage of time would have reduced and then eliminated the pool of persons from which refugees could have been drawn. Indeed, the adoption of the 1967 Protocol provides a clear affirmation that the 1951 *Convention* was not simply an instrument of the early Cold War years, but was designed to do rather more in terms of providing a framework of protection than simply aid those caught up in struggles between East and West.

Regional actors also have the option of adopting an approach to defining refugees in a particular region in a way that is broader than the approach in the 1951 *Convention*. The most striking example comes from Africa. Article 1.2 of the 1969 OAU *Convention on the Specific Aspects of Refugee Problems in Africa* provides that the term 'refugee' shall 'also apply to every person who, owing to external aggression, occupation, foreign domination or events seriously disturbing public order in either part or the whole of his country of origin or nationality, is compelled to leave his place of habitual residence in order to seek refuge in another place outside his country of origin or nationality'. Of particular importance is the reference to 'events seriously disturbing public order', which in practice has expanded the scope of refugee protection in Africa.[30] Similarly, section III.3 of the 22 November 1984 *Cartagena Declaration on Refugees*, adopted by the 'Colloquium on the International Protection of Refugees in Central America, Mexico and Panama', held in Cartagena,

Colombia, recommended for use in the region a definition of refugees that went beyond that in the 1951 *Convention* to include 'persons who have fled their country because their lives, safety or freedom have been threatened by generalized violence, foreign aggression, internal conflicts, massive violation of human rights or other circumstances which have seriously disturbed public order'. An interesting implication of these formulations is that poor countries can be just as generous as rich countries in assisting the vulnerable,[31] and sometimes even more so.

Yet just as some states have sought to expand the definition of refugee, there have been commentators who have seen the definition as problematically broad. One line of argument that has been advanced is to the effect that the 1951 *Convention* was a creature of the Cold War, and that it is dysfunctional in other circumstances, especially those prevailing when borders are not as brutally policed as was the case with communist borders during the period of the 'Iron Curtain'.[32] Some have even gone so far as to recommend that states denounce the 1951 *Convention*,[33] although no state-party has done so. There have also been specific suggestions as to how the definition of refugee might be narrowed, with one suggestion being to limit its coverage to persecution *by states*.[34] Nothing, however, has come of such suggestions, at least in any direct or explicit sense, and it is not hard to see why. While many conventions contain provision for amendment by a meeting of the 'states-parties' that have ratified or acceded to them, the 1951 Convention instead contains a provision in Article 45 that 'Any Contracting State may request revision of this Convention at any time by a notification addressed to the Secretary-General of the United Nations', and that 'The General Assembly of the United Nations shall recommend the steps, if any, to be taken in respect of such request'. Poorer, developing countries not only accommodate the bulk of the world's refugees, but also remain in a majority in the General

Assembly. They have little interest in assisting wealthier, developed countries to narrow the definition of refugee in a way that would do little to reduce the burdens inescapably carried by countries of first asylum, but assist the rich in washing their hands of asylum seekers arriving at their borders.

The deeper threat to the 1951 *Convention* is that countries will profess loyalty to its provisions, but in practice either violate them or interpret them in a deliberately rigid or narrow fashion so that the rights of refugees are compromised. Australia has been perhaps the most egregious source of such threats,[35] and a concrete example of this arose in Australian policy after 1999. In that year, the Australian government determined that those refugees who had reached Australia by boat but had then been found to be refugees would only be issued 'Temporary Protection Visas'. Article 28.1 of the *Convention* provides that 'The Contracting States shall issue to refugees lawfully staying in their territory travel documents for the purpose of travel outside their territory, unless compelling reasons of national security or public order otherwise require, and the provisions of the Schedule to this Convention shall apply with respect to such documents'. Paragraph 13.1 of the Schedule states that 'Each Contracting State undertakes that the holder of a travel document issued by it in accordance with article 28 of this Convention shall be re-admitted to its territory at any time during the period of its validity'. Yet it was a condition of the 'Temporary Protection Visa' that if a holder left Australia, he or she would not be able to re-enter.

The practical ramifications of this kind of breach of the *Convention* can be seen from the following case. In 2001, a refugee from Iraq, Ahmad al-Zalime, was living lawfully in Australia with a Temporary Protection Visa. Because of another limitation imposed on Temporary Protection Visa holders, he was unable to sponsor his wife, Sondos Ismail, and his three daughters,

Eman, Fatima and Zahra, to join him. In spite of his pleas, they boarded a rickety vessel in Indonesia—a boat which came to be known as SIEV-X—in the hope of being reunited with their loved one.[36] On 19 October 2001, the boat sank between Indonesia and Australia, and Mr al-Zalime's three daughters were drowned. Prime Minister Howard stated on television that he felt 'compassion' for Mr al-Zalime, but his 'compassion', as it turned out, did not extend to authorising Mr al-Zalime to re-enter Australia if he travelled to Indonesia to grieve with his wife, who had survived the disaster. When this restriction was finally 'relaxed' in 2014, it was via a labyrinthine provision that a refugee with such a visa 'must not enter any other country unless (i) the Minister is satisfied that there are compassionate or compelling circumstances justifying the entry; and (ii) the Minister has approved the entry in writing'.[37] The limitations of this 'relaxation' are all too obvious: if a refugee has a truly desperate need to travel to another country, for example to visit a dying relative, the chances that appropriate approval could be extracted in a timely fashion from the relevant minister are close to zero.

Refugee protection under other branches of law

There is now a rich literature on what is called 'complementary protection'. The idea itself is relatively simple: 'In legal terms, "complementary protection" describes protection granted by States on the basis of an international protection need outside the 1951 Convention framework. It may be based on a human rights treaty or on more general humanitarian principles, such as providing assistance to persons fleeing from generalized violence'.[38] Where complementary protection becomes complicated is simply in the diverse range of sources that exist under various strands of law.

Refugees may first of all be entitled to protections under the 'laws of armed conflict', or 'international humanitarian law'.[39]

Just as acute refugee movements can be driven by large-scale conflicts, refugee camps may be located in places that are dangerously exposed to entanglement in ongoing strife. Non-combatants in refugee camps may be just as entitled to protections under international humanitarian law as other non-combatants, especially the protections of the Fourth Geneva Convention of 1949. There is, however, one notable complicating factor, namely that refugee camps on occasion have come to function also as operating bases for combatants,[40] which in the eyes of other belligerents may make such camps seem legitimate military targets, with the risk that innocent refugees will be caught in the crossfire. Refugees are, and always have been, extremely vulnerable to manipulation by forces with agendas of their own.[41]

Refugees also have a range of human rights in the international legal sense that are covered by instruments such as the *European Convention for the Protection of Human Rights and Fundamental Freedoms* (1950), the *International Covenant on Civil and Political Rights* (1966), the *International Covenant on Economic, Social and Cultural Rights* (1966), and the *Convention on the Rights of the Child* (1989). These instruments are important because they may provide mechanisms for the consideration of individual grievances that are not available under the 1951 *Convention*. For example, the First Optional Protocol to the *International Covenant on Civil and Political Rights* provides for the Human Rights Committee in Geneva to receive complaints about alleged violations of the *Covenant*, and in August 2013, the Committee found that the indefinite detention of thirty-seven refugees with adverse security assessments, all but one of them Tamils from Sri Lanka, was 'arbitrary' within the meaning of the term in Article 9(1) of the *Covenant*, and amounted to 'cruel, inhuman or degrading treatment' under Article 7.[42] Some states are prepared to ignore findings from a 'Committee', but the European Court of Human Rights, which has functioned as a permanent fulltime body since 1998, is much harder to ignore: as McAdam puts it, 'In addition to the Court's jurisprudence having substantial persuasive influence at the international level, it has enormous precedential value in domestic proceedings'.[43]

A third body of international law of considerable importance relates to torture. Torture as a tool of repressive states has a long and gruesome history,[44] but the twentieth century witnessed unprecedented efforts to prohibit it, culminating in the *United Nations Convention Against Torture and Other Cruel, Inhuman or Degrading Treatment of Punishment* (1984). These suffered a significant setback in the twenty-first century, as the US Central Intelligence Agency resorted to a program of torture of detainees in the wake of the 11 September 2001 terrorist attacks in New York and Washington DC. Nonetheless, as the US Senate Select Committee on Intelligence formally found, 'the program caused immeasurable damage to the United States' public standing, as well as to the United States' global leadership on human rights in general and the prevention of torture in particular'.[45] As a result, the setback in the campaign against torture may not prove as serious as was initially feared. The 1984 *Convention* in Article 1.1 defines torture as:

> any act by which severe pain or suffering, whether physical or mental, is intentionally inflicted on a person for such purposes as obtaining from him or a third person information or a confession, punishing him for an act he or a third person has committed or is suspected of having committed, or intimidating or coercing him or a third person, or for any reason based on discrimination of any kind, when such pain or suffering is inflicted by or at the instigation of or with the consent or acquiescence of a public official or other person acting in an official capacity. It does not include pain or suffering arising only from, inherent in or incidental to lawful sanctions.

Importantly, Article 3.1 provides that 'No State Party shall expel, return ('refouler') or extradite a person to another State where there are substantial grounds for believing that he would be in danger of being subjected to torture'. In contrast to Article 33.1 of the 1951 *Convention*, where the prohibition on *refoulement* is qualified by the provision in Article 33.2, in the 1984 Convention the prohibition on *refoulement* is absolute and unqualified.

A final body of relevant law contains a prohibition on geno-cide.[46] The 1948 *Convention on the Prevention and Punishment of the Crime of Genocide* in Article 2 provides that: 'genocide means any of the following acts committed with intent to destroy, in whole or in part, a national, ethnical, racial or religious group, as such: (a) Killing members of the group; (b) Causing serious bodily or mental harm to members of the group; (c) Deliberately inflicting on the group conditions of life calculated to bring about its physical destruction in whole or in part; (d) Imposing measures intended to prevent births within the group; (e) Forcibly transferring children of the group to another group'. It is doubt-ful whether this adds to the concept of 'persecution' in the 1951 *Convention*, although it may assist in interpreting that undefined term. What it does do, however, is allow refugee protection to be rapidly extended to those who have fled genocide.

Status determination by states

As we saw in Chapter One, a person can be a refugee without being certified as such by the authorities in a state. But that said, in order to enjoy the protection of a state, a refugee may have to take a range of steps prescribed by that state to establish refugee status. The starting point in such procedures will typically be a definition of 'refugee' embedded in the state's domestic law; in most cases this will be based on an international legal definition such as that in the 1951 *Convention*, but sometimes with local twists or qualifications added. Beyond this, a range of issues can arise relating to the identity of a claimant and the circumstances that could confront the claimant in his or her country of nationality if he or she were obliged to return. It is particularly in addressing these issues that decision-makers can prove defective, and this is a major reason why tensions often exist between immigration bureaucracies and refugee advocates.

One problem is simply the politicised character of refugee status determination. If, in a democracy, public opinion is hostile to refugees, governments are quite likely to follow suit, and this can easily trickle down to the level of bureaucratic decision-making. For example, on 9 April 2010, three Australian cabinet ministers in a joint statement claimed that 'The Taliban's fall, durable security in parts of the country, and constitutional and legal reform to protect minorities' rights have improved the circumstances of Afghanistan's minorities, including Afghan Hazaras', and announced that the government had suspended the 'processing of new asylum claims by Afghan nationals for a period of six months.'[47] The processing suspension did not stop Afghans from approaching Australia by boat to seek protection, but one group who seemed to get the government's message comprised immigration officers doing primary determinations of protection visa applications: when processing resumed, the initial success rate for Afghan applicants went from 77.9% in 2009–2010 to 37.7% in 2010–2011. However, the 'overturn rate' for Afghans in 2010–2011 when independent reviewers scrutinised primary rejections was 78.7%, the highest for any country in the caseload. In 2010–2011, the final success rate for Afghan applicants was 89.3%.[48] It seems more than likely that from April 2010, large numbers of Afghan asylum applications were rejected at first instance not because the situation in Afghanistan had actually improved, but because it had been made crystal clear to primary decision makers what their political masters wanted, and some at least responded to this signal.

Refugees, of course, often have to flee their homes without a neat portfolio of documents to establish their identities and circumstances. A question that can therefore arise is whether they come from the places they claim. The danger here is that spurious approaches to dealing with this question may be grasped by decision-makers, even if there are huge questions about their methodological validity. One example is the enthusiasm with which bureaucracies have made use of 'language testing', premised on the view that by listening to an asylum seeker's speech, one can assess his or her place of origin. This view has been subject to detailed and telling criticism by professional linguists;[49] one specialist has warned that 'for the time being, linguists producing Language Analysis Reports, as well as the governments using them in decisions about asylum seeker's applications, should be acutely aware of the current limitations of the scientific basis for this work'.[50] Furthermore, the secretiveness of the private companies such as Skandinavisk Språkanalys AB that supply reports based on this approach has also come in for criticism. Nonetheless, such approaches continue to be used, although increasingly in the face of skepticism from courts of law, such as the Supreme Court of the United Kingdom in *Secretary of State for Home Department* v. *MN and KY (Scotland)* [2014] 4 All ER 443.[51]

Decision-makers are only human, and it is often human failings that account for the occasional indefensible decisions in asylum cases. Decision-makers faced with large caseloads may be tempted to 'cut-and-paste' from one decision to the next, although they risk embarrassment if they do so too blatantly: in *MZZZW* v. *Minister for Immigration and Border Protection* [2015] FCAFC 133, the Full Court of the Federal Court of Australia cuttingly observed that 'Submissions based on "high volume" decision-making can tend to suggest applicants, whose claims relate to matters of liberty and personal safety, are entitled to some kind of "short cut" version of administrative justice with patched together decisions. We fail to see where or how the terms of the Migration Act suggest that is the kind of review the

Act contemplates'. Decision-makers may be under-prepared or ill-qualified, by dint of either background or personality, to cope with the kind of cases that come before them, and may cope especially poorly with cases involving historically-marginalised groups such as women, victims of sexual violence, and sexual minorities.[52] A recent US case of an applicant denied asylum, that of a former interpreter for US forces in Afghanistan, Samey Honaryar, highlights how weak can be a decision-maker's grasp of the prevailing realities in the country from which an applicant for asylum has fled. The journalist Elizabeth Rubin attributed Honaryar's experience to 'a toxic mix of bureaucracy, fear, prejudice and, most poignantly, his naïve faith in American honor'.[53] A detailed study of the Canadian Immigration and Refugee Board documented a range of further failings that can come into play; with ignorance, hyper-scepticism, loss of sensitivity and denial all playing roles.[54] The last of these, namely denial, is a particularly insidious problem since it can be a subconscious reaction to the horrors that are often embedded in refugees' stories, as well as a bureaucratic response to the huge social differences that often exist between refugees and those who are assessing their claims.[55]

Nonetheless, decision-makers need to be held to very high standards of proficiency, for the human consequences can be disastrous if a decision-making process miscarries in the sphere of refugee protection. Again, a recent Australian case highlights the risks involved. On 26 August 2014, an Afghan Hazara from the Jaghori district of Ghazni province, Zainullah Naseri, was deported from Australia to Afghanistan. His case had been assessed in December 2012 by a member of the Refugee Review Tribunal, Paul Millar, who concluded 'The Tribunal is only considering the route for the applicant to make a journey from Kabul back to his native area. In those circumstances, the Tribunal accepts that the applicant is at risk as a Hazara of suffering harm in making that journey but the Tribunal finds that the level of risk does not reach the threshold of a real chance'.[56] Not all decision-makers were as relaxed as Millar,[57] and the dangers of Millar's approach were starkly illustrated when Mr Naseri attempted to return to his home district. He was seized by six Taliban, tortured and—on the strength of his Australian driver's licence and pictures in his mobile phone of the Sydney Opera House and Harbour Bridge—accused of being an infidel. Only by a stroke of good luck, namely the outbreak of fighting in the immediate vicinity that distracted the Taliban's attention, was he able to escape.[58] In the same month as Mr Naseri was attacked, an Australian of Afghan origin, Sayed Habib Musawi, was seized from a bus travelling between Kabul and Ghazni, and subsequently tortured and murdered by the Taliban.[59]

One particular area where misunderstanding can regularly surface relates to assessments of the credibility of an applicant for protection. An egregious example related to an applicant named Moqbool Hussain, who claimed to come from the Hazarajat region of Afghanistan. The Refugee Review Tribunal in Australia held that 'On the basis of the applicant's lack of familiarity with the part of Afghanistan from which he claims to have come, his lack of knowledge of recent events in Afghan history, and his inability to nominate significant national days or to fix any date within the Afghan calendar, the Tribunal finds that the applicant is not from Afghanistan and has not lived there all his life until he came to Australia'. Specifically, the Tribunal considered it 'reasonable to expect that an Hazara from Afghanistan would have known something of the history of his own people, and that he would have at least some awareness of a significant, and relatively recent event, such as the withdrawal of Soviet troops from Afghanistan', an event which the applicant had stated occurred before he was born in 1981. 'When told by the Tribunal that the Soviet forces had withdrawn in 1989 when he was eight or nine years old', the decision maker went on, 'the applicant continued to insist that he had not been born at that time'.

The Tribunal member, in drawing this conclusion, seemed quite unaware that the Soviets' withdrawal from the Hazarajat considerably preceded their withdrawal from Afghanistan as a whole. As Henry S. Bradsher put it, the Soviets 'stopped military operations in the Hazarajat in 1981 and held only two token garrisons in central Afghanistan until 1987'.[60] Given the likely age of the applicant, his insistence that he had not been born at the time of the Soviet withdrawal was not at all inconsistent with his claimed Afghan nationality if he has indeed been a resident of the Hazarajat. The Tribunal member also stated that the applicant 'showed a lack of familiarity with the Afghan calendar, and was unable to place any event, including his birth, within the Afghan calendar even when the Tribunal attempted to assist him to do so'. Yet very few Afghans know their birth date with any degree of certainty. In Afghanistan, there has never been a central system for the registration of births, deaths, and marriages, and one's date of birth is simply not a salient event in Afghan culture in the same way as it is in a Western country. Furthermore, in the Hazarajat, any notion of 'the' Afghan calendar needs to be treated with the greatest of caution. No fewer than three different types of calendar are used in different parts of the Hazarajat: the Arabic Lunar calendar (*hisab-e mah*) with some Hazara modifications; the Afghan solar calendar (*hisab-e burj*) based on zodiac signs; and the traditional Hazara animal calendar.[61] The inability of certain Hazaras from the Hazarajat to locate key dates within the *hisab-e burj* would not be remotely surprising to a specialist on Afghanistan. Without benefit of counsel, the applicant sought in person to challenge the decision before the Federal Court of Australia, but since the Court could only overturn a decision on the basis of an error of law rather than of fact or interpretation, he was unsuccessful. Nonetheless,

Justice Carr, plainly uncomfortable with how things had proceeded, concluded that

> it would be considered, by right-minded persons, to be unconscionable
> and unthinkable if the respondent were to cause the applicant to be
> removed to Afghanistan. A very significant basis of the Tribunal's deci-
> sion was that as the applicant was not a national of Afghanistan he
> would not be required to return there. In my view, to remove the appli-
> cant to Afghanistan without giving him an opportunity to make a fresh
> application for a protection visa would be to make a mockery of
> Australia's compliance with the Refugees Convention.[62]

On occasion, ill-considered decisions can be overturned
through processes of judicial review, although the classic tools of
judicial review such as the writs of *certiorari* and *mandamus* are
designed primarily to address procedural errors by decision-
makers rather than gross errors of judgment. Judicial oversight
nevertheless remains of critical importance if the rights of refugees are to be protected. One reason is that properly-constituted
courts should be immune from the political pressures that on
occasion can shape bureaucratic decision-making. But another
reason is that if bureaucratic decision-makers are insulated from
the threat of judicial oversight, it is likely that over time they will
become indifferent to whether their decision-making meets the
requirements of the law or not, and to the need to achieve the
highest standards of quality in decision-making. Scandal is the
likely result, as for example occurred when the Australian
Immigration Department mistakenly seized and deported an
Australian citizen, originally from the Philippines, who was dis-
oriented after a car accident.[63]

Ordinary language understandings of 'refugee'

While we may speak of 'ordinary language understandings',
people in the real world speak many different languages, and

there is no reason to assume that all languages have a word that coincides precisely with the ordinary language usage of the word 'refugee' in English.[64] Apparent 'equivalents', for example the French word *réfugié*, may actually differ subtly in their meaning when used by native speakers. Even in a purely etymological sense, differences abound. For example, on a literal reading the English word 'refugee' refers to someone who is a recipient of 'refuge'—that is, the focus is on the protection that is made available to someone in need. In Russian, by contrast, the word used as an equivalent for refugee is *bezhenets* (in the masculine form) and *bezhenka* (in the feminine). These words derive from the verb *bezhat'*, which means 'to run', and relate directly to the noun *bezhenstvo*, which means 'flight' or 'exodus'. The emphasis in Russian is on the process of movement rather than what happens at the destination.[65]

That said, everyday understandings of what is a refugee may overlap with legal definitions, but have lives of their own. They are shaped as much by images contained in mass media and by casual conversations as by any careful conceptual analysis. Those fleeing war or natural disasters probably fall most easily into everyday understandings of what is a refugee, although ironically the 1951 *Convention*, on a literal reading, covers neither category of person. One of the explanations for this lies in the phenomenon of the refugee camp, which can function simultaneously as a means of both shelter and confinement and control.[66] The teeming masses of humanity that inhabit such settlements, manifestly in a situation which few Westerners would envy and often pathetically grateful for any help they receive, fall more neatly into a category of 'good' or 'deserving' refugee than the troublesome political exile living in an urban apartment, and seeking to have his or her rights as a refugee properly recognised. Yet large refugee camps are likely to contain people who are not refugees in any legal sense of the term, and even those who are refugees under international law may have little prospect of securing any individualised appraisal of their status, of a kind that might open the door to resettlement elsewhere. In a real sense, therefore, refugees in camps are contained, and that can be exactly what many people outside the camp would want them to be.

Two other usages of 'refugee' are becoming more common, and deserve attention. First, the term 'environmental refugee' has surfaced, in part reflecting the reality that territories may become uninhabitable because of natural phenomena such as drought or desertification, but more recently in the context of climate change, where rising sea levels could threaten the very existence of low-lying island or archipelagic states such as the Maldives, the Marshall Islands, Kiribati and Tuvalu.[67] At present, there is no disposition on the part of policymakers to treat such threats as giving rise to refugee status; in September 2015, the Government of New Zealand deported Ioane Teitiota to Kiribati after the Supreme Court rejected his final appeal against removal. Mr Teitiota had based his claim to stay in New Zealand on the proposition that his homeland, Kiribati, was 'facing steadily rising sea water levels as a result of climate change', with the fear that 'over time, the rising sea water levels and the associated environmental degradation will force the inhabitants of Kiribati to leave their islands'.[68] His claim was not upheld, but the Supreme Court did remark that

> both the Tribunal and the High Court, emphasised their decisions did not mean that environmental degradation resulting from climate change or other natural disasters could never create a pathway into the Refugee Convention or protected person jurisdiction. Our decision in this case should not be taken as ruling out that possibility in an appropriate case.[69]

Related to this is the idea of 'survival migration', originally coined by the scholar Alexander Betts, but with considerable potential to seep into everyday discourse. The term refers to people who are outside their country of origin because of an existential threat for which they have no access to a domestic remedy or resolution ... It is based on the recognition that what matters is not privileging particular causes of movement but rather clearly identifying a threshold of fundamental rights which, when unavailable in a country of origin, requires that the international community allow people to cross an international border and receive access to temporary or permanent sanctuary.[70]

In particular, the idea of survival migration recognises that people may have excellent reasons for fleeing not just from persecution, but also from the effects of environmental change, food insecurity, and state fragility. An implication of Betts's work is that international protection regimes as they currently stand may be defective not because they cover too many people (as politicians on the far right sometimes imply), but because they cover too few.

Philosophical definitions of 'refugee'

A stipulative definition of a term cannot be 'wrong', but it can be unhelpful if it formulates a term in such a way as to preclude a focus on important and interesting issues. This has led a number of scholars to formulate definitions of 'refugee' that open up new lines of inquiry. One of the most notable efforts has been that of Andrew Shacknove, for whom a refugee is a person 'whose government fails to protect his basic needs, who has no remaining recourse than to seek international restitution of those needs, and who is so situated that international assistance is possible'.[71] A definition of this kind can give rise to many further questions. In this case, an obvious one relates to the nature of 'needs', a term which is far from straightforward.[72] Nonetheless, definitions of this kind are important because they highlight that whilst legal definitions such as that in the 1951 *Convention* may help define the boundaries of a state's responsibility towards refugees under international law, other kinds of definition may be required to identify the classes of persons to whom moral responsibilities may be owed, either by states, or by individuals within states. Addressing such issues of course requires substantive argumentation rather than simply the supply of definitions,[73] but clarity at the outset always helps.

Contemporary political philosophy has had less to say about refugees than one might have expected, perhaps because refugee issues sit uneasily between domestic politics and international relations. This is not, however, to say that it is irrelevant to our understanding of refugees and their plight. On the contrary, whether one is concerned with classic values such as liberty or justice, or with wider 'republican' ideas of non-domination, or with conceptions of human flourishing more broadly, it is not hard to see how the ways in which refugees are treated can constitute a challenge to the credibility of those who claim to be concerned with the freedom or the dignity of the individual. At a time when political figures easily adopt the claim that refugees are entitled to no more than relief from the immediate threat of persecution, it is important not to forget that how we treat those we define as refugees may tell us little about them, but a great deal about ourselves.

EXILE AND REFUGE

A BRIEF OVERVIEW

It is tempting to see the world as an extremely violent place, but this would be an oversimplification. The more complicated reality is that large numbers of people lead peaceful and largely untroubled lives, while others experience the horrors of war, terrorism and conflict on an almost daily basis. And between these two groups, there is quite a large group of people for whom there are few protections against a sudden upsurge of violence or instability. This last situation was powerfully captured in Thomas Hobbes's definition of war in his great work *Leviathan*, first published in 1651. Hobbes had witnessed the English Civil War, and had a rather clear view of what war could involve:[1]

> For WARRE, consisteth not in Battel onely, or the act of fighting, but in a tract of time, wherein the Will to contend by Battel is sufficiently known: and therefore the notion of *Time*, is to be considered in the nature of Warre; as it is in the nature of Weather. For as the nature of Foule weather, lyeth not in a showre or two of rain, but in an inclination thereto of many dayes together: So the nature of War, consisteth not in actuall fighting; but in the known disposition thereto, during all the time there is no assurance to the contrary.

The history of human displacement and forced migration drives home the importance of Hobbes's broad definition of war. It is all too easy to see refugee movements as driven by war in a narrower sense. But the reality, both historically and contemporaneously, is much more complex. Some of the individual cases noted in Chapter One point to this conclusion. This chapter reinforces that conclusion by identifying some notable historical examples of refugee movements at the macroscopic level. Violence, and the threat of violence, come in diverse shapes and sizes. At the end of the 1980s, Zolberg, Suhrke and Aguayo famously characterised refugees as 'persons whose presence abroad is attributable to a well-founded fear of violence, as might be established by impartial experts with adequate information'.[2] One of the lessons of history is that a well-founded fear of violence, like a well-founded fear of being persecuted, can be triggered by many different factors. Understanding this is a key to adequate early warning of refugee crises. In a survey of 'early-warning factors', Schmeidl argues that forced exodus depends on root (systemic) causes, proximate causes, and intervening factors.[3] All of these are apparent in the cases discussed in this chapter.

Political violence, marginalisation, and the human experience

The metaphor of the 'social contract' has long figured in analyses of either the origins or the justification of the state, with Thomas Hobbes, John Locke and Jean-Jacques Rousseau among the more famous proponents of the idea. As an historical explanation, however, this image of people voluntarily coming together to create political order has relatively little to commend it, and in a pathbreaking essay, the sociologist Charles Tilly painted a very different picture. 'War', he famously wrote, 'makes states ... Banditry, piracy, gangland rivalry, policing, and war making all belong on the same continuum'.[4] If, therefore, the territorial state is the basic unit in world politics, we should not be surprised if the path that led to the modern system of states turned out to be stained with a great deal of blood, accompanied by human displacement and forced migration on a significant scale.

At the level of societies, boundaries and barriers intended to separate different groups often prove more permeable than one might think.[5] As refugees from the Middle East reached Germany in 2015, many (although by no means all) ordinary Germans mobilised to offer them a welcome they probably did not expect.[6] The logic of state formation, however, historically involved different approaches, and an extreme example came in the form of what Heather Rae has called

> pathological homogenisation', a term she uses 'to designate a number of different strategies that state-builders have employed to signify the unity of their state and the legitimacy of their authority through the creation of an ostensibly unified population. These strategies range from attempts to legally exclude minority groups from citizenship rights, to strategies of forced conversion or assimilation, expulsion and extermination.[7]

A classic and famous example was the treatment of the Huguenots in France after the revocation in 1685 of the Edict of Nantes, a proclamation of 1598 that had given autonomy to the Huguenots, who were Protestants of Calvinist stripe amidst a Catholic majority. The Huguenots had long been endangered; the so-called Saint Bartholomew's Day Massacres of 1572 were an indicator of this, and triggered internal strife that the Edict was designed to terminate. The revocation of the Edict was therefore a powerful symbolic act in Huguenot eyes, although it had been sapped of substance in the years immediately before its revocation. An estimated 200,000 Huguenots fled France, mainly for neighbouring Protestant countries, around this time.[8] The Huguenots were reportedly the first recipients of the English label 'refugee'.[9] Other, more recent, examples of pathological homogenisation cited by Rae include the

Armenian genocide of 1915–16, and 'ethnic cleansing' in the Bosnian war of the 1990s.[10]

Even if groups do not fall victim to pathological homogenisation, they can be attacked or marginalised in other ways, either overt or insidious, and on other bases, that also lead to forced migration. Religion and nationalism have historically been powerful forces to this effect, and put together, they can be particularly potent: Gertrude Himmelfarb once chillingly referred to the 'dark and bloody crossroads' where religion and nationalism meet.[11] One of the most insightful students of the history of nationalism, Sir Isaiah Berlin, observed that nationalisms have been 'responsible for magnificent achievements and appalling crimes'.[12] The same point could be made about religions. Each ideology has the potential to create 'in groups' and 'out groups', and when this happens, the consequences can be very disturbing, especially if political entrepreneurs emerge to whip up hatreds.[13] Political nationalism entails the aspiration of a national group to possess and rule territory of its own,[14] and this can lead to a destructive logic that was formulated in the 1990s by the political scientist Vladimir Gligorov: 'Why should I be a minority in your state when you can be a minority in mine?'[15]

With respect to religion, a different logic can be at play, although with equally repressive consequences. The idea of salvation for those whose earthly conduct justifies it can easily lead to the claim that those who are benighted must be saved from the consequences of their errors. This can lead to reigns of religious terror from which people will naturally seek to flee.[16] It is important to note at this juncture that 'religion' is a notably complex term. Religious belief can encompass a range of convictions about the sacred, the divine, the origins of existence, and the next world.[17] Undoubtedly in human history, large numbers of people have experienced persecution because their articulated beliefs about such matters have not coincided with those of the dominant powers. Galileo in the seventeenth century, who had offended the Roman Catholic hierarchy by defending the Copernican view that the earth orbited the sun, provides an obvious example. In addition, however, one can also speak of communities defined by religious labels, and while some members of these communities may be active believers, this is not necessarily the case. In Northern Ireland, for example, the term 'Protestant' could be applied to ferocious preachers such as the Reverend Ian Paisley but also to self-proclaimed 'Protestants' whose strictly religious beliefs might have been quite obscure. Finally, religious labels can be attached to individuals who might neither entertain religious beliefs, nor see themselves as members of religiously designated communities. In Nazi Germany, the 1935 Nuremberg Laws sought to define 'Jews' according to formal criteria that could be used for purposes of bureaucratic administration, with results as frightening as they were bizarre.[18] Because of the complexity of the idea of religion, it is quite dangerous to work back from religious labels such as Jew, Christian, Muslim, or Hindu to try to infer anything about the behaviours that might be expected from individuals. This kind of collectivist, essentialist thinking has been at the heart of some of the greatest cruelties in human history.

When groups of people are actively demonised, it may seem unduly weak to describe what is happening simply in terms of the existence of differences within complex societies. This is one factor that has led sociologists to use the expression 'the Other' to try to capture the way in which particular groups can be shunned, scorned, and pushed to the fringes of society, if not beyond its boundaries. As Seidman puts it:[19]

> a sociology of otherness aims to understand how non-normative statuses and identities are positioned outside of a normative civil order. Otherness signals a condition of systemic symbolic exclusion. Further, because the Other is also represented as a grave social threat, symbolic exclusion is

typically accompanied by systemic patterns of social exclusion (for example ethnic and racial apartheids, Jewish, black, and gay ghettos, or refugee camps) ... The Other is represented not merely as deficient or eccentric, but as defiled or fundamentally debased and grotesque. The Other inhabits an existential space between the human and non-human ... To the extent that the Other is imagined as powerful and threatening chaos and calamity, political mobilization may be considered warranted to defend civil life.

Conceptions of 'the Other' have of course played a significant role in the targeting of vulnerable groups. Probably no group has experienced this more than the Jews, with the Holocaust providing an awful warning of what the consequences of dehumanising 'the Other' can be. Diaspora groups such as Jews or Roma, minorities almost by definition, may be at particular risk, and it is no surprise that Theodor Herzl's famous 1896 book *Der Judenstaat* ('The Jewish State'), arguably the key text of modern Zionism, aimed at overcoming this problem as far as Jews were concerned, with the creation of the state of Israel in 1948 being the result.[20] But it pays to be alert to how the idea of 'the Other' can worm its way into other contexts as well, and Seidman's passing reference to refugee camps highlights the possibility that refugees who by dint of country of origin and background may seem very different to the population of the receiving country may come to be seen not as fellow humans in need of help, but rather as the Other, to be isolated and rejected.

Exile and ideology from the seventeenth century to the early twentieth century

Just as the violence surrounding much state formation can lead to the exodus of peoples, so also can the movement of peoples contribute to the founding of new states. One example is the United States of America. Until the eighteenth century, America was indisputably a territory and a continent, but it was not a state. It did, however, house a range of colonies, which became parties to the Declaration of Independence of 4 July 1776, the Revolutionary War, and finally the drafting of the US Constitution in 1787. The European populations of the colonies had begun to arrive centuries earlier, and while it would be an exaggeration to see the bulk of them as fleeing persecution, some at least were escaping from looming disorder in which they might otherwise have become entangled. They were all of them 'boat people': as John F. Kennedy put it, 'America has always been a refuge from tyranny ... Every time a revolution has failed in Europe, every time a nation has succumbed to tyranny, men and women who love freedom have assembled their families and their belongings and set sail across the seas'.[21]

The Pilgrim Fathers who landed at Cape Cod in the *Mayflower* in 1620 had found themselves at odds with the Church of England, and although they were Puritans rather than Roman Catholics, recent English history, during the reigns of both Mary Tudor (1553–1558) and Elisabeth I (1558–1603), conveyed the message that being religiously heterodox was a dangerous stand to take. In addition, at the time when the *Mayflower* sailed, England was teetering on the verge of a new period of political dislocation. The Pilgrim Fathers and other colonists who followed them managed to avoid direct entanglement in the English Civil War that culminated in the execution of King Charles I in 1649. The Civil War had complex roots and at heart involved a power struggle between the Crown on the one side, and the House of Commons and the common law on the other. But this in turn pitted the notion of the Divine Right of Kings against Puritan ideas that at the time were more congenial to the Parliament. As the historian Lawrence Stone put it, 'For precisely one hundred years, from 1621 to 1721, it was as if a seismic rift had opened up within the English political nation—a kind of

San Andreas Fault'.[22] When earthquakes strike, it pays to be elsewhere. And ironically, for some 'Loyalists', the American Revolution itself was a disagreeable earthquake, and around 60,000 left for Canada, Nova Scotia, or England.[23]

Not of course that the new United States was an untroubled polity. The Civil War of 1861–65 provided agonising proof of that, and the explosive issue of slavery in Southern states contributed materially to its outbreak. What is often forgotten is that slavery also contributed to a remarkable movement out of the United States, which resulted in the establishment of the African country of Liberia. Founded in 1822 by the American Colonization Society, it became a republic in 1847, with its capital in Monrovia, named after former American president James Monroe. The migrants to Liberia comprised some free Americans of African origin, but also former slaves who had been freed from that status by the process of manumission. Only a minority of African-Americans were attracted to the idea of returning to Africa, but the willingness of members of this minority to do so spoke to their doubts as to whether they would ever be fully accepted in America even outside the slaveholding territories of the Southern states. The case of Liberia also highlighted a danger which is often not sufficiently noted, namely that a space in which a persecuted group might live safely can come to be seen by the persecutors as a place to which further members of that group might be expelled. This was illustrated in 1938 when US Senator Theodore Bilbo, a fanatical white supremacist from Mississippi, proposed the involuntary deportation of the entire African-American population to Liberia.[24] This wild idea fortunately obtained little traction, but it had something in common with an idea with which the Nazis toyed in 1940, namely that European Jews could be expelled to an SS police state on the Indian Ocean island of Madagascar.[25]

It is important to note that these population movements that brought Europeans to North American and African-Americans

back to West Africa were driven not just by calculations of interest, but by the force of ideas and ideologies, which mandated the
casting off of oppression—however defined.[26] Indeed, one can
argue that without the reinforcement that ideologies can provide,
many forms of repression would simply not have materialised.
The French Revolution of 1789–1793 provided an early indica-
tion of how potentially bloody the consequences of ideas preach-
ing the virtue of wholesale political transformation could be, not
least for revolutionaries themselves; if ever there was a case of
revolutions devouring their children, this was it. What made this
particularly poignant was that a range of the expressed values of
the French revolutionaries—notably the ideas of liberty, equality,
and fraternity—originated in the intellectual ferment of the
eighteenth century that came to be known as the Enlightenment.
As an intellectual movement, the Enlightenment was notable for
the promotion of both individualism and rationalism, as well as
elements of cosmopolitanism, with ideas of human rights and of
critical reflection figuring as key elements.[27]

The French Revolution, however, showed how ideas of this kind
could be perverted once they were deployed in the arena of concrete political competition. Furthermore, innovations such as the
Enlightenment moment can produce counter-movements that take
a destructive turn. This was indeed what happened, with the contribution of the Romantic Movement to the development of
nationalism being the most arresting development.[28] Before the
Reformation and the Westphalian settlement, there was relatively little space for nationalist ideas to take shape, given the
obeisance (or lip-service) paid to the idea of a united Christendom.
Enlightenment thinking offered one kind of response to the
Reformation and the Westphalian settlement, but nationalism
offered another. Some of the nationalisms of this time, such as
that of Johann Gottfried Herder, were relatively gentle,[29] but
others such as that of Joseph de Maistre were a good deal more

toxic,[30] and contributed to the rise of Fascism, one of the central totalitarian ideologies generating refugee movements in the twentieth century.[31] The other ideology to play this role was Marxism, and it is ironic that its two most significant progenitors, the German Karl Marx and the Russian Vladimir Ilyich Lenin, both spent time in exile as refugees themselves.

Political exiles often contribute to entirely new ideas about the ways in which states and communities might be constituted, and power exercised—and a bitter reality is that such ideas can be used to justify the most brutal forms of persecution. Karl Marx was born in the Prussian city of Trier in 1818 and died in London in 1883. He had travelled there, in the face of some pressure from the French Government, in 1849, and spent the rest of his life in England. The British government at the time was rather accommodating to political refugees. 'Foreign revolutionaries', Berlin has written, 'were on the whole left unmolested, provided they behaved themselves in an orderly and inconspicuous manner, but neither was any kind of contact established with them. Their hosts treated them with correctness and civility, mingled with a mild indifference to their affairs which once irritated and amused them'.[32] Marx's extensive writings, let alone those of his disciples, defy terse summation,[33] but central to his thought was a very specific definition of freedom in terms of the absence of 'alienation', which itself was not a psychological condition, but an attribute of the capitalist mode of production.[34] As a result, freedom was to be obtained through change in the way in which society was organised. The agent of such change was to be the 'proletariat', or working class. The danger of such a philosophy—a danger that was to become all too clear in the twentieth century—was that it could be used to justify all sorts of repressive measures.

In Lenin's hands, this was exactly what happened. Lenin was born in 1870, was traumatised by the execution of his older brother by the regime of Tsar Alexander III in 1887, and spent the bulk of his life as a fulltime revolutionary. He lived in Western Europe from 1900–1905, returned to Russia in November 1905 when Tsar Nicholas II pardoned political exiles, but moved abroad again in 1908, not to return until April 1917 after the so-called 'February Revolution' had forced the Tsar's abdication. His leadership of Russia from the 1917 'October Revolution' accounts for his enduring fame, but his most significant intellectual contribution arose from a particular twist that he gave to Marxist thought. Contemptuous of the revolutionary potential of the working class, he argued instead for a 'vanguard party' of dedicated revolutionaries to promote the achievement of a socialist society. In practice, this hugely amplified the authoritarian dimension of Marx's thought.[35] It is therefore hardly surprising that once Lenin had genuine power to wield, his regime produce the largest refugee movements by far that the world had witnessed up to that moment.

While Marx's influence on day-to-day politics was extremely limited during his lifetime, this was less true of members of another ideological tendency that flourished in the nineteenth century. When citizens in the twenty-first century express a fear of terrorism at the hands of refugees, they replicate a fear of a nineteenth century movement that used similar tactics, namely anarchism. Anarchist movements have little contemporary significance, and the key members of the nineteenth century movement—figures such as Pierre-Joseph Proudhon, Mikhail Bakunin and Petr Kropotkin—left little behind in the way of coherent theory that could guide future generations. Nonetheless, the apprehension that anarchists managed to generate, especially at the elite level, was truly remarkable, not least because their notion of 'propaganda of the deed',[36] an idea derived from Bakunin, endorsed attacks on figures associated with existing political orders. They, and some others influenced by their ideas, had more than trivial success in striking violently at the very top of a number of polities. In 1881, Tsar Alexander II of Russia, a relatively enlightened monarch who had been responsible for the emancipation of serfs from 1861, was assassinated by populists associated with the Narodnaia volia ('People's Will') group. Rather than triggering the fall of the monarchy, the assassination brought to power a new Tsar, Alexander III, who was a good deal more repressive than his predecessor. This did not, however, stop the anarchists in their tracks. President Carnot of France was assassinated in Lyon in June 1894; Empress Elizabeth of Austria was stabbed in Geneva in September 1898; King Umberto I of Italy was shot in Monza in July 1900; and perhaps most dramatically of all, US President William McKinley was killed in September 1901 by an American anarchist of Polish origin who appeared to have been galvanised by the spectacle of Umberto's murder. Even though the assassin was born in the US, Congress reacted with a 'border control' measure excluding from entry to the United States any person 'who disbelieves in or is opposed to all organized governments'.[37] In the wider history of refugees, anarchists are significant not because they created large refugee flows, but because they prompted panicked state responses that find echoes in twenty-first century political rhetoric directed at refugees as potential sources of danger, even though the overwhelming majority of refugees are not terrorists or assassins.

One other strand of ideological thought, utopianism, deserves a mention here, as it too has found echoes in recent times. The name 'Utopia' was coined by Thomas More in a book published in 1516 that depicted an imaginary society with features that might nonetheless be realisable. Many utopias have been imagined since.[38] One of the clearest analytical characterisations of utopias has been provided by the philosopher Leszek Kolakowski:[39]

First, we shall talk about utopias having in mind not ideas of making any side of human life better but only beliefs that a definitive and unsurpassable condition is obtainable, one where there is nothing to correct any more. Second, we shall apply the word to projections which are supposed to be implemented by human effort, thus excluding both images of an other-worldly paradise and apocalyptic hopes for an earthly paradise to be arranged by sheer divine decree. Consequently, conforming to the second criterion, the revolutionary anabaptism of the sixteenth century may be included in the history of utopias so conceived, but not various chiliastic or adventist movements and ideas which expect the Kingdom on earth as a result of Parousia. On the other hand, according to the first criterion, I would not describe as utopian various futuristic technological fantasies if they do not suggest the idea of an ultimate solution of mankind's predicament, a perfect satisfaction of human needs, a final state.

Most utopian thinking has been harmless, inspiring such quaint developments as 'New Australia', a short-lived utopian socialist community established in Paraguay in 1893 with 238 settlers.[40] But some utopian thinking has not been innocuous at all. In a critique of Lenin's thought, one critic has argued that 'the monolithic utopia will always founder on the rock of divergent human values'.[41] Unfortunately, much blood can be spilt along the way. The reason why can be found in a categorisation of utopias provided by Robert Nozick:[42]

We may distinguish three utopian positions: *imperialistic* utopianism, which countenances the forcing of everyone into one pattern of community; *missionary* utopianism, which hopes to persuade or convince everyone to live in one particular kind of community, but will not force them to do so; and *existential* utopianism, which hopes that a particular pattern of community will exist (will be viable), though not necessarily universally, so that those who wish to do so may live in accordance with it.

This is directly pertinent to modern times, because the movement in Iraq and Syria known as 'Islamic State' or 'Daesh', a movement from which refugees continue to flee in large numbers, bears virtually all the hallmarks of imperialistic utopianism.

Russian and German refugees between the World Wars

The outflow of Russian refugees in the wake of the Bolshevik Revolution of October 1917 differed from all prior mass movements in that by the time it gathered pace, a new international organisation, the League of Nations, had been established as a result of the Versailles conference to foster joint action on the part of the states that had become members. The Russian Revolution had an immense psychological impact on states in Western Europe, not least because the stated expectation of the revolutionaries was that their actions should be replicated in other states. This was profoundly unsettling for elites that were only just emerging from the carnage of the First World War.

The ruthlessness of the new rulers was apparent from the execution of the Tsar and his family in 1918, but it was not something that they showed any great interest in disguising. Lenin was committed to the view that 'not a single problem of the class struggle has ever been solved in history except by violence',[43] and willingly applied this general maxim to specific cases—for example when he wrote to a colleague in 1922 that it 'is precisely now and only now, when in the starving regions people are eating human flesh, and hundreds if not thousands of corpses are littering the roads, that we can (and therefore must) carry out the confiscation of church valuables with the most savage and merciless energy'.[44] But terror had come much earlier. In August 1918, an attempt on Lenin's life became the trigger for what was known as the 'Red Terror', and on 4 September, the Commissar for Internal Affairs issued a proclamation complaining of the 'extraordinarily negligible number of serious repressions and mass shootings of White Guards and bourgeoisie by the Soviets', adding that there 'must be a decisive end to this situation' and that 'a considerable number of hostages must be taken from among the bourgeoisie and the officers'.[45] The instrument for such measures was the Extraordinary Commission for Combating Counterrevolution and Sabotage, known from its acronym as the *Cheka*. Headed by Feliks Dzerzhinskii, it was 'an instrument of terror and class vengeance, not a routine bureaucracy'.[46] An historian of the *Cheka*, George Leggatt, calculated that the *Cheka* and its associated bodies were responsible for perhaps 140,000 executions during the six years under Lenin, and a further 140,000 deaths, as opposed to executions, during 1918–21.[47]

It was no wonder that refugees fled Russia, and they fled in very large numbers indeed. The exact number will never be known, but the most common estimate is more than one million people. While most made their way to Western Europe, some 200,000 travelled to Harbin in China. Most of them were not aristocrats; indeed, according to one pathbreaking study, 'the overwhelming majority of refugees were single men of military age'.[48] Many found themselves in a terrible situation. As Hannah Arendt put it, 'once they had left their homeland they remained homeless, once they had left their state they became stateless; once they had been deprived of their human rights they were rightless, the scum of the earth'.[49] It was to address this humanitarian crisis that the League of Nations in September 1921 called upon the renowned Norwegian polar explorer, Fridtjof Nansen, to accept an appointment as League of Nations High Commissioner for Russian Refugees in Europe. Nansen was rightly described as one of the League's 'mightiest personalities',[50] and his achievements were quite remarkable. He was helped (although those seeking to flee persecution were not) by the Bolsheviks' imposition of stringent controls on exit from 1922; but the problem he was left to manage was nonetheless enormous. Nansen accepted no salary, and was obliged to raise money from private sources in order to cover the expenses of his work; he had no core relief budget. (When Nansen won the Nobel Peace Prize in 1922, he donated the money to humanitarian relief.) His greatest achievement was the development of the so-called 'Nansen passport', a travel document to allow refugees to move from one country to another and thereby overcome the problem of separation of families that is so often associated with urgent flight by refugees, as well as find work in states where it might be available.[51] An even greater achievement was to secure from a significant number of states a commitment to recognise the Nansen passport, and ultimately an agreement from at least some states to allow a return visa to be attached to the Nansen passport too. What Nansen did not do, however, was develop an elaborate bureaucratic structure for the provision of assistance to refugees; he was an extraordinarily dynamic individual who achieved remarkable things, but he left a huge gap when he died in 1930. The League of Nations sought to fill that gap by establishing the Nansen International Office for Refugees.

The need for ongoing multilateral mechanisms for addressing refugee problems was about to be exposed in a horrifying fashion by the treatment of Jews in Germany following the rise of Hitler and the Nazis in 1933. This quintessential case of fascism in power supplies an awful warning of how dreadful can be the consequences of inadequate responses to refugee challenges as they emerge. Hitler had never made any secret of his obsessive hatred of Jews, and anti-Semitism figured in the Nazi party platform from 1920 onwards.[52] This was to culminate in the Wannsee conference of January 1942 at which the Holocaust was planned from a logistical point of view. The operation of death camps such as Auschwitz saw millions of Jews murdered.[53] But long before Wannsee, Jews had suffered in all sorts of ways under Nazi domination. The 1935 Nuremberg laws provided a vestige of 'legality' for what was being done, although the rule of law as a constraint on the power of the state and its minions had broken down long before they were promulgated. Brown-shirted 'storm troopers' in the so-called Sturmabteilung (SA), a Nazi paramilitary, were able to beat up Jews with total impunity, and played a major role in the 9–10 November 1938 pogrom known as *Kristallnacht* (from the shattered window glass lying in the street after attacks on shops owned by Jews). Unsurprisingly, exit was a very attractive option for German Jews who could manage it, and some 400,000 did so between Hitler's coming to power and the outbreak of the Second World War; according to statistics provided by Skran, some 144,000 moved to other European states, 90,000 to Palestine, 100,000 to the US, and 66,000 to other countries.[54] Most emigrated through official channels, although their savings were taxed at a punitive rate. A mark of the cynicism of the Nazi authorities was a January 1939 circular that argued in favour of emigration of poorer Jews as that 'would increase antisemitism in the western countries, in which Jews have found refuge ... It is emphasized that it is in the German interest to pursue the Jews as beggars over the borders, for the poorer the immigrant, the greater the burden on the receiving country'.[55]

Confronted with the mounting flow of refugees after Hitler became Chancellor of Germany, the League of Nations sought a dynamic individual of Nansen's ilk to address the problem. A courageous American, James G. McDonald, accepted an appointment as High Commissioner for Refugees Coming from Germany, serving from October 1933 until his resignation in December 1935. He arrived quickly at the conclusion that the refugee problem demanded a political response, and that 'quiet diplomacy' would not work. This was eventually reflected in his resignation letter, in which he wrote that when 'domestic politics threaten the demoralization and exile of hundreds of thousands of human beings, considerations of diplomatic correctness must yield to those of common humanity'.[56] His letter, however, had little impact on the position of the League and its key members, and as Skran put it, 'McDonald has the distinction of being the only refugee administrator in the Interwar Period to publicly criticize the German government for its treatment of Jews and other "non-Aryans", and to call for international intervention to deal with the root causes of the refugee exodus'.[57] His successors, Sir Neill Malcolm and Sir Herbert Emerson, showed little interest in the root causes of outflows from Germany, and in a way this was understandable given the politics of the time. The United States was not a member of the League of Nations, and within America there were strongly isolationist tendencies that President Franklin D. Roosevelt had to handle with some care. Furthermore, the British Government, under Prime Ministers Stanley Baldwin (1935–1937) and Neville Chamberlain (1937–1940), was not eager to challenge Germany. Chamberlain, indeed, pursued a policy of appeasement of Germany until the German occupation of Prague in March 1939 that exposed the fatal flaws of his approach. This unhappy period of British and European history, punctuated by the German reoccupation of the Rhineland in 1936, the incorporation (*Anschluss*) of Austria into Germany, and the notorious Munich conference in 1938, was one of the least propitious for those seeking to protect refugees.[58]

In an attempt at circuit-breaking, President Roosevelt took the lead in convoking the July 1938 Evian Conference on refugees from Germany, at which some thirty-two states were represented. Golda Meir, later to serve as Prime Minister of Israel from 1969 to 1974, was an observer, but was not permitted to speak. Even the kindest commentator would not have described it as a success, and a recent critic concluded that it 'was widely regarded as a fiasco'.[59] The only state that offered a significant number of resettlement places was the Dominican Republic, and the interventions from some states were deeply chilling: T.W. White, the Australian Minister for Trade and Customs, stated that 'as we have no real racial problem, we are not desirous of importing one'.[60]

It is easy to forget just how pervasive were sweeping anti-Semitic attitudes in Western countries in the 1930s, rather along the lines of the sweeping anti-Muslim rhetoric that one encounters in parts of present-day Europe and America.[61] The majority of those who perished in the Holocaust were not German Jews who could have been rescued in the 1930s, but Eastern European Jews, especially from Poland, who fell within the Nazi net only after the outbreak of the Second World War. Nonetheless, with more concerted efforts, more Jews could have been saved before the war broke out, and the failure to provide them with assistance when they needed it remains a dark stain on the history of the 1930s. On 19 August 1938, a British Magistrate, one Herbert Metcalfe, complained that 'The way stateless Jews from Germany are pouring in from every port of this country is becoming an outrage. I intend to enforce the law to its fullest'.[62] Metcalfe later denied that he was anti-Semitic, and claimed that his remarks had been directed against 'aliens'. Had he not specifically mentioned Jews, his denial might have been more credible. His casual attitude helps us understand why less was done to help refugees from Germany than could have been done,[63] and serves as a grim reminder that there can be issues more morally significant than the minutiae of immigration regulations and processes. The British government also resisted efforts by Jewish refugees to reach Palestine,[64] and even the outbreak of war did not soften the bureaucratic approach. In 1942, the British refused permission for the *Struma*, a vessel that had sailed from Romania with over 790 Jews on board, to proceed to Palestine from neutral Turkey. On 24 February 1942, it was torpedoed by a Soviet submarine. Only one of the passengers, David Stoliar, survived.[65] As late as 1944, a Foreign Office official could write 'In my opinion a disproportionate amount of time at the Office is wasted on dealing with these wailing Jews'.[66]

Postwar refugee resettlement

The scale of human displacement as a result of the Second World War was vast, but its exact scale will probably never be known; one estimate puts it at a staggering 40 million people.[67] A great deal of the displacement was internal, especially in the Soviet Union, and was managed by the Soviet authorities without external involvement. The Soviet authorities during the war also deported entire 'nationalities' about whose loyalty they were suspicious, and it was only during the 1950s that the opportunity arose for them to return to their ancestral lands.[68] One such group was the Chechens, and the experience left a legacy of bitterness that helps explain why Chechnya was to prove such a thorn in the side of the Russians after 1991.[69] What was striking, however, about the phenomenon of human displacement as a result of the Second World War was that despite its scale, it proved quite within the capacity of the wider world to respond with resettlement solutions, although it took some time to do so. One of the reasons was that the International Refugee Organization, discussed in Chapter Two, proved to be an effective instrument for the management of resettlement for those in greatest need. Another was that a range of states were prepared to step up to assist, giving rise to a genuine exercise in 'burden sharing'. The result was that the war did not leave a dangerous legacy in the form of warehoused refugees; instead, refugees were for the most part able to put down new roots in the countries to which they had relocated. They could move on.

This stood somewhat in contrast to another major example in the post-war period of forced population movement, namely that associated with the partition of the Indian subcontinent in 1947 into the states of India and Pakistan. For very large numbers of ordinary people, this proved to be a catastrophic experience. As one study has put it, 'Partition was accompanied by the largest uprooting of people in the twentieth century'.[70] According to Gatrell, 'around 7.5 million Hindus and Sikhs and 6 million Muslims crossed the newly created borders of India and Pakistan between 1947 and 1951'.[71] Figures cited for the scale of mortality range from 200,000 to 2 million, with very little specific evidence available to distinguish between the two,[72] but as Talbot and Singh remark, 'Whatever the numbers, immense human suffering occurred in a peacetime situation in which governments demonstrated a lamentable inability to provide basic security for minority communities'.[73] With time, those who were displaced were able to resettle physically in the newly-formed countries to which they had moved, but the material and psychological consequences of partition should not be underestimated. Many of those who were displaced lost all their assets, and the memory of partition, compounded by the more recent experience of Pakistan's loss of East Pakistan when Bangladesh emerged as a state in 1971, continues to contribute to the deep hostility that divides India and Pakistan to this day. It also remains a source of pain for many individual Indians and Pakistanis.

The legacy of another major postwar movement also continues to be felt, namely that of Indochinese refugees who fled from South Vietnam and Cambodia after communist takeovers of those countries in April 1975. The fall of the Cambodian capital Phnom Penh in early April 1975 led to the emergence of the genocidal ultra-leftist Khmer Rouge regime, which by the time it was overthrown by the Vietnamese invasion of Cambodia in December 1978 had presided over the deaths of several million Cambodians.[74] The Khmer Rouge regime shut off Cambodia from the outside world, but with its overthrow, large numbers of Cambodians—ultimately close to 1 million—seized the opportunity to flee to neighbouring Thailand, where a humanitarian crisis rapidly took shape.[75] Clustered near the town of Aranyaprathet, the Cambodian refugees found themselves pawns in a geopolitical struggle that pitted Thailand and other ASEAN states, backed by the USA, against communist Vietnam. What facilitated this was that one portion of the refugee population was made up of former Khmer Rouge cadres and their families,[76] who not only were committed to resisting the Vietnamese-backed regime, but also very often intimidated those refugees who were not Khmer Rouge supporters. Some refugees from Cambodia made their way to other countries, but the refugee problem on the Thai-Cambodian border persisted through the 1980s, and was resolved only when repatriation proved possible following the signing of the December 1991 Paris Accords on Cambodia, which came about as part of the wider post-Cold War disposition to seek negotiated settlements for 'regional problems'.[77]

The end of the Vietnam War that came with the fall of Saigon in April 1975 was also to be the genesis of significant refugee outflows. A searing episode in US foreign involvement, Vietnam highlighted the perils for any great power trying to manage a complex world with blunt instruments.[78] A stark assessment of the consequences of the war's ending as it did was given by Henry Kissinger, US Secretary of State at the time: 'Hundreds of thousands of South Vietnamese, including all those who had been in the government or armed forces, were herded into so-called reeducation camps—a euphemism for concentration camps—where they stayed for the better part of a decade. Tens of thousands fled as boat people'.[79] By the end of 1986, some 1.1 million had left.[80] Many were not welcomed in the region: in 1978–79, Malaysia 'put its "push-off" policy into full effect, rejecting more than 50,000 Vietnamese who attempted to land, and threatening to send away 70,000 more who were already in camps'.[81] Faced with this, in 1979 key states adopted a 'burden sharing' approach at a meeting in Geneva.[82] As Suhrke put it, 'One major actor, the United States, was moved by humanitarian and political reasons to put pressure on other states, set the rules for collective action, and took its own "fair share"'.[83] However, even the robust commitment from Washington could not sustain the approach, and in 1989 it was succeeded by the so-called Comprehensive Plan of Action, pursuant to which Vietnamese asylum seekers would receive temporary protection in the countries in which they initially arrived, with a commitment from traditional resettlement states to take those found to be refugees under the 1951 *Convention*. This was premised, however, on the need to return to Vietnam those who were not found to be refugees in a process of individual status determination. Some questions arose about the quality of status determination procedures,[84] but approximately 80,000 refugees were resettled in this way. What had led the 1979 approach to unravel was that it offered a rare example of a situation where 'pull factors' genuinely came into play: 'the generous assistance and preferential treatment for Indo-Chinese refugees had a magnet effect, attracting large numbers of people out of the embattled and impoverished countries of Indo-China'.[85]

As time has passed, the role of UNHCR in fostering resettlement of refugees has only increased, and resettlement is now one of three 'durable solutions' to refugee problems that UNHCR routinely identifies. The first is voluntary repatriation of refugees in conditions of safety and security. For many refugees, this is the principal solution in which they are interested, since it avoids some of the dislocation of communities and personal costs associated with relocating to another and unfamiliar country. Voluntary repatriation can be managed by states or international organisations, but it can also occur spontaneously, as a reflection of refugees' own perceptions of the situations evolving in their countries of origin. For example, the collapse of the Communist regime in

Afghanistan in April 1992 triggered the largest and fastest repatriation of refugees in UNHCR's history, and it was essentially spontaneous in character: by the end of 1992, fully 1.4 million Afghans had repatriated during the course of the year.[86] Unfortunately, in many cases voluntary repatriation in safety and security is not remotely feasible for a refugee population, and may be exceedingly unlikely for the foreseeable future. Through bitter experience, Western governments have learned in recent decades that when states have been severely disrupted, there is no easy route back to stability: countries such as Somalia and Iraq provide distressing examples to this effect. In those circumstances, either integration in a country of first asylum or resettlement to a third country provide alternative options. But that said, countries of first asylum are often wary of offering integration opportunities to refugees on their soil. Doing so might seem to foreclose the possibility of voluntary repatriation of those refugees at some point in the future, and in addition, countries of first asylum are themselves often relatively poor states with significant problems of their own to manage, and limited capacity to respect in a meaningful way the rights of refugees set out in the 1951 *Convention*. Furthermore, if their political systems are only weakly institutionalised, they may fear the impact of a large refugee population on their own political life; this was one reason why the Hashemite Jordanian regime of King Hussein struck against Palestinian groups in 1970, an episode that came to be immortalised with the label 'Black September'.

Yet postwar experience shows that while populations for whom resettlement countries feel some kind of moral responsibility, such as displaced persons in Europe or Indochinese refugees, can be easily resettled, others are much less welcomed.[87] In a dramatic demonstration of this point, in 1984 the Executive Committee of UNHCR labelled third country resettlement the 'least desirable and most costly solution'.[88] The danger, however, of shying away from third country resettlement is that the phenomenon of 'refugee warehousing' may surface. This term refers to the existence of protracted refugee situations where several generations can find themselves trapped in an environment where their basic needs might (just) be met, but where there is little in the way of a meaningful future, and refugees themselves are at the mercy of powers and forces almost entirely beyond their control, even if the situations have their own dynamics and change over time.[89] Populations of this sort that come to mind include refugees from Somalia, Sudan, Burma, Afghanistan and Bhutan. Some 'warehoused' refugees may live in camps, but others may eke out a meagre existence in urban areas. (It is a misconception that all refugees are to be found in camps; in Turkey, for example, the vast majority of Syrian refugees do not live in camps.) The political risk that can arise in such situations is that if a sense of hopelessness and despair becomes pervasive within the refugee population, younger people in particular may be susceptible to recruitment by radical forces that offer violence as a solution to the problems that the refugee experience has thrown up. Perhaps the classic example of this problem was the emergence of the Taliban from 1994. Contrary to what is sometimes asserted, the Taliban were not a reflection of Afghan traditional society (and some were not even Afghan, but Pakistanis, or radicals from other parts of the world). Drawn from orphanages in refugee camps, the Afghans in the Taliban movement were a prime example of the breakdown of traditional mechanisms of socialisation. Most of them had never known anything remotely like typical village life in Afghanistan; instead, they were the product of religious training colleges (*madrasas*) in Pakistan that preached an idiosyncratic version of the Deobandi school of Islam that had its origins in India in the second half of the nineteenth century.[90] Those tempted to respond to current refugee movements into Europe with the suggestion that refugees should be warehoused in countries such as Turkey would do well to reflect on whether this could be a recipe for the development of a political Vesuvius. This is especially a problem if preference in third-country resettlement is then given to families at the expense of singles: a warehoused refugee population without family ties would likely strike recruiters for radical movements as a particularly inviting target.

Internal conflict and refugee movements in the late twentieth and early twenty-first centuries

In recent times, internal or transnational conflicts have left significant legacies in the form of substantial refugee populations. These lie at the heart of the challenges that European states currently confront. To show why these problems are not about to disappear, it is useful to look at the genesis of some of these specific refugee flows.

For the last two decades of the twentieth century, the largest single population of refugees in the world consisted of Afghans who had left their country following the communist coup in Afghanistan of April 1978, and the Soviet invasion of Afghanistan in December 1979.[91] Assessing the exact number of refugees was virtually impossible, since some went unregistered, while others were registered twice.[92] UNHCR's estimate is that there were some 600,000 Afghan refugees in Pakistan and Iran by the end of 1979; that within a year this figure had risen to 1.9 million; and that by 1 January 1990 the number was 6.2 million, with a real possibility that it was even higher.[93] Pakistan at the beginning of 1990 was estimated to house 3.272 million of these refugees. Pakistan was not a party to the 1951 *Convention* but on the whole proved a generous host in terms of the provision of shelter and food, although achievements in the area of education for refugees were much less impressive,[94] highlighting some of the problems of warehousing noted earlier. The 'Refugee Tented Villages' which were set up to accommodate the refugees rapidly develop their own political lives, with traditional leaders and Afghan political parties vying for influence.[95] Pakistan as host-country also had its own political agendas where the refugees were concerned. In 1947 when the subcontinent was partitioned, Afghanistan was the only country to vote against the admission of Pakistan to the United Nations. This reflected dissatisfaction in Kabul that ethnic Pushtuns in the North West Frontier of India had only been given the option of joining either India or Pakistan and not of reuniting with their ethnic kin in Afghanistan from whom they had been separated by the drawing of the so-called 'Durand Line' in 1893.[96] A consequence was that from 1947 until around 1978, relations between Muslim-majority Afghanistan and Muslim-majority Pakistan were for the most part quite tense, while Afghanistan enjoyed cordial relations with Hindu-majority India. When Pakistan became a host for large numbers of Afghan refugees, it was determined that Afghan nationalism of the kind that had underpinned the tense relations of the past would not be encouraged to flourish on Pakistani soil. Instead, Pakistan's Inter-Services Intelligence Directorate (ISI) openly favoured Islamist political parties in the Afghan resistance to the Soviet invasion—parties such as the Hezb-e Islami of Gulbuddin Hekmaytar—in the belief that they would be less likely in the future to be animated by an ethnic and territorial issue.[97]

As noted earlier, there was a vast spontaneous repatriation of Afghan refugees in 1992 following the collapse of the communist regime in Kabul. This did not, however, put an end to the Afghan refugee problem.[98] Pakistan, finding that the Hezb-e Islami was unpopular and unable to secure and hold territory, found a new surrogate in the Taliban movement, described by Pakistan's Interior Minister as 'our boys'.[99] With Pakistani help, the Taliban took over Kandahar in 1994, Herat in 1995, and finally Kabul in 1996, but their pathogenic eccentricities ensured that they received neither strong normative support in Afghanistan nor international recognition, and their regime was overthrown with relative ease by the US following the September 2001 terrorist attacks. Many Afghans had fled the Taliban's repressive regime, and many returned to Afghanistan after 2001, but vulnerable minorities resumed their flight as the Taliban reappeared in rural Afghanistan from around 2003–2004. As of mid-2015, UNHCR estimated that Pakistan continued to host 1.5 million Afghan refugees, and Iran a further 951,000.[100]

During the 1990s, European countries were much more transfixed by the Balkans than Southwest Asia, let alone 'remote' areas such as the Great Lakes region of Africa. The immediate cause of refugee movements was fallout from the disintegration of Yugoslavia, a state which itself had been established in 1919 in the wake of the breakup of the Austro-Hungarian Empire. Initially a patchwork monarchy (known until 1929 as the 'Kingdom of Serbs, Croats, and Slovenes'), after the Second World War and the triumph of Marshal Tito's partisans, it became a communist state, albeit of a more independent character than the core Eastern Bloc states within the Soviet sphere.[101] When Tito died in 1980, the tensions between the different communities in Yugoslavia began to surface, and they became much more acute at the end of the 1980s when the Serbian leader, Slobodan Milošević, resorted to nationalism as a substitute ideology for Marxism, which had taken a fearful battering following the ascent to power in the USSR of Mikhail Gorbachev. The disintegration of Yugoslavia was an ugly spectacle. While clear boundaries had been drawn between 'republics' and 'autonomous regions' within the Yugoslav federal system, within these different units there were often mixed populations, with quite a lot of intermarriage. The Republic of Bosnia and Herzegovina, admitted to UN membership in 1992, was particularly vulnerable because its population contained Bosnjak Muslims, Croats, and a well-organised Serb minority seeking to carve out space for itself. The country was wracked by brutal conflict,[102] which a UN Protection Force (UNPROFOR) proved unable to halt,[103] and it was only when the hideous July 1995 Srebrenica massacre led to NATO's 'Operation Deliberate Force' that the Serbs were brought to the negotiating table and the December 1995 Elysée Treaty provided a modicum of stability. Internal displacement was on a grand scale, and huge numbers of refugees fled to neighbouring European countries. When the Elysée Treaty was signed, there were between 900,000 and 1.2 million Bosnian refugees in different parts of the world.[104] By mid-1997, solutions had been found for about one third of them, with Germany, hosting 315,000, the main country of refugee outside Bosnia's immediate neighbourhood. More have returned since, and fewer than 20,000 refugees now remain.[105] But with all the turmoil wrought by war, the very notion of 'going home' is a complex one for former refugees,[106] and major issues from the time of war, especially relating to transitional justice, have remained largely unaddressed.[107]

This is even more the case with the comparatively recent experiences of refugees from Iraq and Libya. More than a decade has passed since the disastrous US invasion of Iraq in March 2003, but the burdens of this enterprise continue to shape both the politics of the Middle East, and the lives of large numbers of Iraqis who found themselves caught up in turmoil and disarray as Washington discovered that military intervention is a singularly blunt instrument for finessing political engineering in the aftermath of the displacement of a long-standing dictatorship.[108] Some 377,700 Iraqi refugees are currently the focus of UNHCR's attention.[109] The Libyan case is in some respects just as daunting. While the Libyan revolution that overthrew Colonel Muammar al-Gaddafi in 2011 had internal roots, wider events in the Arab world, especially Tunisia and Egypt, served as triggers, and international involvement came when the new 'Responsibility to Protect' doctrine, discussed in more detail in Chapter Seven, was invoked by the UN Security Council in Resolution 1973 of 17 March 2011 to authorise states to take 'all necessary measures' to protect civilians.[110] The outcome has not been a happy one. Internally, Libya remains deeply divided; regionally, developments in Libya catalysed a major crisis in neighbouring Mali, culminating in a French intervention;[111] and people have been displaced in large numbers.[112] Flight to safe neighbouring countries is difficult; only 9536 refugees and asylum seekers from Libya were recorded in mid-2015. Internal displacement, however, accounted for 434,869 Libyans.[113]

While the Iraq conflict and the Libyan revolution undoubtedly contributed to the general political climate in which the Syrian civil war broke out, in its scale the Syrian refugee crisis dwarfs any other in the contemporary world. As of mid-2015, UNHCR was assisting 4,023,972 Syrian refugees, and a further 7,632,500 Syrians were internally displaced.[114] The implications for Syria's neighbours are of course enormous. Turkey found itself hosting 1,838,848 refugees; Lebanon 1,172,388; and Jordan 664,102.[115] Given the ferocity of the antagonisms that divide the different parties in the Syrian conflict, as well as the well-documented and large-scale atrocities that have punctuated its course, it is exceedingly difficult to envisage a negotiated settlement in the foreseeable future. Beyond this lie further questions. How could Syria be reconstructed to the point where life for returnees would be livable? Can cruelly-damaged people realistically be expected to make new lives in the very places where their old lives were ruined? Some may be prepared to do so, but for others it would be psychologically catastrophic even to make the attempt. And what are the implications for refugees of the substantial presence in much of Syria's territory of the fanatical 'Islamic State' movement? There are no obvious answers to these questions, but that in itself suggests that the Syrian refugee crisis is likely to be with us all for a very considerable period of time.

The figures that UNHCR has produced on displacement from and within Syria help put into context the apprehension in Europe about refugee movements during the course of 2015. The vast majority of refugees from Syria and Afghanistan, the two main source countries of the 2015 flows, are being housed not by European countries, but by Turkey, Lebanon, Jordan, Pakistan, and Iran. In mid-2015, UNHCR estimated that there were 14,441,674 refugees worldwide in the legal sense of the term; of these, 1,625,002, or 11.3 per cent, were located in Europe. By contrast 7,853,396 were in Asia and 4,419,845 in Africa.[116] When one includes internally displaced persons and others of concern to UNHCR, the figures are even more striking. Of 57,959,702 in total, Europe houses 4,673,766, or 8.1 per cent, whereas Asia houses 28,420,724 and Africa 17,067,308.[117]

Europe, in other words, is not the centre-stage of a global refugee crisis. The number of refugees who arrived in Europe in 2015 was the equivalent of less than *five days* of growth in world population.[118] Regionally, it is Africa and Asia that are most affected. States such as Lebanon and Jordan, with smaller populations and lower per capita incomes than most major European powers, have much stronger bases for fearing how they might be affected by refugee flows, but this has neither made them noisy complainants about refugees, nor led them, until recently, to close their doors to people in desperate need. Indeed, one of the reasons that refugees have been moving on from these countries is not hostility from the locals, but rather that a lack of adequate funding for UNHCR from wealthy countries has meant that surviving in refugee camps, even with UNHCR assistance, is becoming more and more difficult. The outgoing UN High Commissioner for Refugees, António Guterres, made this point forcefully in 2015:

Mr Guterres said the reasons for the massive movement are easy to find in the teeming refugee camps of Turkey and Jordan. More than 80 per cent of families there are below the local poverty line, and only half of the children are in school. The U.N. refugee agency is able to help only about 20 per cent of families in the Jordanian camps—and they receive only $1 per person per day. In September, the World Food Program was forced to drop 229,000 Syrian refugees from its voucher program in Jordan, continuing a series of cuts that Mr. Guterres said provided a trigger for the mass movement toward Europe.[119]

This is not to say that there is not a crisis in Europe over refugees. It is, however, a multidimensional political crisis.[120] It is in some states mainly a domestic problem, with governing parties fearing that they might lose votes to populists on the far right of the political spectrum. For Europe in a corporate sense, it is an intramural crisis in so far as powerful temptations for some states to be 'free riders', always a danger when one is faced with collective action problems,[121] threaten the notion of a cohesive and co-operative Europe. Most fundamentally, however, it is a crisis of the Westphalian order, and it is to the relationship between the system of states and the phenomenon of the refugee that I turn in the next chapter.

4

STATES AND REFUGEES

Without states, refugees as we broadly understand the term would not exist. In a very thoughtful study, Emma Haddad argues that refugees 'are not the consequence of a breakdown in the system of separate states, rather they are an inevitable if unanticipated part of international society. As long as there are political borders constructing separate states and creating clear definitions of insiders and outsiders, there will be refugees'.[1] While one can argue in parallel that refugees reflect imperfections in the operation of a system of assigned responsibility, Haddad's argument has great force, and a number of important implications. One is that the problem of refugees, as so often in the world of politics,[2] is one to be managed rather than solved. While 'durable solutions' may be achieved for specific groups of refugees, the issue as a whole is intimately bound up with the character of the international system more broadly. Another is that to understand some of the difficulties that refugees face in the course of their journeys, it is necessary to identify rather specifically some of the features that have been associated with 'sovereign states' of the broadly Westphalian variety. As we shall see, much of the suffering of refugees is a product, and a fairly direct one, of attempts by states and bureaucracies to control the lives of vulnerable people who have no reason to think that states and bureaucracies have their interests at heart. This ineluctable tension plays out in many different ways, some of which are explored in more detail in this chapter. Its unhappy message is that when one is in grave danger, it is perilous to rely for rescue on states and bureaucracies, and individual initiative may be the better path to take.

The Westphalian system

On 23 May 1618, in an event that came to be known as the 'Defenestration of Prague', two eminent Bohemians who served the ruling Catholic Habsburg dynasty, Jaroslav Borita von Martinitz and Vilém Slavata, were flung by Protestant conspirators from a window of the Hradčany castle, followed moments later by Slavata's secretary, Philipp Fabricius.[3] All survived, and Fabricius carried news of the affront to Vienna, where steps to put down the Bohemian revolt were initiated. Thus began the Thirty Years War, the most destructive conflict that Europe had experienced up to that point. It was a complex conflict, one reason why it lasted so long. The Peace of Westphalia that terminated it was undoubtedly a fundamental development in the history of Europe. It put an end to the idea of a united Christendom. One who realised this immediately was Pope Innocent X, who in an adjectival outburst rarely matched anytime since, described it as 'null, void, invalid, iniquitous, unjust, damnable, reprobate, inane, and devoid of meaning for all time'.[4]

Yet the Peace of Westphalia was important not so much because of what it said, but because of what it presaged. The Treaties of Münster and Osnabrück on literal reading do not offer explications of sovereignty, and as one scholar has pointed out, in the Latin language in which they were written there was no specific equivalent of the word sovereignty.[5] Yet they did import a focus on territoriality, challenging fundamentally what has been called 'the preexisting nonterritorial, heteronomous system of rule'.[6] And as time went by, older ideas of sovereignty, which in the writings of essayists such as Jean Bodin were firmly absolutist in content,[7] came to be replaced by more nuanced ideas which reflected different usages of the term surfacing in both philosophical works and evolving political rhetorics and discourses.[8]

One of the most influential modern attempts to flesh out the complexities of the idea of sovereignty has been undertaken by Stephen D. Krasner:[9]

> The term sovereignty has been used in four different ways—international legal sovereignty, Westphalian sovereignty, domestic sovereignty, and interdependence sovereignty. International legal sovereignty refers to the practices associated with mutual recognition, usually between territorial entities that have formal juridical independence. Westphalian sovereignty refers to political organization based on the exclusion of external actors from authority structures within a given territory. Domestic sovereignty refers to the formal organization of political authority within the state and the ability of public authorities to exercise effective control within the borders of their own polity. Finally, interdependence sovereignty refers to the ability of public authorities to regulate the flow of information, ideas, goods, people, pollutants, or capital across the borders of their state.

The vital point to note here is that Krasner neither argues that all these usages crystallised at the same time, nor suggests that they necessarily developed hand-in-hand, although some are obviously related to others. The reason this is so important is that harsh policies towards refugees are frequently underpinned by references to control of borders as central to sovereignty. But Krasner's account suggests that this is far from being the case. Not only are there other dimensions of sovereignty of very considerable historical significance, but, as we are about to see, borders except as formalistic markers of jurisdiction typically did not register prominently in the thinking of Princes, not least because until the advent of modern systems of regulatory bureaucracy, rigorous border control was simply beyond the capacity of rulers.

The Peace of Westphalia was a settlement about borders, not about border control. That came much later. As one scholar put it, it was 'only in the twentieth century that the full consolidation of the Westphalian culture of border control occurred'.[10] Under the Treaty of Münster, subjects were actually guaranteed a right to emigrate, a continuation of the *jus emigrandi* recognised in the 1555 Peace of Augsburg.[11] This was not automatically matched by a right of entry, but in the Europe of that time, entry was not easily denied. In order to run a system of border control, it is necessary at the very least to have a system of physical monitoring at the frontiers of a country to regulate population movement, and it is also necessary to have a system of documentation of subjects so that those who are involved in physical monitoring can distinguish those who are subjects from those who are not, by reference to some authoritative identifier. Even in the twenty-first century, complex issues relating to documentation continue to arise with great frequency.[12] Indeed, the obsession with documentation in Western states has frequently led to document fraud, poignantly depicted in the forged papers of the actress Anna Schmidt, played by Alida Valli in Carol Reed's brilliant 1949 film *The Third Man*. In earlier centuries, challenges of documentation were overwhelming. It was for this reason that the modern passport emerged as a tool for identifying subjects and facilitating their being controlled. And it, in turn, was a creature of the development of the modern bureaucratic state.

As was noted in the previous chapter, Charles Tilly's work highlighted the role of violence in state formation. The consolidation of the state, however, depended upon a range of further developments. One was the formulation of ideas about what a consolidated state might attempt to do. There was of course no one set of ideas, since the roles of the state are a central focus of debate in political theory, and differences of opinion over the appropriate scope and strength of the state can be quite fiery.[13] Nonetheless, at an abstract level one can identify certain functions that distinguish the state from other power-holders; in the words of Joel S. Migdal, these include 'the capacities to *penetrate* society, *regulate* social relationships, *extract* resources, and *appropriate* or use resources in determined ways'.[14] Discharging these functions requires achievement on two specific fronts. First, a state must secure a stream of fungible revenue that allows it to engage in complex budgeting and prioritisation of state activities. This is only possible once the state moves from 'in kind' to 'in cash' taxation. Second, a state must develop a set of administrative agencies that are able to undertake complex tasks. The development of modern states with secure revenue streams and effective agencies for policy implementation for the most part came well after the Peace of Westphalia, although Westphalia played an important role in triggering the process.[15] Even in major powers in Western Europe, some of the key developments did not materialise until the late eighteenth or nineteenth centuries,[16] and modern bureaucracies of the kind theorised by the German sociologist Max Weber,[17] based on formal hierarchy, precise role definition, and skilled professional recruitment, were relatively late arrivals on the scene.

It is therefore unsurprising that modern passports were also relatively late arrivals on the scene. According to Torpey, the passport 'arose out of the relatively inchoate international system that existed during the nineteenth century'.[18] Where refugees were concerned, however, the problem they faced was not so much the emergence of the passport (although some refugees can find it very difficult to obtain one), but the complementary expansion of the system of visas, that is, state-issued permits for entry to a country that a traveller was required to carry over and above a passport. These were used in the 1930s to block movement by Jewish refugees who possessed passports; the Swiss government responded to the 1938 *Anschluss* of Germany and Austria by imposing visa requirements on Austrian passport holders.[19] More broadly, the visa system served at the time to affirm a distinction between more and less 'civilised' states,[20] a distinction that has now been formally expunged by the UN Charter's affirmation of the sovereign equality of states and practically by processes of decolonisation—although it arguably retains some traction even to the present, at least at the level of popular opinion.

The requirement for visas allows the selective exclusion from authorised or approved routes of migration of those whom states would prefer not to have to accommodate. Unfortunately, potential refugees tend to be right at the top of the list. The twenty-first century has witnessed the systematic closure of 'legal' routes of egress for the poor, the vulnerable, and victims of persecution. Technologies of control have expanded the capacity of agents of rich states to engage in exclusion. One example of this is the phenomenon of carrier sanctions, where airlines can face penalties if they allow a person to board a flight when that person has not been electronically cleared in advance by agencies of the country into which he or she wishes to fly. Another is the Australian practice from 2013 of using vessels of the Royal Australian Navy to turn boats back to Indonesia without the passengers having had any opportunity to raise an asylum claim. Another is simply not to locate diplomatic or consular posts where visas could be lodged in countries where persecution is rife and the number of applications would likely be large. As James C. Hathaway has put it, 'Most refugees today cannot travel to the developed world to seek recognition of their international legal right to protection'.[21] To this one might add that states often have no qualms about treating even the neediest refugees as deviant or criminal if they have sought to circumvent such systems of regulation. In Matthew J. Gibney's words, 'We have reached the *reductio ad absurdum* of the contemporary paradoxical attitude towards refugees. Western states now acknowledge the rights of refugees but simultaneously criminalize the search for asylum'.[22] In a globalising world, control measures directed against the acutely vulnerable can seem almost like sovereignty's last gasp.[23]

The human consequences of this web of controls can be deeply disturbing. The recent experience of a young married couple in Afghanistan from different ethnic backgrounds, faced with the very real threat of a so-called 'honour killing', helps highlight the nature of the problem. Wary after Alan Kurdi's death of using the services of a people smuggler, they nonetheless found themselves unable within Afghanistan to find any 'legal' route of escape.[24] The surreal dimension of this kind of situation was brought out by another case around the same time. Hassina Sarwari, a rights activist from Kunduz, faced extremely serious Taliban threats. As correspondent Rod Nordland put it, she 'would like to leave Afghanistan, but has not received a visa despite her pleas to officials at the American and German Embassies in Kabul. Instead, she received the unofficial advice to flee like everyone else, and then apply'.[25] Such Kafkaesque situations seem to arise with distressing frequency in the everyday lives of refugees.

Bureaucracy and its failings

Broad policy settings in many countries will be determined by politicians who occupy the top positions of executive government, but where refugees are concerned, their day-to-day practical experiences involve little interaction with actors at this level. States are typically stratified and networked in complex ways, and Migdal has identified four distinctive elements. First are the trenches, consisting of 'the officials who must execute state directives directly in the face of possibly strong societal resistance'. Second are the dispersed field offices, that is, the 'regional and local bodies that rework and organize state policies and directives for local consumption, or even formulate and implement wholly local policies'. Third are the agency's central offices, the 'nerve centers where national policies are formulated and enacted and where resources for implementation are marshaled.' Fourth are the commanding heights, the 'pinnacle of the state' where the 'top executive leadership' is to be found'.[26] It is those who occupy the trenches and possibly the dispersed field offices that refugees are most likely to encounter, and they may well also find themselves encountering certain pathologies of bureaucracy at these levels, often originating from an agency's central offices, that may make life for them very uncomfortable.

Max Weber, in his writings about bureaucracy, stressed its intimate involvement with rationality,[27] and much subsequent organisational theory has focused on ways in which particular patterns of administrative organisation can allow large-scale and complex tasks to be carried out in a timely manner and at much lower cost than might otherwise have been the case.[28] Yet at the same time, there has also been a recognition that bureaucracies themselves are highly political spaces, venues for competition as well as cooperation, where political goals may be achieved or frustrated, and political careers made or broken. Bureaucratic actors may have objectives of their own, and agencies may have interests to pursue or protect.[29] In addition, as one eminent observer put it, the 'conditions in which administrators are expected to implement policy'—including incomplete specification of ostensible policy, conflicting criteria for application, incentive failures, conflicting directives, limited competence, and inadequate administrative resources—'compel them to join in the policy making process'.[30] Exactly how this plays out will crucially depend on the bureaucratic cultures that exists in particular agencies. This also shapes refugees' experiences. In a justly famous study, Tom Burns and G.M. Stalker distinguished between 'mechanistic' and 'organic' approaches to organisation,[31] with the former based on rigid fidelity to procedure and predesignated spheres of responsibility, and the latter based on goal achievement and creative problem solving. Immigration bureaucracies tend to be highly mechanistic in their operations, while what refugees typically need is organic approaches to address their problems.

Two historical cases, one quite famous and the other much less well known, show how dangerous the phenomenon of bureaucratic rigidity can be. The first involved a merchant vessel, the M.S. *St Louis*, which sailed from Hamburg for Havana on 13 May 1939 with over 900 Jewish refugees on board. With *Kristallnacht* a recent memory, the passengers had every reason to wish to escape from the reach of the Third Reich before it was too late. The US, however, had a strict set of immigration quotas, embodied in the Immigration Act of 1924 (the 'Johnson-Reed Act'). Unable to disembark most of his passengers in Havana, Captain Gustav Schröder headed for Miami, but there he encountered the barrier of the quota system. On 4 June, an official of the US State Department stated that 'The German refugees ... must await their turn ... before they may be admissible to the United States'.[32] Reluctantly, for he at least understood the danger his passengers faced, Captain Schröder headed back to Europe. Over a quarter of those who were returned, to the Netherlands, Belgium and France, were subsequently murdered in the Holocaust. Not surprisingly, this tragic episode earned the sobriquet of the 'Voyage of the Damned'. Captain Schröder was subsequently honoured with the title 'Righteous Among the Nations' by the Yad Vashem World Center for Holocaust Research, Education, Documentation and Commemoration. At the heart of the *St Louis* tragedy was a lack of political will: as one recent commentator has put it, President Roosevelt 'was unwilling to confront xenophobic public opinion, a vaguely anti-Semitic State Department, and an isolationist national mood'.[33]

The less widely known example, again relating to quotas, was recounted by William Russell from his time as an employee of the US Embassy in Berlin at the end of the 1930s:[34]

> A small woman, dressed in black and wearing thick spectacles, moved forward to the desk. 'My husband is in the concentration camp at Dachau,' she said simply, in a low voice. 'Tell me what I can do to help him get out.'
>
> 'What's his registration number?' Joe asked.
>
> 'Eight thousand four hundred and ten, Polish quota,' the woman said.
>
> 'I'm sorry,' Joe answered sympathetically. 'There are thousands of applicants registered before your husband. He has at least eight years to wait.'
>
> The expression on the woman's face showed that she did not believe Joe's words. 'But you will just have to do something,' she insisted. 'He will die there. If war comes, they will never let him out of that place.'
>
> Joe shook his head slowly.
>
> The little woman began to cry as she gathered up the letters which she had spread out on the desk. She fumbled with the papers and when she had them all in her pocket-book she walked away.
>
> It was like that all day, every day, in our Embassy.

The cases of the *St Louis*, and the unnamed couple in Russell's story, point to the dreadful consequences of treating humanity and compassion as goods to be rationed by bureaucratic means. It was in part to avoid further cases such as that of the *St Louis* that the non-*refoulement* obligation was written into the 1951 *Convention*. Yet the mindset that leads to such results is not one that has disappeared, and it lives on in some countries with programs for selective resettlement of refugees. Australian bureaucrats are much given to deriding refugees who arrive without prior authorisation as 'queue jumpers', even though international protection mechanisms and resettlement programs as they currently operate do not offer a place in a queue but a ticket in a lottery. The continual resort to this kind of language finally prompted an exasperated former Secretary of the Australian Department of Immigration and Ethnic Affairs, John Menadue, to remark that the idea of a queue 'was invented by bureaucrats in Canberra',[35] and UNHCR's Gary Troeller to point out that 'Resettlement must remain a complement to, and not a substitute for, the right to seek asylum. The right to seek and enjoy asylum from persecution is a fundamental human right which has universal import and application'.[36] The reason why the cases of the *St Louis* and of the Berlin Embassy stand out as cases of bureaucratic as well as political rigidity is that, as we shall see shortly, bureaucrats who are so minded can often find creative ways of subverting inhumane policy settings. In these cases there was little evidence that any made much attempt to do so. If Nazi officials, in Hannah Arendt's famous phrase, embodied the banality of evil,[37] too many Western officials also accepted the seductive German notion that an order is an order (*Befehl ist Befehl*), and thereby came to embody the banality of obedience.

Bureaucratically-run resettlement programs are often marketed as helping the 'neediest' refugees, but it would be unwise to take this claim at face value. Too often, they embody subtle biases in favour of people who know how to deal with bureaucracies. Menadue, from his years of experience, remarked that the 'poor, unskilled, illiterate and non-English-speaking refugee with no links to Australia and stuck in a squalid camp may be in the greatest need of resettlement and have superior claims to "refugee status", but they are unlikely to be on our priority list'.[38]

At a conference attended by this writer, a senior UNHCR official who had been posted in Africa told the story of a visit from a Western bureaucrat. After initial pleasantries, the visiting bureaucrat said 'What we are looking for are English-speaking engineers'. His face fell when he heard UNHCR's reply: 'We can give you some non-literate women who have been raped'.[39] The lesson here is that need is not necessarily the main criterion on which states and bureaucracies will focus in selecting which refugees to help. Several concrete examples bring this out.

One common feature of managed resettlement programs that can militate against their helping the neediest is prioritisation of applications by those who have sponsors—typically family members—in the country to which they wish to resettle. The appeal of such an approach from the point of view of governments and bureaucracies is that some of the costs and responsibilities of resettlement can be transferred from the state to the sponsors. Thus, under Australia's 'Special Humanitarian Programme', there is a formal requirement for sponsorship by a 'proposer', typically a close family member, and the airfares to Australia for those lucky enough to get a visa are not covered by the government, but have to be paid either by the applicants or their sponsors. The 'Special Humanitarian Programme' in 2015–2016 occupied 5000 places out of 13750 in the 'Humanitarian Programme' as a whole, or 36.4 per cent. Thus, more than a third of 'resettlement' places were effectively inaccessible to any refugees who did not already have close family in Australia—irrespective of considerations of need. In any case, dealing with 'Special Humanitarian Programme' applications has historically been a glacially-slow process; this writer has in his possession a letter dated 31 May 2001 sent to an Afghan applicant in Pakistan informing her that the average processing time for such visas was 122 weeks 'if all the requested documentation has been provided and there are no unexpected processing difficulties'. Canada also makes use of a sponsorship system; indeed, a refugee cannot apply directly for resettlement in Canada, but must either be referred by UNHCR or privately sponsored, with the sponsor providing financial support throughout the period of sponsorship. Again, sponsorship can be a difficult obstacle for the neediest refugees to overcome. The US, by contrast, largely focuses on refugees referred for resettlement by UNHCR, but on occasion allows particular categories of refugee to approach a 'Refugee Resettlement Center' directly. In 2015, it committed to boost its intake from 70,000 to 100,000, mainly in response to the Syrian crisis.[40] But that said, the actual resettlement of Syrian refugees proved painfully slow, and a 31 March 2016 report recorded that in the first six months of Fiscal Year 2016, only 1285 Syrian refugee admissions to the US had occurred.[41]

Bureaucratic resettlement can also work to the disadvantage of the sick or the disabled. Normally for reasons of cost, countries may shy away from helping such refugees, even though they may be amongst the neediest in a refugee population. This proved a major preoccupation for UNHCR in the second half of the 1950s. As of mid-1957, there were still 53,400 refugees in camps in Europe, left over from the Second World War,[42] with many suffering from disabilities that had made them unappealing candidates for resettlement in the eyes of states. Through effective diplomatic cajoling from the High Commissioner, Auguste R. Lindt of Switzerland, these refugees were finally resettled and the camps closed. Within their individual programs, however, states have had the capacity to discriminate. Australia again provides a prime example: until at least 2010, routine health checking potentially disadvantaged the most vulnerable refugees in serious ways.[43] A case cited in the report of a parliamentary committee inquiry shows just how:[44]

Two young Rwandan women of mixed Hutu and Tutsi ethnicity fled war and genocide in their country, leaving family behind and arrived in Australia in 2003.

Both sisters were in their twenties and had endured significant trauma as a result of genocide, they had been displaced from their homelands and separated from family. During this time they also suffered discrimination as a minority group because of their mixed ethnicity. As young women they had also been targeted by ever present groups of soldiers who utilised rape as a weapon of war.

In 2004 an application was lodged for their mother to join them in Brisbane. The application took approximately four months to be processed, but was ultimately rejected. Their mother had failed to meet the Health Requirement according to the legislation. The health problems identified were the result of civilian attack during the civil war. She had suffered serious gunshot wounds to both her legs, resulting in disfigurement and permanent disability.

Subsequently, the sisters applied for a family visit visa for their mother, but this too was rejected on the basis of her disability.

None of this should be especially surprising. Those seeking protection or resettlement as refugees do not vote in national elections of resettlement countries, while those forces hostile to refugees in such countries may be both vociferous and well-organised. On occasion, courageous political leaders may be prepared to stare down such forces, but others will opt to appease them. It is important also to note here that what matters is not just the numbers of people who take up a particular positions, but also the intensity with which they cling to them. In national elections in democratic countries, many voters will be taken for granted by political parties, since their partisan commitments are unlikely to shift. While it is important to mobilise one's natural supporters to vote, political competition may focus on a relatively small number of swinging or floating voters, whose political orientations may be quite different from those of the bulk of the electorate. If swinging voters are hostile to refugees, they may disproportionately shape political discourse, even if a much larger number of voters do not share their views. This can have the effect of distorting the agenda of issues in democratic elections, and this in turn is likely then to shape the orientation of the state at the level of the commanding heights as well as through different layers of bureaucracy. The political theorist Chandran Kukathas has put it rather starkly: 'If refugees and asylum seekers are to be welcomed into any society, and shown a measure of hospitality, this will not be because the polity is welcoming but because society is so. Hospitality is, as Homer shows us in the *Odyssey*, a human relation rather than an institutional one'.[45]

Individual initiatives

All that said, of course, very large numbers of people *have* been resettled by states in the post-war period. But more frequently than one might wish, states have been missing in action when action is required, and it is in such circumstances that the initiatives taken by courageous individuals can prove decisive in providing life chances for people whose prospects might otherwise have been very grim. Oskar Schindler provides a famous example.[46] Some people, it seems, have a predisposition to be what the psychologist Steven Baum calls 'rescuers', people in whom one can find 'extraordinarily high levels of altruism, courage, and independent mindedness'.[47] And in communities marked by high levels of trust, rescuers may find partners whose contributions allow them to rescue people on a relatively large scale, such as one saw with the efforts to spirit Jews in occupied Denmark into neutral Sweden during the Second World War.[48]

Rescuers can be found in both fiction and fact. In December 1942, Warner Brothers released a black-and-white film entitled *Casablanca*, which went on to win that year's Academy Award for best picture. It has since gone on to become one of the most beloved movies of all time, and it is a movie about refugees and people smuggling.[49] Ugarte, an Italian people smuggler, memorably played by Peter Lorre, has contrived the murder of two German couriers carrying 'Letters of Transit' signed by General Weygand. He leaves them for safekeeping in the hands of café owner Rick Blaine, played by Humphrey Bogart, but is then killed after being arrested by the pro-Vichy police, themselves acting to impress a visiting Nazi officer. Also in Casablanca, seeking to escape to the United States, is Victor Laszlo, a leader of the anti-Nazi underground in Europe, and his wife Ilsa, played by Paul Henreid and Ingrid Bergman. At the film's climax, Rick, who had been embittered at the earlier end of a romance with Ilsa at a time when she thought Victor was dead, hands them the Letters of Transit, and they leave on the Lisbon plane, bound for America. Several things are striking about the film. One, not apparent from the screenplay, is that a large number of the cast members were themselves exiles or refugees from Nazism,[50] some of them refugees *sur place*, others forced to flee in dire circumstances. They included Paul Henreid, Conrad Veidt, Helmut Dantine, S.Z. Szakall, Peter Lorre, Curt Bois, and Marcel Dalio. Another is that the hero, Rick, engages in behaviour which in the twenty-first century would likely see him charged with multiple offences in Western democracies, including document fraud and the facilitation of people smuggling. The audience forgives him such infractions because the cause in which he acts is so plainly just. A third is that Ugarte, whose endeavours ultimately allow Laszlo and Ilsa to escape, is quite explicitly motivated by self-interest, something brought out in his exchange with Rick:[51]

Ugarte: You despise me, don't you?

Rick (*indifferently*): If I gave you any thought, I probably would.

Ugarte: But why? Oh, you object to the kind of business I do, huh? But think of all those poor refugees who must rot in this place if I didn't help them. That's not so bad. Through ways of my own I provide them with exit visas.

Rick: For a price, Ugarte, for a price.

Rescuers could be found not just in fiction but in the real world. As the Second World War approached its end, officials of neutral Sweden stepped up efforts to rescue Jews. Count Folke Bernadotte of the Swedish Red Cross had the distasteful experience of having to negotiate with the murderous Reichsführer-SS Heinrich Himmler.[52] One of the most famous of all was a 32-year-old Swedish diplomat, Raoul Wallenberg, who arrived in Budapest on 9 July 1944 and set out to do all he possibly could to assist remaining members of the Jewish population, who were in grave danger of attack from the fascist Arrow Cross movement even though deportations had been halted the day before Wallenberg's arrival by decree of the Hungarian Regent, Admiral Horthy.[53] The situation became even more acute in October 1944 when the Arrow Cross seized power in Budapest, allowing deportations to resume. Wallenberg distributed Swedish 'protective passes', and Swiss diplomat, Charles Lutz, issued Swiss documents of similar ilk, in order to try to save Jews from the attention of both the Hungarian fascists, and Adolf Eichmann, who had returned to Budapest on 17 October with a view to continuing his ghastly program of mass deportation and extermination. More than 7500 protective documents were issued in just a few days.[54] Lutz has been credited with saving more than 62,000 lives, and like Wallenberg was designated 'Righteous Among the Nations' by Yad Vashem. For tragic reasons, however, it was Wallenberg who won the greater fame. Summoned to a meeting with Soviet occupiers following the fall of Budapest to the Soviet Army in January 1945, he disappeared, and to this day it is not clear exactly what happened to him, although it is almost certain that he perished in Soviet custody, whether through neglect or some other and more sinister cause. Wallenberg has been very widely honoured. Honours and recognition came more slowly to Lutz. While his colleagues in Budapest strongly supported his activities, some in Switzerland saw what he was doing as a threat to the principles of Swiss neutrality.[55]

Another example of a rescuer who saved thousands of refugees through individual initiative was the Japanese diplomat Chiune Sugihara, who served in the Lithuanian city of Kaunas in 1939–40. What made his endeavour quite remarkable was that unlike Switzerland and Sweden that were neutral states, Japan had close relations with Nazi Germany and Fascist Italy. Sugihara issued thousands of visas to Jews, in express contravention of his government's commitment to cooperate with Germany. The political scientist John G. Stoessinger, who in 1956 published *The Refugee and the World Community*, was one of those whom Sugihara saved. When his consulate was finally closed, he continued to issue visas even from his train window as the train began its trip to Berlin. After the war, he lost his job in the Foreign Ministry, and lived in rather straightened circumstances until his death in 1986, although shortly before he died he too was recognised by Yad Vashem as 'Righteous Among the Nations'. But not long before he died, he remarked that he was motivated by 'the kind of sentiments anyone would have when he actually sees the refugees face to face'.[56] Not everyone was so moved; in fact, the British Ambassador in Tokyo, Sir Robert Craigie, in December 1940 wrote to the Japanese Foreign Minister, Yosuke Matsuoka, to warn of the 'dangers of personification' that could see the escaping Jews seeking to enter Palestine.[57]

On some notable occasions, organisations of rescuers have emerged. The Emergency Rescue Committee, forerunner of the International Rescue Committee,[58] was one of the most remarkable. Following the fall of France in June 1940 and the establishment of the puppet Vichy regime under Marshal Pétain, a young American journalist, Varian Fry, was despatched to Marseilles as representative of the US-based Emergency Rescue Committee to try through the Centre Américain de Secours to assist refugees seeking to escape from the advance of Nazism.[59] As a history of his endeavours put it, 'It was absolutely legal to help refugees survive while they were in France. It was absolutely illegal to help refugees who did not have all their papers in order to get out of France. But that was exactly what Varian intended to do'.[60] He was not alone. For some months, he enjoyed the support of the young Albert O. Hirschman, who went on after the war to become one of the world's leading economists.[61] Furthermore, Dr Frank Bohn, of the American Federation of Labor, was involved in aiding the escape of labor leaders.

However, Fry did not enjoy the support of the US State Department. It is easily forgotten that until the bombing of Pearl Harbor in December 1941, the US maintained cordial relations with Vichy. The State Department's verdict on Fry's work was unambiguous: 'This government cannot countenance the activities reported of Dr. Bohn and Mr. Fry and other persons in their efforts in evading the laws of countries with which the United States maintains friendly relations'.[62] And indeed, Fry and Hirschman operated consciously outside the law of Vichy France. When Hirschman died in December 2012, the Institute for Advanced Study at Princeton, where he had been a Professor since 1974, recorded that he 'traded currency on the black market, obtained forged documents and passports, devised ways to transmit messages by concealing strips of paper in toothpaste tubes and arranged for ships to transport—often illegally—many of the refugees'.[63] It is worth reflecting that had the wishes of the State Department prevailed, a number of luminous figures in European culture whom Fry and his team helped save—figures such as Hannah Arendt, Marc Chagall, Marcel Duchamp, Lion Feuchtwanger, Arthur Koestler, Heinrich Mann, and Franz Werfel[64]—might well have died at the hands of the Nazis. People smuggling can be altruistic as well as commercial.

Norms of family obligation can also lead people to become rescuers. One such example was the Iraqi Ali Al Jenabi, a victim of torture under Saddam Hussein who fled his homeland as a refugee. Unable to secure 'orderly' resettlement, he agreed to work for a people smuggler who agreed to transport one member of his family to Australia on each voyage he assisted. His boats arrived safely, and all but one of the passengers were found to be refugees. Yet in Australia, he was imprisoned for four years, and—despite being found to be a refugee, and no security threat—left in limbo with a 'Removal Pending' Bridging Visa.[65] Even to have a timely decision made on his protection visa application, Mr Jenabi was obliged to petition the Federal Court of Australia, where the judge criticised what he called 'an egregious failure by the Minister to obey the Parliament's command', and agreed to issue an 'order in the nature of mandamus' which would 'add the prospect of contempt of court by the Minister if the Minister were not to comply within the time fixed in the order'.[66] The lesson here is chilling. Once a panic about 'people smuggling' sets in, politicians can rapidly lose any sense of moral compass, and prove relentless to the point of viciousness in striking against any who have bypassed 'normal' bureaucratic channels—even though the situation a refugee confronts is often anything but normal.

People smuggling: a product of state inaction

In the 1948 film *A Foreign Affair*, Marlene Dietrich, who had been a refugee from Nazism and entertained Allied troops during the Second World War,[67] memorably performed a song by refugee composer Friedrich Holländer entitled 'Black Market':

> No ceiling, no feeling. A very smooth routine.
> You buy my goods, and boy my goods are keen

Refugees, so often thrust to the fringes of society, have every reason to know about black markets.[68] The expression, often used interchangeably with 'informal economy' and a host of other terms, captures an economic phenomenon of considerable significance: if the supply of a good for which there is significant demand is prohibited or the good is legally available only in limited amounts, an illicit supply is likely to be offered to meet the demand that cannot be otherwise satisfied. The ubiquity of black markets in such situations is an affirmation in practice of the power and effectiveness of markets as devices for providing information and for allocating resources.[69] Attempts to stamp out black markets rarely meet with much success.[70] People smuggling is a classic black market phenomenon. As Morrison has put it, 'the imposition of visa restrictions on all countries that generate refugees is the most explicit blocking mechanism for asylum flows and it denies most refugees the opportunity for legal migration'.[71] To put it bluntly, refugees have been driven *by governments* into the arms of people smugglers.

It is important to recognise that people smuggling is not the same as people trafficking or 'trafficking in persons', which is stringently defined in Article 3 (a) of the December 2000 *Protocol to Prevent, Suppress and Punish Trafficking in Persons, Especially Women and Children*, supplementing the *United Nations Convention Against Transnational Organized Crime* as

> the recruitment, transportation, transfer, harbouring or receipt of persons, by means of the threat or use of force or other forms of coercion, of abduction, of fraud, of deception, of the abuse of power or of a position of vulnerability or of the giving or receiving of payments or benefits to achieve the consent of a person having control over another person, for the purpose of exploitation. Exploitation shall include, at a minimum, the exploitation of the prostitution of others or other forms of sexual exploitation, forced labour or services, slavery or practices similar to slavery, servitude or the removal of organs.[72]

People smuggling is not conducted 'for the purpose of exploitation' in this specific sense. Rather, a separate *Protocol against the Smuggling of Migrants by Land, Sea and Air*, supplementing the *United Nations Convention against Transnational Organized Crime*, defines 'smuggling of migrants' in Article 3 (a) as 'the procurement, in order to obtain, directly or indirectly, a financial or other material benefit, of the illegal entry of a person into a State Party of which the person is not a national or a permanent resident'.[73] Article 3 (b) makes it clear that '"Illegal entry" shall mean crossing borders without complying with the necessary requirements for legal entry into the receiving State'.[74] It does not purport to make it illegal to seek asylum under international law; after all, Article 14.1 of the 1948 *Universal Declaration of Human Rights* provides that 'Everyone has the right to seek and to enjoy in other countries asylum from persecution'. It is also notable that to constitute smuggling, activity must be undertaken 'in order to obtain, directly or indirectly, a financial or other material benefit'; thus, someone motivated by norms of reciprocity or altruistic motives who does not seek to make a financial or material benefit is arguably not a smuggler at all.

Some basic data illuminate very clearly why people smuggling is so ubiquitous a phenomenon. According to UNHCR's projection, in 2015 some 1,150,000 refugees were in need of resettlement; but in the same report, UNHCR noted that in 2014, only 73,331 UNHCR resettlement departures occurred.[75] Furthermore, as noted earlier, resettlement programs do not necessarily target the most desperate refugees. For example, in 2014, some 8,395 of the 73,311 refugees resettled were Bhutanese, and while no one could begrudge them the chance for a new life, few informed observers would have seen them as the neediest refugees in the world: a study by Susan Banki concluded that 'relative to refugee camps in other countries, the Bhutanese refugee camps in Nepal are of a reasonable quality, and relative to health and education systems in rural Nepal, they are of a high quality'.[76] Banki also offers a rather dispiriting explanation of why the Bhutanese have been chosen for resettlement: that 'there was a need to find refugee populations that would allow Western countries to fill their resettlement quotas without turning to those populations viewed as potentially dangerous—that is, the Middle East refugees'.[77] The number of Bhutanese resettled in 2014 actually exceeded the numbers of both Syrians (7,021) and Afghans (only 3,331).[78] In such circumstances, no one should be surprised that Syrians and Afghans made up 70 per cent of those who arrived in Europe in 2015: a rational Syrian or Afghan would have concluded by then that the chance of securing resettlement through allegedly 'orderly' means was negligible.

The tardy performance of developed countries in making resettlement places available also helps explain the ferocity of their attacks on people smuggling. People smuggling in effect holds parties to the 1951 *Convention* to account, by presenting them at their borders with refugees whose needs they have recognised in principle, but whom they would prefer not to have to help. The result has been a barrage of superheated rhetoric directed against people smugglers, on a scale out of all proportion to both their numbers and their activities. On 17 April 2009, the then Australian Prime Minister, Kevin Rudd, in a doorstop interview described people smuggling as 'the world's most evil trade', and people smugglers as 'the vilest form of human life' and 'the absolute scum of the earth' who should 'rot in hell'. Given the existence of alternative candidates for vilification, such as those involved in human trafficking for purposes of sexual servitude, or organised distribution of narcotics, or the use of slave labour, this language might seem somewhat extreme. While there is evidence that at certain points in the smuggling 'chain', those being smuggled, especially child refugees, can be highly vulnerable to exploitation,[79] those deciding to accept the offer of a smuggler's services typically have a higher level of personal autonomy than someone being trafficked or enslaved. Most who use smugglers would certainly prefer an alternative means of egress if states had not acted systematically to close such alternatives off. And an incidental oddity in the fierce denunciation of the morality of smugglers, especially when it comes from politicians who otherwise preach the value of free markets, is that the logic of markets is that producers need not be driven by moral sentiments. As the great philosopher and political economist Adam Smith put it, it is 'not from the benevolence of the butcher, the brewer or the baker, that we expect our dinner, but from their regard to their own self interest'.[80]

One might have thought that states would wish to have nothing whatsoever to do with people smugglers, but the picture is rather more complex. For example, in October 2015 an Amnesty International report provided substantial testimony to the effect that in May 2015, Australian officials had paid more than US$30,000 to the crews of vessels carrying asylum seekers to return to Indonesia.[81] *Prima facie*, such activity could itself amount to people smuggling and be the subject of a prosecution under the Australian *Criminal Code*, although it is only with the approval of the Attorney-General that a prosecution for such an offence can be undertaken. An expert legal opinion (of which a former Judge *ad hoc* of the International Court of Justice was a lead author) concluded that the payments to the crew members were 'inconsistent with Australia's obligations under the People-Smuggling Protocol (2000) and the Refugees Convention (1951)' and noted that 'Payment by Australian authorities to people-smugglers involves providing a financial benefit for engaging in an illicit trade, as well as an incentive to continue doing it'.[82] The Australian Government responded to the controversy by asserting that Australian officials had done nothing illegal. Notably, however, section 14(1) of the *Intelligence Services Act* 2001 provides that 'A staff member or agent of an agency is not subject to any civil or criminal liability for any act done outside Australia if the act is done in the proper performance of a function of the agency.' From Indonesia's point of view, the payoffs were alarming not so much because of the specifics of the episode itself, but rather because they opened up the possibility that on land, Australia might have been attempting to pay off the heads of crime syndicates with much larger sums, which could end up helping to fund other activities in which such syndicates might be involved, such as bribery of police, drug trafficking or sexual enslavement.

Paying off people smugglers is just one potential approach that states may take to try to minimise flows of refugees towards their frontiers. Increasingly we have witnessed the use of martial terminology to frame such campaigns, whether we are speaking of 'Operation Sovereign Borders' in Australia, or of attempts to 'smash' people smuggling,[83] or mount a war against it. A 'war against people smuggling', however, is no more likely to eliminate people smuggling than a 'war against drugs' will eliminate narcotics, or a 'war against terrorism' will end the resort to terror. As long as root causes of refugee flight remain unaddressed, those in danger will have recourse to market forces as a means of making their escape, and market forces are immensely strong and resilient. Concentrated local campaigns to obliterate particular people smuggling networks will most likely have a classic 'balloon squeezing' effect.[84] The more sophisticated smugglers will simply shift into alternative income generating activities such as human trafficking, and refugees will be driven into potentially even more dangerous routes of escape than they might otherwise have had to use. These kind of local campaigns do not stop people drowning; rather, they ensure that if people drown, they drown somewhere else.

A certain amount of cynicism may thus be in order when one appraises the responses of political leaders to the tragedy of human mortality. In 2013, for example, there were 1.25 million road traffic deaths worldwide,[85] vastly exceeding the number of deaths amongst refugees being moved by people smugglers. Yet there was little or no sense of crisis generated by this frightening statistic, and certainly no suggestion that car manufacture was the world's most evil trade, or reckless drivers the vilest form of human life. The painful reality is that most people remain largely indifferent to the deaths of those whom they do not know, or with whom they have no connection of identity. As the racketeer Harry Lime put it in *The Third Man* while riding the giant ferris wheel in the Prater amusement park in Vienna: 'Look down there. Would you feel any pity if one of those dots stopped moving forever?' Governments understand this, and have no qualms about dehumanising refugees when it suits them to do so.[86] Therefore, when political leaders show sudden bursts of empathy with refugees they have been doing their best to keep at arms' length, it pays to ask what is really going on. Occasionally something like an answer bubbles to the surface. In 2009, the opposition Liberal Party of Australia had strongly attacked the government over the arrival of boats, claiming that lives were being put at risk. But thanks to Wikileaks, we now know that on 13 November 2009, the US Embassy in Canberra sent a cable to Washington headed 'Australia Searches for Asylum Seeker Solution', and in a section headed 'Opposition smells blood', the author wrote that 'A key Liberal party strategist told us the issue was "fantastic" and "the more boats that come the better"'.[87]

The campaign against people smuggling is an intensely political one. It reflects the ferocity of contention in democratic polities, and the search by political parties for issues they can use to thrash their opponents. It also reflects the desire of states and bureaucracies to appear strong even as processes of globalisation relentlessly sap their capacity to act unilaterally. It has very little to do with saving lives at sea. It is not the minority of refugees who drown that pose a challenge for policymakers; it is the majority who do not.

5

ROOTS OF REFUGEE 'CRISES'
IN A GLOBALISED WORLD

In 1991, following the ejection of Iraqi forces from Kuwait in the UN-sanctioned 'Operation Desert Storm', US President George H.W. Bush spoke optimistically of the prospects of a 'new world order'. Bush was a measured and insightful occupant of the White House, and not given to flights of fantasy.[1] Unfortunately, however, his hopes were not realised. On the contrary, a more pessimistic picture, of a turbulent and fractured world,[2] has dominated much of the quarter of a century since Bush gave voice to his vision. Disorder has been the order of the day, and this has fundamentally shaped the environment generating refugee flows. Some manifestations of disorder are a direct product of decisions taken by sentient policymakers, such as the use of coercion by rulers, or the US move to invade Iraq in March 2003, which in its strategic recklessness has been compared to Hitler's invasion of the Soviet Union in June 1941.[3] Others are much more a result of processes of sociopolitical and sociocultural change in world politics that cumulatively alter the environment in which potential refugees choose whether to move or whether to stay put. Together, they present a potential for instability that makes extremely unlikely the dwindling, anytime soon, of substantial refugee movements. They are not all necessarily root 'causes' of refugee movements in a direct sense, but rather a mélange of contributing and enabling factors. This chapter explores some of these problems in more detail.

State disruption and violent conflict

Since the end of the Cold War, a great deal of effort has been devoted to understanding the problems confronted by what have been called 'collapsed', 'disrupted' or 'failed' states.[4] If the state is the predominant institution charged with providing protection to citizens, an erosion of its ability to do so has serious implications for refugee movement; only by exit might ordinary people be able to escape the rampage of predatory non-state actors that can thrive in an environment in which the state is unable to provide security. Hobbes provided a grim picture of the extreme form of such a condition in his book *Leviathan*:[5]

Whatsoever therefore is consequent to a time of Warre, where every man is Enemy to every man; the same is consequent to the time, wherein men live without other security, than what their own strength, and their own invention shall furnish them withall. In such condition, there is no place for Industry; because the fruit thereof is uncertain: and consequently no Culture of the Earth; no Navigation, nor use of the commodities that may be imported by Sea; no commodious Building; no Instruments of moving, and removing such things as require much force; no Knowledge of the face of the Earth; no account of Time; no Arts; no Letters; no Society; and which is worst of all, continuall feare, and danger of violent death; And the life of man solitary, poore, nasty, brutish, and short.

Fortunately, more states are disrupted than fully failed or collapsed in such a way as to give rise to all the gruesome problems that Hobbes's account implies. But that said, severe state disruption can create just as much misery and horror for ordinary people as might total disintegration. In addition, states can be disrupted in a number of different ways, and these can have ramifications for refugee movements as well.

One contributing factor to state disruption can be the so-called 'rentier state' problem. States can be dangerously over-dependent on unstable external sources of revenue such as foreign aid or income from the sale of a natural resource such as crude oil or natural gas. If anything happens to disrupt the flow of such revenue, the state may be unable to fund some of its basic functions, let alone meet the expectations of crucial social groups that may have become dependent on the state for advancement. A classic example of a rentier state running into strife was Afghanistan in the late 1960s and early 1970s,[6] and the ultimate consequence was a communist coup in April 1978 that led to grave disarray from which the country is yet to recover almost four decades on. Refugees began to leave the country in 1978; the numbers went up in 1979; and following the Soviet invasion in December 1979, the Afghan refugee population rapidly became the world's largest, a status it retained until the Syrian conflict proceeded to create an even larger refugee population in the second decade of the twenty-first century.

A further potent source of state disruption is fragmentation at the elite level. Unified political elites with a shared understanding of the 'rules of the game' are a critical component of a stable political order. In the absence of a sufficient degree of elite unity, the results can be distinctly unpleasant, as the following account of elite disunity suggests:[7]

> Communication and influence networks do not cross factional lines in any large way, and factions disagree on the rules of political conduct and the worth of existing political institutions. Accordingly, they distrust one another deeply; they perceive political outcomes in 'politics as war' or

zero-sum terms; and they engage in unrestricted, often violent struggles for dominance. These features make regimes in countries with disunified elites fundamentally unstable, no matter whether they are authoritarian or formally democratic. Lacking the communication and influence networks that might give them a satisfactory amount of access to government decision making and disagreeing on the rules of the game and the worth of existing institutions, most factions in a disunified elite see the existing regime as the vehicle by which a dominant faction promotes its interests. To protect and promote their own interests, therefore, they must destroy or cripple the regime and elites who operate it. Irregular and forcible power seizures, attempted seizures, or a widespread expectation that such seizures may occur are thus a by-product of elite disunity.

A good example of this kind of problem surfaced in Somalia at the beginning of the 1990s. Mohamed Siad Barre, who had led a coup in 1969, was driven from power in Mogadishu in January 1991, by which time he was 71 years old; and he fled the country in May of that year. In April 1990, a group of prominent Somalis had called for democratic reform but instead were imprisoned by Barre's regime. The elite was fragmented on the basis of an array of complex factors including clan loyalties, and the country slid into civil war, from which it has arguably not yet escaped.[8] Several major interventions authorised by the UN Security Council failed to put the country on a stable path,[9] and as of mid-June 2015, over one million Somalis were refugees outside the country, the majority of them in Kenya, Yemen, and Ethiopia.

Another reason states can run into difficulty is meddling by neighbours, which in its most extreme variant can amount to a 'creeping invasion'. This occurs when a middle power uses force against the territorial integrity or political independence of another state, but covertly and through surrogates, denying all the while that it is doing any such thing; and this use of force is on a sufficient scale to imperil the exercise of state power, by the state under threat, on a significant part of its territory, and is designed and intended to do so. A classic example was Pakistan's conscious instrumentalisation of the Taliban movement from 1994 as a way of preventing Indian influence from developing in Afghanistan after the collapse of the Communist regime in April 1992.[10] Ahmed Rashid has estimated that 'Between 1994 and 1999, an estimated 80,000 to 100,000 Pakistanis trained and fought in Afghanistan',[11] and senior officers from Pakistan serving in Afghanistan at that time reportedly numbered in the hundreds.[12] In late 2001, this time with US complicity, Pakistan had to mount an airlift from Kunduz in northern Afghanistan to extract Pakistanis who had been trapped in that enclave during 'Operation Enduring Freedom'.[13]

The phenomenon of creeping invasion highlights a rather depressing feature of power politics: that for some states, it is preferable that other states be in disarray, rather than stable and secure but aligned with other actors. When this is the case, of course, it is almost certain that refugee flows will result. But the problem does not stop here. States that employed creeping invasion as a tool run the risk of creating a Frankenstein's monster that can then turn on its creators. In the case of Pakistan, a predictable consequence of its nurturing of the Afghan Taliban was that at some point a *Pakistani* Taliban would emerge. This indeed happened in December 2007 under the leadership of Baitullah Mehsud, and now Pakistan is faced with a threat of extreme violence directed by Pakistani Taliban against vulnerable groups in Pakistani society—the massacre of schoolchildren near Peshawar in December 2014 being but one example.[14] This has also led to refugees fleeing from Pakistan, notably Shiite Muslim Pakistanis from the Pushtun Turi tribe fearful of the radicalism of the Sunni Pakistani Taliban.

Some elites, when faced with indications that not all is going well for them, have historically responded by directing the coercive instrumentalities of the state against those whom they view as enemies. This tactic is most likely to be effective in totalitarian regimes, but has also been frequently employed in an attempt to abort either the complete unraveling of a fragile state, or the erosion of the power of an elite that is already in a parlous condition. Yet while refugee flows are an obvious consequence that can flow from such coercive measures, recent experience suggests that the wider world can be very slow in responding in any meaningful preventive fashion to developments of this kind.[15] One wake-up call that unfortunately succeeded in waking up very few people was Saddam Hussein's gassing of the Kurdish population in Halabja in March 1988.[16] This attack, which occurred in the last stages of the Iran-Iraq war, highlighted the vicious brutality of the Iraqi regime, but it led to no particular outrage on the part of key capitals. Instead, spurious attempts were made to blame the massacre on the Iranians, and from a reputational point of view, Saddam Hussein escaped largely unscathed. It was only when he further violated international norms with the invasion of Kuwait in August 1990 that other states mobilised to confront the challenge that he posed.

An even more distressing example of international neglect came with the Rwandan genocide of April–June 1994. Triggered by a suspicious plane crash that killed the Presidents of both Rwanda and neighbouring Burundi, the massacres organised by extremist members of the Hutu ethnic group and targeting moderate Hutus and ethnic Tutsis killed close to a million people while the world looked on.[17] The Rwandan case also highlighted another problem that can arise in such circumstances. When the advance towards the Rwandan capital of forces opposed to the murderous *génocidaires* finally prompted the killers themselves to flee, they entered eastern Zaire in large numbers, immersed in a wider flow of refugees seeking to escape from the charnel house that Rwanda had become. This created a dilemma for aid agencies, and on ethical grounds, Médecins Sans

Frontières (MSF) withdrew from the camps.[18] The experiences of the Kurds under Saddam, and of the Rwandans, do not bode well for groups such as the Rohingyas in Burma for whom there is every reason also to entertain the gravest fears.[19]

Sometimes state disruption results from invasions that are anything but creeping. The US invasion of Iraq in March 2003, for example, did not bring peace to Iraq; rather, it triggered new and highly destructive patterns of political mobilisation grounded in sectarian identities, of a kind that left many Iraqis with a well-founded fear of being persecuted for reasons of membership of a particular social group. In effect, it activated the 'logic of spoiling'.[20] It is cheaper and easier to be a wrecker than a builder, and those who cannot access power themselves may quite rationally set out to prevent anyone else from exercising power in a peaceful or effective fashion. Once Saddam Hussein and his Sunni Muslim elite (in a Shiite Muslim majority country) were ejected from power, the Sunnis in general, not just those who had actively supported Saddam's regime, had much to fear from a democratisation process that could make them a permanent minority. Their fears were compounded when the head of the US-established 'Coalition Provisional Authority' from May 2003 to June 2004, L. Paul Bremer III, issued a 'De-Baathification' decree and ordered the disbanding of the Iraqi Army. Sunni groups swiftly turned to spoiling, with car bombings and other terrorist strikes an easy approach to employ. This in turn led to the consolidation of militias among the Shia, and a push for entrenched territorial autonomy for the Kurds.[21] As an official US report subsequently put it, 'The liberation model—in which a rapid transfer of power to Iraqi authorities would enable U.S. troops to depart 90 days after the regime's fall—broke down almost immediately after the invasion. Neither the U.S. military nor the civilian leadership was prepared for the complete disintegration of Iraq's government and the subsequent loss of law and order. The looting and chaos it engendered destroyed plans for a rapid transfer of power'.[22]

On the whole, the experiences of recent exercises in state-building to try to overcome the problems of state disruption or fragmentation have not proved especially promising. Larry Diamond pointedly observed that

> The experience in Iraq cautions against the gung ho logic that a country can be quickly transformed from dictatorship to democracy by warfare and occupation. Without an international mandate and coalition for regime transformation, any such mission in the future would no doubt face crippling shortages both of resources and of domestic and international legitimacy.[23]

Rebuilding a state requires complex attempts to design new institutions; win them generalised normative support or 'legitimacy'; and work out ways to fund them.[24] All of these tasks are fraught with difficulty. There is now also a large and critical literature on the limitations of a 'liberal peacebuilding' model focused on democratisation and the promotion of free markets;[25] and an appreciation that, desirable as democracy and markets may be, they are complicated social institutions that cannot be created by the wave of a wand. Since both free elections and free markets can create losers as well as winners—and often *angry* losers—they need to be nested within a framework of rules on which one can rely to ensure that the benefits they can offer are not outweighed by the dangers.

This is why the establishment of a meaningful system of laws subject to the political principle of the rule of law is so important. But equally, the rule of law is extremely difficult to establish rapidly; on the contrary, systems marked by the rule of law tend to be the product of a very substantial period of evolutionary development that cannot be conjured out of thin air.[26] This is why some have argued strongly for postponing rule-governed activities such as elections to the later stages of political transitions—the hope being that by the time they are finally held, a system of rules and an independent judiciary to enforce them will be sufficiently entrenched to protect whatever the outcome of the election might be.[27] But even if this happens, there is no guarantee that a free and fair election will lead to a tolerant political culture, a statesmanlike elite, workable political institutions, or an institutionalised political system.[28] Moves in the direction of liberal peacebuilding may be sufficient to encourage some refugees to return to a thitherto-disrupted state, and plans for repatriation of refugees may be built into transitional arrangements under UN auspices, as was the case in Namibia under UNTAG[29] and Cambodia under UNTAC—although few gave the UN high marks for its handling of rehabilitation in Cambodia.[30] In some circumstances, refugees may simply seize the opportunity to repatriate spontaneously, as they also can do during times of conflict.[31] It is naïve, however, to see the current tool-kit of post-conflict transition as affording a rapid solution to most refugees' problems, or the Cambodian experience of repatriation as one that it would be wise to seek to replicate elsewhere.

Violent conflict is not simply associated with the erosion of state capacity. It can take the form of protracted civil war, with the power of the state on occasion menacingly real. Syria is the nastiest contemporary example of this problem. Triggered by the 2011 'Arab Spring' that displaced longstanding autocratic rulers in Tunisia, Egypt and Libya, the Syrian uprising proved how difficult it could be to dislodge a leader—in this case Bashar al-Assad—intent on clinging to power, supported by an establishment with nowhere else to go, and willing to use even the most revolting forms of brutality to avoid eviction.[32] Assad proved a much tougher nut to crack than the other Arab Spring dictators, and whilst some tracts of Syrian territory came under the control of Assad's opponents, and then of 'Daesh', Assad succeeded in maintaining control of the capital Damascus, and secured ongoing backing, first from circles in Iran, and then, much more significantly, from the Russian Federation and President Putin. It is hard to imagine a situation more calculated to produce refugee flows; and equally, it is extraordinarily difficult to envisage how Syria could be made to function in the future as an effective state protecting its citizens. Too many Syrians have too many awful memories of the last few years for there to be any real hope in this respect. Those who expect otherwise should reflect on how the display of the Confederate flag remains a source of tension in the United States, more than 150 years after the end of the American Civil War.

Armed conflict can pose different kinds of threats to different kinds of victim, although all may end up being categorised as refugees. A positive, albeit depressing, development has been the growth in recognition of how women can suffer in war, with rape and sexual violence interpreted in terms of power rather than biology. The move within the UN to endorse a 'Women, Peace and Security Agenda' is a significant marker of this shift, recognising that 'women and girls experience conflict differently from men and boys'.[33] Women refugees often face daunting challenges in exile, including having to function as single parents or breadwinners. Refugee camps can also be exceedingly dangerous places: a camp with a population the equivalent in size of a small-to-medium city is likely to display all the problems of order that such a city can throw up, and then some more. Furthermore, some elements of the camp population are likely to constitute a *Lumpenproletariat*, in the worst cases intimidating, threatening or even terrorising other camp residents. Yet that said, particular risks may be greater for men than for women, and young men of military age in particular. A notorious example of this was the July 1995 massacre in Srebrenica in eastern Bosnia-Herzegovina, where the Bosnian Serb army systematically massacred some 8000 men and boys. Here was a case where a 'women and children first' approach to protection had little to offer to those who were the main target in the eyes of the attackers.[34] Despite this vulnerability, however, young male refugees are all too often dismissed as 'economic migrants', and overlooked in favour of families when candidates for resettlement are being selected.

The fear of 'terrorism'

Ever since September 2001, when Al Qaeda's attacks on the World Trade Center in New York and the Pentagon in Washington DC mesmerised a global audience, terrorism and the threat that it can pose have been at the forefront of international discussion. Billions of dollars have been spent to confront or contain the threat of terrorism, and the politics and legal systems of a number of states have been adjusted or modified in order to put the threat of terrorism on centre stage. This has been a matter of great concern to some observers preoccupied with the protection of liberty, since states in the name of action against terrorism may be tempted to compromise important freedoms. Benjamin Franklin once remarked that 'Those who would give up essential Liberty, to purchase a little temporary Safety, deserve neither Liberty nor Safety'.[35] This observation, together with Franklin D. Roosevelt's remark in his First Inaugural Address in 1933 that the only thing we have to fear is fear itself, too often has been lost in the post-2001 cacophony. Yet at the same time, in any discussion of modern refugee problems, it is important to pay some attention to terrorism, not only because some ill-judged policies directed against terrorism have actually helped give rise to disorderly situations which force refugees to flee, but also because real threats of terrorism can be a potent, immediate cause of refugee flight.

Even the word 'terrorism' has a fearsome ring to it. This may be one reason why many different attempts to define terrorism can be found in the literature. The French sociologist Raymond Aron argued that one labels as 'terrorist' an 'action of violence of which the psychological effects are out of proportion to the purely physical results'.[36] To this one needs to add two other elements. First, such an action needs to be undertaken to pursue a political purpose, since otherwise terrorism could be conflated with violence for purely criminal purposes, or epiphenomenal violence associated with a wider armed conflict. Second, the target of violence should be non-combatants, rather than members of a security force engaged in actions governed by international humanitarian law. Some have suggested that terrorist violence by definition involves victims chosen at random,[37] but this limitation is unhelpful if one is interested in attacks that can generate refugee flows, since a targeted strike against the leader of a particular community may be an important factor prompting members of that community to seek safety elsewhere.

Visa systems do not provide an especially effective mechanism for excluding potential terrorists from Western countries, as recent experience has shown.[38] Indeed, an Australian case from 2003 suggested that it was probably harder for foreign cheese and salami to enter Australia than a foreign terrorist.[39] But fortunately, terrorism is not by any stretch of the imagination an existential threat to a Western state. Indeed, overreaction by states may be exactly what terrorists themselves seek to produce.[40] The number of people killed or injured in terrorist attacks in Western countries, or in the world at large, is miniscule compared to the mortality associated with traffic accidents. In the United States in 2001, criminal firearm violence claimed 11,348 lives,[41] more than three times the number killed in the September 11, 2001 terrorist attacks.[42] This does not of course mean that the effects of terrorism are trivial. This writer has lost five friends or acquaintances in terrorist attacks,[43] and seen others severely injured. Every death at the hands of terrorists will likely leave an aching void in the hearts of the victim's surviving friends and relatives. Nonetheless, it takes considerably more than a terrorist strike to bring down a consolidated state. Where terrorism is much more existentially threatening is in environments and localities that are already stressed or unstable, and there, the emergence of organised terrorist groups can be the last straw for elements of the population hanging on in the hope that things will get better.

Terrorist attacks may occur for a range of different reasons. There seems to be no single terrorist profile.[44] Some writers have seen violence as somehow a purifying force: the notorious French theorist Georges Sorel comes to mind.[45] Historical experience, however, suggests that reasons related to 'race, religion, nationality, membership of a particular social group or political opinion' are quite commonly at play. The psychologist Fathali M. Moghaddam has offered an insightful account of what he calls the 'staircase to terrorism'. This model posits a range of different stages through which an individual passes before he or she reaches the point at which terrorism becomes a part of the individual's repertoire. The penultimate stage—the 'fourth floor' in Moghaddam's terminology—involves 'a world rigidly divided into "us" and "them", "good" and "evil."'[46] While this can explain violence based on secular ideologies, it also helps explain how sectarian violence can occur. Not all sectarian violence leads to refugee movements. Pakistan during the 1990s was seriously afflicted by clashes between Sunni and Shiite Muslims,[47] but the options for flight at the time were relatively limited. That said, sectarianism has played a very significant role in two major outflows in recent times that have impacted directly on Europe: the outflow of Shiite Hazaras from Afghanistan, and the outflow of diverse peoples fearing sectarian persecution in the context of wars in Iraq and Syria.

Hazaras in Afghanistan have been subject to discrimination and persecution at least since the 'Hazara Wars' of 1891–1893,[48] and there is no reason to believe that the underlying factors—both ethnic and sectarian—fuelling hostility towards Hazaras have dissipated. As was noted in Chapter One, there was a ferocious massacre of this vulnerable minority by the Taliban in Mazar-e Sharif in August 1998. Rupert Colville of UNHCR wrote of it as follows:[49]

> Some were shot on the streets. Many were executed in their own homes, after areas of the town known to be inhabited by their ethnic group had been systematically sealed off and searched. Some were boiled or asphyxiated to death after being left crammed inside sealed metal containers under a hot August sun. In at least one hospital, as many as 30 patients were shot as they lay helplessly in their beds. The bodies of many of the victims were left on the streets or in their houses as a stark warning to the city's remaining inhabitants. Horrified witnesses saw dogs tearing at the corpses, but were instructed over loudspeakers and by radio announcements not to remove or bury them.

The massacre was supervised by Mullah Abdul Manan Niazi, a fanatical Pushtun chauvinist from Shindand. He incited his troops to further action through incendiary speeches denouncing Shiite Muslims as unbelievers. Niazi personally oversaw the selection of prisoners to be moved in containers.[50] It was in the immediate aftermath of this reign of terror that a substantial flow of Hazara refugees from Afghanistan commenced. The overthrow of the Taliban regime and its replacement by an Interim Administration under Hamid Karzai put an end to official discrimination against Hazaras, but did nothing to secure them against Taliban attack in the vast tracts of Afghanistan where the Kabul Government is ineffectual. For example, on 6 January 2004, there was a grisly massacre of Hazara travellers near the border between Uruzgan and Helmand, leading a provincial official, Mohammed Wali Alizai, to suggest that the object of the assailants was 'to stir up ethnic tensions'.[51] Another example came in late June 2010:[52]

Afghanistan, June 25 (Reuters)—The bodies of 11 men, their heads cut off and placed next to them, have been found in a violent southern province of Afghanistan, a senior police official said on Friday. A police patrol discovered the bodies on Thursday in the Khas Uruzgan district of Uruzgan province, north of the Taliban stronghold of Kandahar, said police official Mohammad Gulab Wardak. 'This was the work of the Taliban. They beheaded these men because they were ethnic Hazaras and Shi'ite Muslims,' he said.

Such attacks show no sign of abating. On 6 December 2011, a suicide bomber attacked Shiite Afghans, most of them Hazaras, at a place of commemoration in downtown Kabul during the *Ashura* festival that marks the anniversary of the Battle of Karbala in 680 AD. Almost simultaneously, a bomb in Mazar-e Sharif also killed Afghan Shia. The Kabul bomb killed at least 55 people, and the Mazar bomb four more.[53] And in February 2016, the United Nations Assistance Mission in Afghanistan reported that in 2015,

> UNAMA observed a sharp increase in the abduction and killing of civilians of Hazara ethnicity by Anti-Government Elements. Between 1 January and 31 December, Anti-Government Elements abducted at least 146 members of the Hazara community in 20 separate incidents. All but one incident took place in areas with mixed Hazara and non-Hazara communities, in Ghazni, Balkh, Sari Pul, Faryab, Uruzgan, Baghlan, Wardak, Jawzjan, and Ghor provinces.[54]

Many attacks on Hazaras go unreported in Western media, and escape the attention of foreign missions understandably preoccupied with protecting their own personnel in Kabul.

Sectarianism has also been brutally at play in Iraq and Syria. A combination of circumstances in Iraq led to its dramatic resurgence. In Iraq, the recognition that the Coalition Provisional Authority had no particular legitimacy led to a rapid push for elections. However, in the absence of the detailed demographic data required to produce a legislature based on single-member constituencies, there was little option seen at the time other than to adopt a nationwide 'list' system of proportional representation. This virtually guaranteed, however, that sectarian identities would be the basis of political mobilisation, and this proved to be the case when elections were held in January 2005. The predictable consequence was the formation of militias to defend or promote the interests of different sectarian communities, and Iraq is yet to recover from the consequences. In particular, the government of Nouri al-Maliki, Prime Minister from 2006–2014 and leader of a major Shiite party, ruled very much in the interest of Shia, and this helps explain the rise of Daesh as a political and military force. It was not simply the imperialistic utopianism of the Daesh leadership that gave them some traction, nor their commitment to restoring the Caliphate, which had been abolished in 1924 following the disintegration of the Ottoman Empire.[55] Indeed, one eminent Syrian scholar cuttingly remarked that 'The Caliphate is a public affair linked to the entire Muslim Nation and cannot be settled by a few juveniles'.[56] Critically, Daesh *also* benefited from the shift to its ranks of Sunni Muslims who had previously served as soldiers for Saddam Hussein and felt marginalised under the rule of Maliki.

Where Daesh's ideology has been important is in its repudiation of the legitimacy of existing territorial states. An issue of considerable moment in the history of Islam has been how to reconcile the idea of a universal community of Muslim believers, or *ummah*, with the reality of territorial states with rulers of their own. Contrary to what is often thought, classic Islamic political theory allows some space for territorial pluralism,[57] but Daesh has sought to challenge this notion at every opportunity, taking pride in its ability to control territory in both Syria and Iraq, and declaring other areas as 'provinces' (notably the province of 'Khorasan', spanning Afghanistan and Pakistan). Just as striking, however, has been its violent sectarianism, with Shia being particularly targeted,[58] which has won it support from some Sunni circles.[59] This, in turn, helps explain why Iran has lined up to support Bashar al-Assad in Syria, but it also explains the flight from Syria of millions of refugees.

Transport, the wherewithal to travel, and human mobility

An often-neglected contributor to refugee movements in the twentieth and twenty-first centuries has been simply the growing availability of affordable means of long-distance transport. This is not a cause of forced migration, but it is a critical enabling factor. Until the advent of the Industrial Revolution, opportunities for long distance travel were extremely limited. The two main devices for covering long distances were ships for use at sea, and horses and other beasts of burden over land. These were not of course trivial in their impact. Ships permitted the trade in ancient times that transformed the Mediterranean and led to the emergence of the Phoenicians and the Athenians as major powers, with relations regulated by specific norms and understandings.[60] They also permitted the great voyages of exploration by Spanish, Portuguese, Dutch, French and British explorers, as well as the establishment of colonies dominated by these and other European actors. In the meantime, animal power facilitated trade along the Silk Road, and the conquest of the Eurasian space by the Mongol ruler Chinggis Khan—leading, among other things, to the belief of some Hazaras that they are descended from Chinggis Khan's troops. In a very real sense these means of transport opened up the world, something revealed indirectly through the creation of maps. What the means of travel of this era did *not* allow was the movement, rapidly, of very large numbers of people pursuing private objectives. Ships existed to serve the ends of trade, of naval offence and defence, and of territorial domination. Armies on horseback could support 'conquest empires' such as the Chinggisid and the Timurid, but they could not provide mass transport. The vast majority of the world's population, until relatively recently, were unlikely to travel much out of sight of the towns and villages in which they dwelt, although those who did travel were able to move quite easily.

The Industrial Revolution radically transformed opportunities for human mobility. The emergence of the steamship—most famously Isambard Brunel's S.S. *Great Britain*, which crossed the Atlantic for the first time in 1845—opened the door to truly mass movements of people. It is often forgotten that when the R.M.S. *Titanic* hit an iceberg and sank in the North Atlantic on 15 April 1912, the majority of passengers on board were in Third or 'Steerage' class, including a number of Christians and Muslims from the Ottoman Empire who had boarded the ship at Cherbourg.[61] Continents such as America and Australia saw their populations swell as a result of immigration by ship, fuelled also by events such as the Irish Famine from 1845. Two other developments, however, were arguably of even greater long-term importance. The first was the invention of the automobile, from which then flowed the invention of the bus. Buses have proved to be crucial devices for moving people within and between developing countries, and even in severely disrupted states, it is notable that bus services very often continue to operate despite the extremely adverse environment which they confront. Bus fares tend to be cheap throughout the world, and they allow people with some degree of imagination to travel quite astonishingly long distances at relatively low cost. The second development was the invention, much more recently, of wide-bodied aircraft. Until the 1970s, air travel over long distances tended to be financially beyond the reach of even many citizens of developed countries. The number of seats on planes with narrow fuselages was too low for prices to be generally affordable, and the need to refuel fairly frequently also added to the cost of travel. All this changed with the development of the Boeing 747 and other wide-bodied aircraft. This, together with other changes in the industry, meant that air travel was suddenly accessible to large numbers of people who in the past could never have contemplated flying. As one analyst put it in 2002, 'During the last forty-five years the airline industry has undergone an expansion unrivalled by any other form of public transport. Its rate of technological change has been exceptional. This has resulted in falling costs and fares which have stimulated a very rapid growth in demand for its services'.[62] This in turn meant that people smugglers could move people not just by road or by boat, but also by air.

Complementing this in recent times has been one further very important factor, namely access to higher incomes, or to savings, on the part of some people contemplating exit. In certain situations, refugees are forced to flee with absolutely nothing, and face destitution early in their journeys. But this is not necessarily the case. It is not part of the definition of a refugee that he or she must be destitute. On occasion, anticipatory refugees will liquidate assets in order to hedge against risks that they face during their journeys, and sometimes, the savings of a wider lineage might be 'pooled' in order to allow the particularly vulnerable to escape. Indeed, those who face the threat of complete destitution if they flee may be deterred from making the effort in the first place. In such circumstances, rising real incomes become a potentially-significant enabling factor. That said, global statistics are far too general to provide an illuminating picture of who might move. What is important is the prevailing situation amongst those who might be disposed to flee because of a well-founded fear of being persecuted on the basis of race, religion, nationality, membership of a particular social group or political opinion. In Afghanistan, according to the World Bank, Gross

National Income per capita based on Purchasing Power Parity increased from $890 in 2002 to $2000 in 2014.[63] Even under dictatorships, such as that of Saddam Hussein, there can be periods of prosperity in which ordinary citizens can save or build up assets; and while recent data on Gross National Income per capita in Syria are not available, it is not surprising to find middle-class Syrians amongst those seeking asylum in Europe. They may have both the most to fear from some of the forces at loose in their country, and the wherewithal to attempt an escape.

Globalisation and its impacts

The growing opportunity to travel affordably over long distances is simply one manifestation of the wider effects of globalisation. This phenomenon has created an environment in which the primacy of the 'sovereign state' is challenged not by refugees, but by the costs of seeking to act autonomously when pressures are mounting to conform with rules or norms that reflect globalisation's force. The idea of globalisation is exceptionally complex and multifaceted.[64] The term has been applied to a range of different spheres of international activity. One of the most important is *economic*, and here, 'globalisation' refers to a diverse mix of developments beginning in the early 1970s: the breakdown of the 'Bretton Woods' system of fixed currency exchange rates in favour of floating rates; the emergence of the OPEC cartel as a major determinant of oil prices; the discrediting of protectionism and the entrenching of free trade as a core principle of the World Trade Organization (albeit adulterated to some degree by preferential trade arrangements in particular parts of the world); and the development of real-time financial market trading on a virtually-global basis.[65] This points to a second vital sphere of globalisation, namely developments in *communications technology*. While the telegraph and telephone seemed transformational developments in their day, it was the launch of the satellite Sputnik in October 1957 that inaugurated a genuinely new world of communications, as became clear in June 1967 with the first live global television transmission via satellite. Since then, intercontinental communications have become ubiquitous, not just through television, but through internet-based communications tools such as electronic mail and Skype, and social media platforms such as Facebook and Twitter. A third sphere of globalisation is manifested in what some have called *global governance*, that is, a mix of processes grounded in both bilateral and multilateral engagements by which global policy settings are determined and administered by officials (hopefully) thinking beyond narrow considerations of perceived 'national interest'.[66] To some, this is a threat to democratic states, although arguably such a fear is highly exaggerated.[67]

One of the most significant consequences of globalisation is that images of the wider world are now available to more people than ever before.[68] This is largely a product of the penetration of television as a medium of communication into even remote parts of developing countries. The key point to note here is that the influence of media of this kind can be felt long before every household has access to its own screen. Initially, there may be little more than one television per village, possibly dependent on solar power rather than mains electricity; but this can be enough to induce dramatic social change. Indeed, the force of television as a medium was recognised instantly in 1939 by the writer and MP Harold Nicolson who, while describing it as 'bleary, flickering, dim, unfocused', foresaw that it could 'alter the whole basis of democracy'.[69] Afghanistan provides a good example of how television can alter a society. Some 62.1 per cent of respondents in The Asia Foundation's 2015 survey of Afghan opinion now own a television.[70] When this writer first travelled to Kabul in the 1990s, there was virtually no mains electricity available in the country, and the only television broadcasts were from a tedious state-run channel that few Afghans watched, and which operated for only a limited number of hours each day. Afghan refugees in Pakistan, however, had become used to watching television, and when they returned to Afghanistan after 2001, they were keen to continue doing so, if only as a source of entertainment. The lead in satisfying this need was taken by a group of Afghan-Australian entrepreneurs headed by Saad Mohseni, who began by establishing FM radio stations, and then moved on to establish TOLO television, which swiftly became the most respected and credible outlet in the country for both news and entertainment. This has resulted in its being attacked by the Taliban,[71] but not in its muting its messages. From stations of this kind, even the most casual viewer of Afghan television now has access to pictures of a world that is starkly different from that which they encounter in their everyday lives. Television brings into living rooms images of well-ordered, peaceful and democratic societies to which it attaches specific names. It would be highly surprising if those fearing persecution were not to have such places as their destinations should they opt to leave Afghanistan.

This is also relevant where the issue of messaging is concerned. Key leaders in democratic states have often proclaimed their commitment to assist vulnerable groups, including refugees. The Statue of Liberty in New York Harbor bears the following inscription, a poem entitled *The New Colossus* penned in 1883 by Emma Lazarus when funds to build the statue itself were in the process of being raised:

> Not like the brazen giant of Greek fame,
> With conquering limbs astride from land to land;
> Here at our sea-washed, sunset gates shall stand
> A mighty woman with a torch, whose flame
> Is the imprisoned lightning, and her name
> Mother of Exiles. From her beacon-hand

Glows world-wide welcome; her mild eyes command
The air-bridged harbor that twin cities frame.

'Keep ancient lands, your storied pomp!' cries she
With silent lips. 'Give me your tired, your poor,
Your huddled masses yearning to breathe free
The wretched refuse of your teeming shore.
Send these, the homeless, tempest-tost, to me:
I lift my lamp beside the golden door.

This is one of the best-known works of its kind, but it is by no means unique. The Australian National Anthem, *Advance Australia Fair*, contains in its second verse the lines:

Beneath our radiant Southern Cross.
We'll toil with hearts and hands;
To make this Commonwealth of ours
Renowned of all the lands;
For those who've come across the seas
We've boundless plains to share;
With courage let us all combine
To Advance Australia fair.

There is a considerable irony in the reference to sharing boundless plains with those who've come across the seas: refugees who come across the seas have long been subject under Australian policy to mandatory detention, either in Australia or more recently in offshore facilities in Nauru or Papua New Guinea. The point, nonetheless, is that with relatively few exceptions, states continue to paint themselves, even if hypocritically, as committed to protecting the vulnerable, and in a globalised world, this can be the message that many refugees hear. No matter how hard they may try, it is difficult for countries such as Australia to seem as vicious as the Taliban or Daesh.

It is also important to bear in mind that in a globalised world, refugees may require a significant degree of sophistication to survive, and will not be easily conned by state propaganda. Western states often show little skill in this area. Countermeasures to cope with Daesh's information operations have on occasion proved embarrassingly feeble and ill-conceived.[72] Just as risible was a cartoon booklet used by the Australian Government to try to dissuade Afghan Hazara refugees from seeking to reach Australia.[73] The penultimate page depicted an Hazara man downcast at missing a happy dance scene shown in a 'thought bubble' above his head. The only problem was that the dancers in the 'bubble' were quite plainly ethnic Pushtuns, whom a significant number of Hazaras view as historic oppressors. Hazaras to whom this writer showed the cartoon tended to react with laughter (if they were kind-hearted) and searing scorn (if they were not). There is no evidence publicly available that this campaign offered value for money. And this is not surprising. A study by Dr Roslyn Richardson of Australia's deterrent messaging has shown that refugee audiences are complex and unpredictable, reading messages in a range of different ways. As she concluded, 'Australia's deterrence message is unlikely to have the desired impact while it continues to be based on an understanding of "the audience" that lies in stark contrast to the way refugees see themselves and their journeys'.[74]

Refugees' sources of information have been augmented by one other striking technology of the globalised world, namely mobile phones. Cellphone technology has permitted forms of networking of a kind totally unprecedented in human history.[75] Subscriber Identity Module (SIM) cards not only serve to connect a handset to a telephone network, but can be loaded with credit so that even those with no fixed abode can access a telephone service. Furthermore, as technology has become more sophisticated, the capacity to send and receive text messages and photographs has been built into the mobile phone, which can also function as a high-resolution camera as well as a communications device. Phone users have the opportunity as a result to interact in complex and sophisticated ways with an extraordinarily diverse range of people. Some of these will likely be family members, but the spread of the technology opens the door to much more complex exercises in phone-based coordination, such as the management of people smuggling networks. While tapping a mobile phone conversation may not be especially difficult from a technical point of view, there are many ways in which those who do not wish to be overheard can protect their privacy—by using obscure languages, by speaking in coded language, by borrowing phones from others who may not be suspected of involvement in nefarious activity, or simply by using mobile phone conversations only for innocuous purposes, with suspect purposes being pursued in different ways. On the whole, the empowerment of refugees in flight that results from access to mobile phone technology is yet to be offset by countervailing measures taken by states to reassert their power.

The reassertion of state power is central to an understanding of the politics of immigration and of refugees. Many factors can constrain a state's freedom of action, including international law, regional organisations, and the judiciary,[76] but few states like what is happening. It is therefore unsurprising that from time to time states seek to cooperate in order to realise shared goals of restricting the movement of people. This, however, is not as straightforward an undertaking as might superficially seem to be the case. While states may share a particular objective, they may differ on the question of how best it should be realised, not least because different approaches may carry different costs, and the burden of costs may fall differently on individual states under different models. In those circumstances, what might seem to be a straightforward negotiation to set a common position can prove to be anything but straightfoward. This is central to the discussions that are being pursued in Europe in anticipation of further substantial flows of desperate refugees in Europe's direction. For this reason, it is necessary to appreciate, both conceptually and practically, some of the complexities of modern diplomatic engagement, and how these challenges play out when the central focus of discussion is refugees. These issues are taken up in detail in the next chapter.

6

DIPLOMACY AND REFUGEES

Any attempts by states to deal with complex refugee challenges will almost inevitably require resort to the tools of diplomacy.[1] Diplomacy is a social practice of great antiquity, and provides the mechanisms for effective engagement between states, and increasingly between states and non-state actors.[2] The classic form of diplomacy is bilateral, conducted between two states and commonly underpinned by formal diplomatic relations with either resident or non-resident Ambassadors or High Commissioners being appointed from one state to another.[3] Since the late nineteenth century, bilateral diplomacy has been increasingly complemented by multilateral diplomacy with a multiplicity of participating actors, sometimes in the context of international organisations, but sometimes in the context of loosely-institutionalised processes, or of *ad hoc* meetings or conferences.[4] Diplomacy is governed by a mixture of formal rules, notably those embodied in the *Vienna Convention on Diplomatic Relations* of 1961,[5] and uncodified norms and understandings. While diplomacy has a range of dimensions, including 'representation' and 'reproduction of international society',[6] its central element is arguably 'communication', with negotiation being at the heart of this activity. Effective negotiation very often turns on the ability to strike a bargain, but in some circumstances, the distinct art of persuasion also comes into play.[7] Since it is a social practice, diplomacy has the flexibility to evolve, as it arguably has done dramatically in the face of changes in technology and in the expectations that political leaders have of their diplomatic servants.[8]

Frameworks for negotiation over refugees

The establishment of the Executive Committee of UNHCR by the UN General Assembly put in place one important multilateral forum for negotiations over matters relating to refugees. Meeting annually in Geneva, the Executive Committee provides an opportunity not only for states to express their views, but for a range of advocacy groups to exploit the opportunity to promote their own perspectives from the sidelines. The importance of this should not be underestimated. In multilateral gatherings, a great deal of important discussion can take place outside the formal venues of interaction, in what are sometimes called 'corridor discussions'. At Executive Committee meetings, there is a specific opportunity for NGO statements to be made at a number of points in its deliberations, an undertaking coordinated by the Geneva-based International Council of Voluntary Agencies (ICVA). The Executive Committee's membership includes a number of states (notably Pakistan, Jordan, Lebanon and the United States) which are not parties to the 1951 *Convention* but which are significant players either as countries of first asylum, or significant contributors to resettlement. Yet at the same time, it is important to note that the UNHCR Executive Committee does not provide a venue for the management of refugee crises. To do so, it would need to be permanently on call, since acute time pressure is one of the common features of a crisis.[9] Any committee that meets only for four days in one month of a year is not a management body. What the Executive Committee can do is articulate, through its 'Conclusions', a range of 'soft law' principles with the potential to guide the responsibilities of states when crises come along.

Another multilateral venue in which refugee issues surface, although it is not exclusively focused on refugees, is the International Organization for Migration (IOM). Established in 1951 as the Provisional Intergovernmental Committee for the Movement of Migrants from Europe, it was rebadged in 1952 as the Intergovernmental Committee for European Migration (ICEM), and in 1980 as the Intergovernmental Committee for Migration (ICM) before finally assuming its current form in 1989. Its present Director-General is Ambassador William Lacy Swing of the United States. It is funded almost exclusively by voluntary contributions from member states. It is, however, not a body focused on refugee protection, which remains the responsibility of UNHCR. Rather, its focus is on providing logistical support at the request of its members (currently 162 in number) via an extremely diverse portfolio of projects.

In addition to these organisations, a venue of increasing salience in the Asia-Pacific region is the so-called 'Bali Process on People Smuggling, Trafficking in Persons and Related Transnational Crime'. It has 48 members, including IOM, UNHCR, and the United Nations Office on Drugs and Crime (UNODC); and a range of other countries and agencies, many of them European, participate in its activities. It is nothing if not ecumenical; even North Korea is a member. Despite its multinational character, the Bali Process is very much a creature of Australian initiatives, with the bulk of its funding coming from Australia as well.[10] The background is relatively straightforward: in 2001, at the time of the Tampa Affair,[11] Australia floundered to find a state that would relieve it of the burden of responsibility for those refugees whom the crew of the Tampa had rescued from the waters of the Indian Ocean. Eventually, the Pacific state of Nauru stepped into the breach (for a price), but since it was a microstate, it was not in a position to offer 'relief' for more than a small number of refugees.

The Bali Process therefore served as a mechanism by which Australia could seek in the future to shift its responsibilities into the hands of the wider range of actors. As a result, the Bali process has not proved to be especially impressive when issues have arisen that do not particularly engage the interests of the co-chairs, Australia and Indonesia. An example of this occurred in 2015 when Rohingyas seeking to escape by boat from Burma were left abandoned in the Andaman Sea.[12] Asked whether Australia would help in relieving their desperate plight, the then Australian Prime Minister, who was noted for thinking in slogans, replied 'Nope, nope, nope'.[13] As the former Indonesian Foreign Minister, Dr Hassan Wirajuda put it in early 2016, 'The Bali Process did nothing to respond to the issue of Rohingya, because of the different degree of interest, including the co-chairs of the Bali Process ... It illustrates that Rohingya migrants were not within the purview of the Bali Process, and in fact, a series of ad hoc meetings were initiated by Malaysia, Thailand and Indonesia outside the framework of the Bali Process'.[14] The lesson here is that in the absence of political will, the mere existence of a diplomatic framework for multilateral engagement may count for relatively little.

Diplomatic engagement may also be constrained by considerations of legality, an issue that came to the surface in the aftermath of a meeting of European Heads of State or Government on 7 March 2016 with Prime Minister Ahmet Davutoğlu of Turkey. In a statement issued at the conclusion of the meeting, the Heads of State or Government affirmed a range of principles: 'to return all new irregular migrants crossing from Turkey into the Greek islands with the costs covered by the EU'; 'to resettle, for every Syrian readmitted by Turkey from Greek islands, another Syrian from Turkey to the EU Member States, within the framework of the existing commitments'; 'to accelerate the implementation of the visa liberalization roadmap with all Member States with a view to lifting the visa requirements for Turkish citizens at the latest by the end of June 2016'; 'to speed up the disbursement of the initially allocated 3 billion euros to ensure funding of a first set of projects before the end of March and decide on additional funding for the Refugee Facility for Syrians'; 'to prepare for the decision on the opening of new chapters in the accession negotiations as soon as possible, building on the October 2015 European Council conclusions'; and 'to work with Turkey in any joint endeavour to improve humanitarian conditions inside Syria which would allow for the local population and refugees to live in areas which will be more safe'.[15]

These principles, in some respects simply reflecting long-standing dispositions,[16] nonetheless met with immediate criticism. Amnesty International stated that 'EU and Turkish leaders have today sunk to a new low, effectively horse trading away the rights and dignity of some of the world's most vulnerable people. The idea of bartering refugees for refugees is not only dangerously dehumanising, but also offers no sustainable long term solution to the ongoing humanitarian crisis'.[17] UNHCR's spokesman voiced concern 'about any arrangement that involves the blanket return of all individuals from one country to another without sufficiently spelt out refugee protection safeguards in keeping with international obligations'. He went on that 'An asylum-seeker should only be returned to a third state, if (a) responsibility for assessing the particular asylum application in substance is assumed by the third country; (b) the asylum-seeker will be protected from refoulement; (c) the individual will be able to seek and, if recognized, enjoy asylum in accordance with accepted international standards, and have full and effective access to education, work, health care and, as necessary, social assistance'.[18] Vincent Cochetel, UNHCR's Regional Refugee Coordinator for the Refugee Crisis in Europe, put it very bluntly: 'The collective expulsion of foreigners is prohibited under the European Convention of Human Rights ... An agreement that would be tantamount to a blanket return to a third country is not consistent with European law, not consistent with international law'.[19] These criticisms seemed to hit home, and in a further meeting on 17–18 March, European leaders adopted a (somewhat) modified framework. The new agreement stated that:

> All new irregular migrants crossing from Turkey into Greek islands as from 20 March 2016 will be returned to Turkey. This will take place in full accordance with EU and international law, thus excluding any kind of collective expulsion. All migrants will be protected in accordance with the relevant international standards and in respect of the principle of non-refoulement.[20]

Whether this amounted to much remained a matter for debate. Amnesty International responded blisteringly: 'Promises to respect international and European law appear suspiciously like sugar-coating the cyanide pill that refugee protection in Europe has just been forced to swallow ... Guarantees to scrupulously respect international law are incompatible with the touted return to Turkey of all irregular migrants arriving on the Greek islands as of Sunday. Turkey is not a safe country for refugees and migrants, and any return process predicated on its being so will be flawed, illegal and immoral, whatever phantom guarantees precede this pre-declared outcome'.[21]

The principal treaties dealing with refugee matters are all multilateral, but bilateral negotiation has a role to play in developing non-binding Memoranda of Understanding (MoUs) that can shape the handling of refugee issues on a bilateral basis. In such negotiations, it is important that negotiators have their wits about them. A striking example of what can happen if they do not came in the form of a 'Memorandum of Understanding between the Government of the Kingdom of Cambodia and the Government of Australia relating to the Settlement of Refugees in Cambodia' signed on 26 September 2014. This provided in Article 4 that:[22]

> The Kingdom of Cambodia will offer permanent settlement to persons who:
>
> (a) have undergone a refugee status determination process in the Republic of Nauru and have been determined to be a Refugee, and meet the entry and settlement requirements of the Kingdom of Cambodia;
>
> (b) have been provided with further information by Cambodian competent officials on living conditions, customs, tradition, culture and religion of the Kingdom of Cambodia; and (c) voluntarily accept an offer of settlement as evidenced by written consent, and who travel to the Kingdom of Cambodia voluntarily.

The MoU went on to provide in Article 5 that 'The number of Refugees settled, and the timing of their arrival into Cambodia under this MOU, will be subject to the consent of the Kingdom of Cambodia.'

The striking feature of the MoU was how one-sided it was. Given the wording of Article 5, Cambodia was not obliged to accept any refugees at all. On the other hand, on 25 September 2014, the Australian Minister for Immigration and Border Protection, Scott Morrison, disclosed in a radio interview that 'the Australian Government will be providing over four years $40 million to support various overseas development aid projects. That's on top of the $79 million or thereabouts we currently provide in aid to Cambodia'.[23] By late 2015, a further A$15 million had been committed to fund the scheme.[24] Yet only five refugees had voluntarily availed themselves of the opportunity to move from Nauru to Cambodia.[25] It would be hard to argue that this represented good value for Australian taxpayers' money.

This was despite desperate efforts by Australian officials to talk up the charms of Cambodia to refugees on Nauru.[26] A document circulated on Nauru entitled 'Settlement in Cambodia' stated that Cambodia was 'a safe country, free from persecution and violence,' where one could enjoy 'all the freedoms of a democratic society including freedom of religion and freedom of speech'. Cambodia was said to be a country that did 'not have problems with violent crime', and where police maintained 'law and order'. The document also maintained that 'Cambodia has a high standard of health care, with multiple hospitals and general practitioners'. These claims were at odds with those made by other Australian Government agencies. For example, the Department of Foreign Affairs and Trade warned that

> Opportunistic crime is common in Cambodia ... Assaults and armed robberies against foreigners have also occurred, and foreigners have been seriously injured and killed ... Foreigners have been the target of sexual assault in Cambodia ... The level of firearm ownership in Cambodia is high, and guns are sometimes used to resolve disputes ... Some people were killed and a large number injured in separate protests in Phnom Penh in late 2013 and early 2014 ... Health and medical services in Cambodia are generally of a very poor quality and very limited in the services they can provide. Outside Phnom Penh there are almost no medical facilities equipped to deal with medical emergencies ... In the event of a serious illness or accident, medical evacuation to a destination with the appropriate facilities would be necessary.[27]

It is hardly surprising that an academic commentator concluded that 'As an impoverished country with a poor human rights record, Cambodia is a completely unsuitable host for the resettlement of asylum seekers'.[28] An official of Human Rights Watch put it even more bluntly than this: 'It was a classic Phnom Penh sting job on a donor; get the money upfront but don't concede the operational control over the project—and then stall or obfuscate until you get the outcome you want, which in this case was only a handful of refugees'. He added that Cambodia's Prime Minister, Hun Sen, was 'laughing all the way to the bank'.[29]

When debacles of this sort occur, one possible explanation may lie in the training and experience of the officials involved. In negotiations over refugee issues, it is often not the Foreign Ministry in a country that is the lead agency in handling the negotiations, but rather the ministry or department of government that carries prime responsibility for refugee processing. This can be reflected in the political leadership of delegations. Thus, at the Evian conference in 1938, the British delegation was not led by Viscount Halifax, the Foreign Secretary, but by Earl Winterton, the Chancellor of the Duchy of Lancaster. On occasion, officials from these other ministries or departments have shown great dexterity as negotiators, but this has often been when they have been long-serving staff members who have acquired extensive international experience. Increasingly, however, as lateral recruitment becomes a feature of Western bureaucratic systems, there is a risk that negotiations of some complexity and sensitivity will end up in the hands of naïve officials with inadequate background. This is not just a matter affecting negotiations in the sphere of refugee policy; foreign ministries the world over are struggling to maintain professional standards as other ministries, departments, and agencies stake their claim to roles in international engagement for which they may be ill-prepared.

'Burden sharing' and its dilemmas

One of the main drivers for negotiation over refugee issues is the irregular way in which the burden of responsibility for refugees falls upon states.[30] As noted earlier, refugees in the first instance tend for the most part to flee to neighbouring states that may be nearly as troubled as their own. A sudden and substantial flow of refugees may be destabilising for such hosts. They may lack the resources to provide adequate support to the refugee population; the arrival of refugees may alter the balance of ethnic groups within a state that has experienced serious ethnic conflict in the past; and in weak states they may appear to pose a threat to the state's security.[31] The host states may not even be parties to the 1951 *Convention* or other relevant international instruments; this was the case with Pakistan following the Soviet invasion of Afghanistan. Such states therefore look to more developed countries to assist in sharing the burden of the Westphalian system's inadequacies. Yet as a matter of international law, there is no obligation to share refugee burdens, and it is therefore something to be resolved in the sphere of international politics, through diplomatic engagement. As Gregor Noll has pointed out, this gives rise to a 'multi-actor, multi-level game'.[32] In diplomacy, state negotiators are regularly looking over their shoulders in order to ensure that what they are proposing will not be thwarted by hostile domestic opinion,[33] and one of the difficulties here is that members of the public, and politicians responding to them, may be much more focused on short-term costs than on long-term benefits. Thus, while refugees in the long run may be significant assets for a society, negotiators often focus on ways of minimising short-term costs that they might be obliged to carry. And what can add to the challenge are the broad asymmetries of power in the international system. In many cases, there is little that poorer and weaker states can do to induce wealthier and stronger states to do more to help those in the greatest need.

This is an issue that has been extensively discussed in recent writings.[34] The trigger was an article in 1998 by the Norwegian scholar Astri Suhrke, who depicted refugee protection as a public good—that is, an activity the benefits of which could not be denied to those who declined to contribute to it. The notorious risk that then arises is that of 'free riding'.[35] Suhrke pointed to two historical cases where this dispiriting logic had been overcome. One was post-World War Two resettlement, which she saw as the product of a mixed instrumental-communitarian model, where norms and interests drove resettlement. The other was the resettlement of Vietnamese refugees, the product of a hegemonic scheme underpinned by the power of the United States.[36] In subsequent writings, a number of other insights have surfaced. One is that norms of behaviour can emerge to constrain the disposition to engage in free riding,[37] and that UNHCR can play an important role as a norm-entrepreneur.[38] Another is that UNHCR can play a significant role in issue-linkage. This particular insight has been developed in most detail by Alexander Betts. He argues that the global refugee regime is best modelled as a 'suasion game', in which, in a two-actor model, 'one player is privileged and must be persuaded to participate and the other has little choice but to cooperate'.[39] The effects of these power asymmetries, can, however, be overcome or at least ameliorated, by what Betts calls 'cross-issue persuasion'. As Betts puts it in summary form:[40]

> Rather than contributing to refugee protection in the South for its own sake, Northern states' willingness to contribute has depended upon a belief that there is a substantive causal relationship between refugees in the South and interests in other issue-areas affecting the North such as security, migration, and trade. However, because the material relationship between refugee protection in the South and other issue-areas in the North has been subject to uncertainty or ambiguity, UNHCR has played a significant role in influencing Northern states' beliefs about the causal relationship between issue-areas through a combination of information provision, argumentation, institutional design, and playing an epistemic role.

In elaborating this argument, Betts examines a range of specific cases: the International Conference on Central American

Refugees; the Comprehensive Plan of Action for Indochinese refugees; the 1981 and 1984 International Conferences on Assistance to Refugees in Africa; and the 'Convention Plus' initiative of 2003–2005. Issue-linkage was arguably the key to success in the first two examples; its absence—or a failure to recognise it—shed light on the failure of the second two.

One important qualification, however, needs to be offered to the 'suasion game' model. Power is not an absolute or measurable phenomenon. It is an attribute of relationships, and occasionally situation or context can 'flip' what might seem an obvious asymmetry of power so that the relationship does not operate quite as one might have expected. The basis lies in Francis Bacon's observation that 'It is better dealing with men in appetite, than those that are where they would be'.[41] Sometimes major powers are 'in appetite'. This was of course the case with the European Heads of State and Government who met with the Turkish Prime Minister on 7 and 18 March 2016, and Turkey prima facie could feel well pleased with the concessions to it that were offered. Australia in 2001 also provided an arresting example of how asymmetries in power can be offset. On paper, the asymmetries in power between Australia and Nauru are enormous, and favour the former. When Australia was seeking a state that would agree to relieve it of the refugees who had been on board the Tampa, Nauru came to mind. An eminent specialist on the Pacific wrote, of Australia's so-called 'Pacific Solution', that the 'vulnerable and small societies of the Pacific did not just *happen* to be approached by Australia; they were approached *because* they were vulnerable and dependent on Australia'.[42]

Nauru was a deeply unsavoury state. As a report in *The New York Times* put it, 'Nauru operates as an offshore tax haven and stands accused of laundering around $70 billion in Russian mafia money'.[43] However, Australia's frantic search for a dumping-ground gave Nauru remarkable leverage. Specifically, pursuant to the 'First Administrative Arrangement' with Nauru of September 2001, Australia paid over $1 million to cover outstanding hospital accounts for treatment in Australia of Nauruan citizens.[44] To have committed to cover future hospital accounts in Australia for Nauruans might legitimately have been called 'aid' (since the category of potential beneficiaries would have been defined only by their citizenship), but to pay outstanding accounts from the past would best be described as 'bribery' (since it would relieve a specific group of individuals, including quite possibly members of the Nauruan political leadership, of the burden of private debts).[45] Australia even reportedly lobbied—unsuccessfully—against the application of 'countermeasures' to Nauru arising from its being included on the List of Non-Cooperative Countries and Territories (NCCTs) maintained by the OECD Financial Action Task Force on Money-Laundering. Since all OECD countries would have understood Australia's vulnerability to a state notorious for its financial opacity, it is unlikely that this particular endeavour added to Australia's international standing.[46] Nauru retains its leverage to this day. The collapse of the rule of law in Nauru has been met with almost total silence from Australia,[47] and it remains a major aid beneficiary. In the May 2015 Australian budget, Afghanistan, with an UN-estimated population of 29,825,000, was slated to receive A$78.5 million in aid for 2015–2016 ($2.63 per person per year, or 22 cents a month). Nauru, with an Australian detention centre, and a UN-estimated population of 10,000, was slated to receive A$21.2 million in aid for 2015–2016 ($2,120.00 per person per year, or $176.67 a month).

A state's being 'in appetite' can also have a chilling effect on its human rights advocacy. No one would seriously expect Europe at this juncture to take a strong stand on the erosion of freedoms in Turkey under the regime of President Recep Tayyip Erdoğan. The more likely precedent for it to follow is the Australian relationship with the Sri Lankan regime of President Mahinda Rajapaksa, to which Australia looked for cooperation in preventing an outflow of Tamil asylum seekers in Australia's direction. A great deal of evidence pointed to this regime's having committed major war crimes in May 2009 in its (ultimately-successful) push to obliterate the terrorist 'Liberation Tigers of Tamil Eelam',[48] with the president's brother, Defence Secretary Gotabaya Rajapaksa, being a particularly prominent suspect.[49] There was also evidence of Sri Lankan forces committing extensive acts of rape and sexual abuse against Tamils.[50] Yet at a press conference in Colombo on 15 November 2013, when quizzed about claims that the Sri Lankan regime made use of torture, the Australian Prime Minister offered an almost *pro forma* statement that torture was to be deplored, and then undermined it by saying 'But we accept that sometimes in difficult circumstances, difficult things happen', adding that Sri Lanka was 'advancing towards the goals of justice and freedom under the law'.[51] Immigration and Border Control Minister Scott Morrison subsequently hosted Gotabaya Rajapaksa in Canberra for a bilateral meeting in April 2014. A Sri Lankan Government statement reported that Rajapaksa 'thanked the Government of Australia for the bold decision of not co-sponsoring this year's human rights resolution on Sri Lanka'.[52]

Diplomatic responses that focus on short-term rather than long-term considerations are understandable from a political perspective, but can prove exceedingly dangerous in the long run. In earlier chapters, mention was made of two examples which illustrate this point: the use of refugee camps as operating bases for combatants, and the danger that long-term warehousing of refugees may set the scene for the development in the future of radical groups that may prove very difficult to control. It is therefore tempting to ask how diplomacy might be reformed in such a way as to minimise dangers of this kind. The answer, unfortunately, is that there is no easy solution. Diplomacy is an elaborate social practice, but it is also a human institution, subject to the frailties that flow from human imperfections. Political leaders who set objectives for diplomats maybe unrealistic, naïve or indifferent to the challenge of matching ends and means. Diplomats themselves, even if they have clear ideas of their objectives, may be thwarted by lack of resources, or inconsistencies between objectives defined by political leaderships. Above all, in democracies, political leaders are prone to aspire to re-election, and this creates a strong inbuilt bias in favour of policies designed to fit relatively short electoral cycles. The sophisticated version of this mindset is commonly defended by reference to John Maynard Keynes's 1923 comment 'In the long run we are all dead'[53]—although Keynes's aphorism can be read as a call to act in the present, rather than defer action until it is too late. A more popular version, attributed to the mistress of King Louis XV in eighteenth century France, Madame de Pompadour, was embodied in the words 'After me, the deluge'. Unfortunately, when short-term thinking dominates refugee policy, many may suffer from the deluge that can result— both refugees and non-refugees alike.

The temptation of 'easy options'

In almost any sphere of public policy, political leaders are confronted with the need to make choices between different options that are available to them. This is also true of diplomacy. The danger is that options that seem easiest will be those that are favoured, even in the short-term. Yet this may be at the cost not just of the interests, but also of the rights, of refugees under international law. And the 'easiest' options may be exclusionary policies that enjoy domestic political support, obviating the need for energetic leadership to win domestic support for humane policies that might initially seem likely to encounter significant opposition. This difficulty arises because some refugee situations are truly intractable and do not lend themselves to solution in ways that respect refugees' needs for protection. Several factors come into play in defining a situation as intractable. One may be the strength of the forces that give rise to a well-founded fear of being persecuted. On occasion, vulnerable groups come under attack from richly-resourced and highly-institutionalised coercive instrumentalities that show no sign of disappearing. Where this is the case, it is innocent in the extreme to suggest that the threat which refugees face will necessarily dissipate in a reasonable time. This time element, however, is the second factor that needs to be taken into account. Sometimes, nasty threats *can* dissipate quite quickly. The Rwandan genocide of 1994 came to a conclusion when the *génocidaires* were driven out of the country by forces opposed to them. In 1999, the threat to Kosovar Albanians from forces loyal to the Serbian leader Slobodan Milošević was eventually overcome by NATO's intervention. A third factor is simply whether refugees stand a good chance of promptly securing a durable solution to their plight. Only if these do not materialise can one realistically speak of an intractable refugee situation.

It is when dealing with intractable refugee situations, either existing or prospective, that diplomacy over refugees is likely to prove most contentious. If, for example, diplomatic discussions take place in order to coordinate relief for a particular needy refugee population, the shared goal of providing relief often functions as a lubricant for the discussions themselves. By contrast, negotiations over how to manage an intractable situation tend to have a zero-sum character—one party's gain is another party's loss—and domestic politics may as a result intrude much further into the discussions. An easy option is to privilege domestic opinion over refugees' needs. European leaders face this quandary at present. There is no sign that the factors driving refugees to leave Syria for neighbouring countries are diminishing in force, and with 'durable solutions' on offer for very few, it is more than likely that they will continue to seek, outside any managed framework, to leave countries of first asylum in large numbers. German Chancellor Angela Merkel has shown remarkable generosity towards those fleeing oppression; she leads the Christian Democratic Union and doubtless recalls the Parable of the Good Samaritan. At the same time, her party faces a challenge from the far right-wing Alternative für Deutschland,[54] which polled well in March 2016 elections in several German Länder, securing 24.2% of the vote in Sachsen-Anhalt, 15.1% in Baden-Württemberg and 12.6% in Rheinland-Pfalz. That said, support for refugees remains relatively strong in Germany,[55] but intractable refugee situations can easily create domestic political dilemmas.

One way of addressing serious problems can be to lapse into self-delusion. This is rarely a wise move. In writing about the handling of the 1938 Czechoslovak crisis, now widely regarded as a diplomatic disaster for the British Government, Telford Taylor described it as 'a potent and historically valid symbol of the dangers of not facing up to unpleasant realities'.[56] It is surprising that this failing continues to surface in diplomatic processes, for as the Athenians warned the Melians in ancient times, hope is by its nature an expensive commodity.[57] Nonetheless, there is no shortage of examples of just this kind of thinking coming into play. Sometimes it can surface as part of a wider package of measures. In 1988, following the signing of the Geneva Accords on Afghanistan, the United Nations launched a major program designed to raise funds for refugees returning to their homes from Pakistan and Iran. The only problem was that refugee repatriation did not occur in accordance with the planners' hopes, not least because the Geneva Accords left unresolved a key issue in dispute in Afghanistan, namely the character of internal political authority. By the time a significant repatriation did occur, in

1992 following the collapse of the communist regime, many donor states felt with some justification that they had already made their contributions to assist Afghan refugees some four years earlier, even though the funds contributed at that time had been spent on a range of activities not directly focused on facilitating repatriation. The point here is that it was highly predictable that refugees would not return in 1988; the pretence that they would seemed to be part of a package of measures to augment what momentum had been created by the signing of the Geneva Accords.

This misjudgment was unfortunate, but arguably not especially dangerous in the greater scheme of things. Much more dangerous is the pretense that it is safe for those who have fled a country to return, even though there may be credible evidence that it remains unstable. The irony is that states that routinely make such claims—the United Kingdom's approach to Afghanistan comes to mind—often surround their embassies in the country concerned with multiple layers of security, and use websites to warn their own citizens against travelling there. Thus, the Foreign and Commonwealth Office warns that 'There is a high threat from terrorism and specific methods of attack are evolving and increasing in sophistication. There is a high threat of kidnapping throughout the country ... The security situation throughout Afghanistan remains uncertain, and could change rapidly'.[58] This is an accurate assessment of the situation in Afghanistan, especially in respect of its extreme fluidity; but it is striking that the Home Secretary's view of the situation in Afghanistan is much more sanguine when asylum claims are being considered.[59] The Foreign and Commonwealth Office assessment also differs from that contained in a 'non-paper' from the European Commission and European External Action Service that was leaked to the media in March 2016.[60] This argued that 'Member States have the competence, when processing asylum applications, to declare which areas are safe or not' and that there 'is a need for a common definition of *safe areas* in Afghanistan'.[61] Yet the notion of there being a 'safe area' at all in a country such as Afghanistan is deeply problematic. Kunduz, for example, received substantial assistance over a long period of time thanks to the presence of a German Provincial Reconstruction Team (PRT),[62] but that did not prevent it falling to the Taliban in late September 2015. The situation throughout Afghanistan is simply too unpredictable for any part of the country realistically to be pronounced 'safe'.

If states can choose the easy options of shaping their policies to appease domestic constituencies, or of turning a blind eye to situations that might put refugees and asylum seekers at peril, a third 'easy option' they might pursue diplomatically is to negotiate to pay a third country to assume their responsibilities, so that they can either escape the burden of assisting refugees directly, or deter refugees for approaching them for protection in the first place. This can amount to what some call a strategy of 'vicarious dirty hands'. Australia pioneered this approach with its 2001 'Pacific Solution', and continues to do so by funding offshore detention centres on Nauru, and Manus in Papua New Guinea. The misery to which asylum seekers were consigned in Papua New Guinea was noted in a report from a UNHCR monitoring mission in January 2013:[63]

> UNHCR considers that, at present, all transferees at the Centre are subject to deprivation of liberty in a closed place which amounts to 'detention' under international law ... In accordance with international law, detention that is imposed in order to deter future asylum-seekers, or to dissuade those who have commenced their claims from pursuing them, is inconsistent with international norms, and would be arbitrary ... There was one smaller marquee which had neither a floor nor full sides, meaning the 13 men living there were sleeping with an extremely muddy and wet floor, and had no effective way of keeping mosquitos

out. There were no lights in this marquee, and the roof was leaking. The physical living conditions for the 13 men in this smaller marquee were deplorable ...'.

Worse was to come. In February 2014, an asylum seeker of Iranian origin, Reza Barati, was beaten to death. Reviewing the circumstances, an Australian Senate Committee concluded that it was 'clear from evidence presented to the committee that the Australian Government failed in its duty to protect asylum seekers including Mr Barati from harm', and that it was 'undeniable that a significant number of local service provider staff, as well as a small minority of expat staff, were involved in the violence against transferees'.[64] The conditions on Manus remained a threat to life and limb. Another young Iranian, Hamid Kehazaei, died on 5 September 2014 after contracting a simple septicaemic infection that could not be adequately treated.[65] Dr Peter Young, who spent three years as Director of Mental Health for the Australian Government's contractor International Health and Medical Services, described the detention centre environment as 'inherently toxic'.[66] Finally, in April 2016, the Supreme Court of Justice of Papua New Guinea ruled unanimously that the detention of asylum seekers and transferees was contrary to their constitutional right of personal liberty guaranteed by s.42 of the *Constitution*, and ordered that both 'the Australian and Papua New Guinea governments shall forthwith take all steps necessary to cease and prevent the continued unconstitutional and illegal detention of the asylum seekers or transferees at the relocation centre on Manus Island and the continued breach of the asylum seekers or transferees Constitutional and human rights'.[67]

There is an additional problem associated with 'outsourcing of responsibility', namely that the state to which the outsourcing occurs may not be able adequately to process claims for refugee status, or provide adequate protection to those found to be refugees. For example, it is by now well established that sexual orientation can found a claim for refugee protection on the basis of 'membership of a particular social group'.[68] In Papua New Guinea, however, section 210 of the 1974 *Criminal Code* criminalises certain consensual male homosexual acts. Asylum seekers removed from Australia (where no such provisions exist) to Papua New Guinea might be unable safely to articulate and substantiate their claims for asylum, since the very act of doing so might entail the provision of 'confessional evidence' on the strength of which a prosecution for violation of section 210 could follow.

While there was no suggestion that prolonged detention explicitly formed part of the European plan to outsource the housing of refugees to Turkey, this particular case equally highlights some of the dangers of 'easy options'. Quite apart from the issue, noted earlier, of a potential political volcano being established on Europe's doorstep through the warehousing of refugees deprived of much hope, there are other flaws in the approach that were noted in a stinging comment by Alexander Betts initially prepared for the Spanish newspaper *El País*. As well as noting legal and human rights problems, Betts focussed on the crucial issue of Turkey's internal politics:[69]

[T]he Turkish commitment is only possible because of particular dynamics within Turkish politics. The distribution of Erdogan's support base, the shared religion of most Turks and Syrians, the Alawite population in the South-East, the desire of Erdogan to please the international community make it possible to Turkey to host so many Syrians. But this could change. Until now, the Turkish government is quick to blame the Kurds for all terrorist attacks in mainland Turkey. But what if a bomb were to go off in Istanbul? As soon as that perception changes, will the Turkish electorate continue to welcome Syrians?

Refugee issues almost always play out in a complex and difficult political environment, and it is easier to divert refugees from one place to another than to solve refugee problems.[70] Diplomats concerned with refugee issues should disabuse themselves of the notion that there are any 'quick fix', 'rabbit out of a hat' solutions to complicated refugee problems. There are not. Any solution that seems too good to be true more than likely *is* too good to be true.

Refugees as agents

Refugees are often completely overlooked as agents to be taken into account where diplomacy is concerned. There are a number of reasons why this is the case. First, refugees themselves, especially those in flight, may be almost wholly preoccupied with surviving on a day-to-day basis. In such circumstances, they may have little time for voicing their concerns about wider policy. While refugee camps may have consultative committees to allow administrators to sense the mood of the resident populations, it is highly unlikely that issues of global refugee policy will figure all that much on the agendas of discussion. Second, refugees are far from being a homogeneous collective. Refugee populations may be severely divided on the basis of both social structure and attitudes. In such circumstances, identifying 'representative' refugee voices may be quite difficult. Third, to some degree effective diplomatic conversation depends upon participants having assimilated a range of norms of engagement which cannot necessarily be expected of refugees; there is therefore a risk that refugees and their diplomat interlocutors may fail to engage effectively because, metaphorically speaking, they are employing quite different languages.

Indeed, far from being treated as purposive agents, refugees may be manipulated to serve the interests of other actors. The EU-Turkey agreement provides an obvious example: not for nothing did Human Rights Watch respond with the warning that 'Refugees should not be used as bargaining chips'.[71]

Unfortunately, there is no shortage of comparable historical examples. When General Zia ul Haq of Pakistan welcomed Afghan refugees following the Soviet invasion of Afghanistan, it was not simply humanitarian impulses that drove his behaviour; Zia consciously set out to position Pakistan as a 'frontline state' in order to rescue his country from the isolation into which it had slipped following the execution in 1979 of the former Pakistani Prime Minister Zulfikar Ali Bhutto. Zia was also extremely careful to ensure that Pakistan could exercise firm control over the Afghan refugee population. As an officer deployed in Jordan, he had been witness to the clash in 1970 between the Hashemite monarchy of King Hussein and the Palestinian groups that were driven out in the events of so-called 'Black September'; and he was determined that Pakistan would not undergo any similar experience. In order to ensure this, a body was established known as the 'Commissionerate for Afghan Refugees of the Northwest Frontier Province', and it was this body, rather than international agencies, that played the lead role in managing what came to be known as 'Refugee Tented Villages, or RTVs. A well-oiled public relations mechanism was put in place to showcase these to visitors, with the more militarised elements of the refugee population being kept well out of sight.

Refugees can be manipulated in one other notable fashion, namely to strike fear in a population disposed to be suspicious of refugees. In Chapter Three, it was noted that Nazi Germany sought to stoke anti-Semitism in western countries by making Jewish refugees a burden on the receiving states. Much more recently, a report has suggested that German intelligence chiefs Hans-Georg Maaßen and Guido Müller warned the German government that Russia was seeking 'to destabilise Germany by fuelling tensions over migrants through its "easily influenced" Russian-German population'.[72] This came hard on the heels of a claim in testimony before the US Senate Armed Services

Committee by General Philip M. Breedlove, NATO's Supreme Allied Commander for Europe, that 'Russia and the Assad regime are deliberately weaponizing migration in an attempt to overwhelm European structures and break European resolve ... this is bringing great pressure on the nations of Europe'.[73] There could be other possible interpretations of Russian policy, but General Breedlove's is by no means out of the question given the authoritarian character of Putin's Russia.[74]

Refugees can nonetheless exercise considerable power in certain circumstances. As a category, of course, 'refugees' do not constitute an actor. To be an actor, it is necessary to be able to make decisions and undertake actions, and as a global category 'refugees' can do neither. Individual refugees, however, can be powerful in their own ways. They can contribute to the setting of agendas for the treatment of refugees, and can be moral voices of great power, as Thomas Mann proved during his years of exile from Germany. Furthermore, groups of refugees can be very significant actors indeed.[75] Refugees are often left to survive on their own devices, and may cooperate in order to achieve shared goals. In the individual stories of refugees who have recently arrived in Europe, there are many that focus on assistance that they have received not from agents of a state, but from other refugees making the same journey. In March 2016, refugees trapped at the closed border between Greece and Macedonia took the initiative to cross a fast-flowing river in order to try to move north, and photographs taken at the scene at one point showed a team of refugees helping others to cross, with the beneficiaries holding onto a rope and being assisted along the way by refugees standing in the river. This is a benign example of refugee power, although Macedonian police reportedly then blocked their path.[76] A less benign form comes when groups of refugees take up arms to try to recover control of their countries from agents of persecution. This was proposed by the Polish foreign minister where Syria is concerned,[77] but missed the point that refugees who are pressured to take up arms, as opposed to those who volunteer to do so, are unlikely to be reliable members of a cohesive force. Furthermore, while members of the Polish resistance fought courageously during the Second World War, they were unable to prevent millions of Poles being killed, or Soviet domination of their country for decades after the end of the war.

It is also important to note that refugee camps tend to develop their own hierarchies of power or authority if they are in place for any length of time, and can be the venues for intense competition between different political forces. This was certainly the case with Afghan refugee camps in Pakistan during the 1980s. Very often the decision to leave Afghanistan had been a collective decision taken by a village council, and members of the council joined other village members in going into exile. Once in Pakistan, however, they found their traditional authority challenged from a number of different directions. One phenomenon, found not just in refugee camps but in Afghan society more broadly, was the threat to traditional leaders posed by younger Afghans with military training who had skills more directly germane to the ongoing campaign in Afghanistan against Soviet forces. Another, however, was the favouring by the refugees' Pakistani hosts of Islamist political groups such as Gulbuddin Hekmatyar's Hezb-e Islami, which saw refugee camps as a major recruiting venue. The radical ideologies of such groups were often at odds with the views of the more traditional village leaderships, and this set the scene for tensions. In other parts of the world, power has been exercised in refugee camps not so much by organised political forces, but by what one might almost call 'camp militias', that is, thuggish groups setting out to ensure positions of dominance by intimidating more vulnerable refugees, and extracting resources from them. Sometimes the political and the thuggish can come together: for example, a political group may be resistant to the idea that refugees in the camp should repatriate to their country of origin, and a camp gang may provide the muscle required to ensure that this does not happen. Refugee camps can be very violent places indeed, with the resort to violence stimulated by a range of complex institutional and social factors, including the orientations of the host state.[78]

Finally, on occasion, refugees may play crucial roles to complement the diplomatic strategies of international organisations. A fascinating example is that of Palestinian refugees. In the course of the events that led to the establishment of the State of Israel in 1948, some 700,000 Palestinians were uprooted. The circumstances remain controversial to this day, but a 1988 study by the Israeli historian Benny Morris attributed the bulk of the displacement to Israeli attacks.[79] These events of course preceded the establishment of UNHCR as an agency committed to refugee protection, and the International Refugee Organization had only limited and concrete responsibilities. To fill the gap, the United Nations General Assembly in Resolution 302(IV) of 8 December 1949 established a specific body, the United Nations Relief and Works Agency for Palestine Refugees in the Near East (UNRWA), to help deal with the Palestinian refugee population.[80] It is headed by a Commissioner-General, currently Pierre Krähenbühl of Switzerland, who in 2014 succeeded Filippo Grandi of Italy, now the UN High Commissioner for Refugees.

UNRWA is substantially funded by voluntary contributions from UN member states, but the disposition of states to contribute naturally varies over time and according to specific circumstances within a donor country. It was in the face of a challenging financial environment that a crisis broke out that saw a remarkable symbiosis taking shape between the core mythologies held dear by the Palestinian refugees, and the diplomatic objectives of UNRWA in seeking to secure continuing support. Obliged in August 1997 to implement a series of emergency austerity measures, UNRWA became the focal point for intense diplomatic engagement that culminated in additional funding that defused the crisis. Palestinian refugees reacted vigorously to what they saw as a threat to core interests. In a detailed study of the crisis, Robert Bowker identified two key themes in refugees' reactions: 'First, the measures announced by the agency were generally portrayed as an attempted abandonment of the international community's responsibilities toward the refugee community that would place additional burdens upon needy families ... Second, the measures were widely interpreted in the Palestinian media and among Palestinian refugee political figures as being part of a more extensive political conspiracy'.[81] The robustness of the Palestinian response sent a diplomatic signal for which there was a receptive audience; as Bowker again observed, 'Although Western donors in general wanted the refugees and host governments to appreciate the budget-driven realities facing them and the agency, most of them were more concerned— indeed were primarily concerned—to avoid the prospect of deepening political unrest within the refugee community'.[82] This proved to be a decisive factor in the short-term amelioration of the crisis. UNRWA is not much loved by some supporters of Israel,[83] who resent what they see as the agency's nurturing of Palestinian political aspirations, but it has proved remarkably resilient in the face of a range of challenges. One reason it has survived is that the tools of diplomacy have consolidated the confluence of interest between the agency itself, a number of the donors who fund it, and the refugees it assists.

7

REFUGEES, INTERVENTION
AND THE 'RESPONSIBILITY TO PROTECT'

Refugee movements on a large scale are usually associated with overt acts of persecution, and serious human rights abuses. These terms, however, can seem overly-tepid labels for certain kinds of horror. Somehow it jars to refer to the killings of the Holocaust, or of the genocides in Cambodia and Rwanda, simply as examples of human rights abuses. The reason is not just that attempts to eliminate an entire category of people are shocking—this can be a small-scale activity if the category itself is small—but rather that the genocides that capture attention and create large-scale movements are likely to be mass activities, involving organised and coordinated murder, underpinned by patterns of hatred and hostility that challenge optimistic conceptions of what it means to be human. Many acts of homicide in everyday life are carried out by people acting under the pressure of intense emotional confusion, and in the heat of the moment. By contrast, there is something very dark about mass atrocity crime that chills the blood of witnesses and leaves the survivors traumatised, with empty eyes and a fear of the nightmares that intrude in what should be restful sleep.

When one contemplates the magnitude and the horror of some serious refugee crises, especially those triggered by mass atrocity crime, an obvious possible response could be that nothing short of military intervention offers any prospect of effectively addressing the root causes of people's displacement. And indeed, in certain circumstances it is very hard to see how anything *less* than a military intervention could bring relief to people who are suffering. Those who embark on the course of killing large numbers of their fellows have crossed their Rubicon: it is highly unlikely that they will be diverted from their paths by statements of condemnation, or threats that they might be subject to legal action. The very mindset that can sanction mass atrocity crime is unlikely to be amenable to dissuasion. That said, it is easily overlooked that one of the objectives of the Westphalian settlement was to put an *end* to rampant interventionism, which had had devastating consequences for the people of Europe.[1] Furthermore, the palpable need in some circumstances for dramatic action does not of itself answer the question of what form such action might take. The use of force in international affairs is a complex matter from legal, political and operational perspectives, and in order to appraise when and if so how armed force might be used for the benefit of refugees, it is necessary to explore these complexities in more detail.

The use of force

Until the twentieth century, the use of force as a tool of statecraft was seen not a violation of international law, but as a 'right of sovereign states',[2] and power balancing was seen as the pre-eminent tool for preventing armed conflict.[3] This began to change after the First World War, and an important development was the 1928 *General Treaty for the Renunciation of War as an Instrument of National Policy*, known popularly as the 'Pact of

Paris' or the 'Kellogg-Briand Pact'. Article I provided that 'The High Contracting Parties solemnly declare in the names of their respective peoples that they condemn recourse to war for the solution of international controversies, and renounce it, as an instrument of national policy in their relations with one another'. Article II provided that 'The High Contracting Parties agree that the settlement or solution of all disputes or conflicts of whatever nature or of whatever origin they may be, which may arise among them, shall never be sought except by pacific means'. The Pact was not successful in creating a binding norm, but it set the scene for 'waging aggressive war' to be included in the indictment of German defendants in the Nuremberg Trial of 1945–46,[4] and it also contributed to a new framework of the law governing the use of force that was incorporated in the 1945 *Charter of the United Nations*.[5]

The *Charter* opens with a general prohibition in Article 2.4: 'All Members shall refrain in their international relations from the threat or use of force against the territorial integrity or political independence of any state, or in any other manner inconsistent with the Purposes of the United Nations'. It goes on to outline various powers of United Nations Security Council. Article 41 states that 'The Security Council may decide what measures not involving the use of armed force are to be employed to give effect to its decisions, and it may call upon the Members of the United Nations to apply such measures. These may include complete or partial interruption of economic relations and of rail, sea, air, postal, telegraphic, radio, and other means of communication, and the severance of diplomatic relations'. Article 42 provides that 'Should the Security Council consider that measures provided for in Article 41 would be inadequate or have proved to be inadequate, it may take such action by air, sea, or land forces as may be necessary to maintain or restore international peace and security. Such action may include demonstrations, blockade, and other operations by air, sea, or land forces of Members of the United Nations'. Importantly, Article 51 adds that 'Nothing in the present Charter shall impair the inherent right of individual or collective self-defence if an armed attack occurs against a Member of the United Nations, until the Security Council has taken measures necessary to maintain international peace and security'.

This framework is not entirely irrelevant to refugee issues, since refugee movements might be seen as giving rise to a 'threat to the peace' of the kind that could engage the attention of the Security Council. On the face of it, however, action to protect refugees or prevent further refugee flows can only be carried out if authorised by the Security Council—and the risk that arises is that steps to secure the Council's authorisation could be blocked through exercise of the so-called 'veto power' by any one of the five permanent members of the Council: the United States, the United Kingdom, France, Russia and China. Should this happen, some other ways of using armed force in defence of refugees might need to be sought.

One potential candidate is peacekeeping. Indeed, it has been argued that states by contributing to peacekeeping operations might engage in 'implicit burden sharing' where refugees are concerned.[6] The activity of peacekeeping was not contemplated when the *Charter* was being drafted. Rather, it emerged as a creative response to international needs. Some date it from the establishment of the United Nations Truce Supervision Organization (UNTSO) in the Middle East in 1948; others look to the roles of UN Secretary-General Dag Hammarskjöld and Canadian Secretary of State for External Affairs Lester B. Pearson in crafting the United Nations Emergency Force (UNEF) in 1956 following the Suez crisis. Classically, peacekeeping involved the deployment of lightly-armed personnel, drawn ideally from neutral or unaligned states, authorised to use their weapons only in self-defence, and tasked with contributing to peace by separating combatants, verifying ceasefires, and engaging in other activities to facilitate the building of trust between former adversaries.[7] Central to such operations was the consent of the states on the territory of which the deployments were to occur. Some operations of this kind have proved extremely durable; for example, the United Nations Peacekeeping Force in Cyprus (UNFICYP) has been running since March 1964. Over time, peacekeeping has evolved in a range of significant ways, to the point where the generic term 'peace operations' is now commonly in use.[8] This process took off with the UN missions in Namibia in 1989 and Cambodia in 1992–93, and saw the UN involved in the reconstitution of political authority through the overseeing or the running of elections for constituent assemblies, as well as in the facilitation of refugee repatriation, the promotion of human rights, and efforts to build the rule of law, sometimes in the context of full-scale UN transitional administrations.[9]

Peacekeeping is an appropriate tool to use in appropriate circumstances; it runs into difficulties when political leaders who should know better seek to use it either to disguise their lack of will to do anything more kinetic, or as a way of addressing problems to which it is not an appropriate response. A famous example of this problem came in the Balkans in the 1990s with the mission known as the UN Protection Force or UNPROFOR. The muted approach of UNPROFOR to the circumstances it faced on the ground was emblematic of this kind of mismatch. There are many candidates for the title of 'low point of the mission', with the July 1995 Srebrenica massacre usually topping the poll, but a sign of things to come was the murder in January 1993 of the Bosnian Deputy Prime Minister, Dr Hakija Turajlić, who was shot by a Serb militia member when he was seated in a UN-badged armoured personnel carrier; the UNPROFOR soldiers on the scene neither apprehended the killer nor returned fire.[10] As Professor Rosalyn Higgins, subsequently President of the International Court of Justice, pointedly observed in 1993, 'Leaving all considerations of law and UN practice on one side, the reality is that we have chosen to respond to major unlawful violence, not by stopping that violence, but by trying to provide relief to the suffering. But our choice of policy allows the suffering to continue'.[11]

It should always be borne in mind that peacekeeping is a creature of international politics, and the foundations of a mission can crumble for political reasons. In 1967, one of the factors that triggered the Six Day War in the Middle East was the withdrawal at the behest of President Nasser of Egypt of the United Nations Emergency Force. Since the Force was deployed on Egyptian but not on Israeli territory, the effect of its removal was to create a corridor for a potential Egyptian attack on Israel. Unsurprisingly, the Israelis did not wait to be attacked, but struck first, and with devastating effect. Nasser subsequently sought to blame the UN leadership, especially Secretary-General U Thant and Under Secretary-General Ralph J. Bunche, for the misfortune that he had brought upon himself. The key point from the case, however, was simple: once the essential prerequisite of consent had been withdrawn, the UN had no option but to remove the mission; to have done otherwise would have been a direct affront to the principle of state sovereignty to which the UN was formally committed.[12] A somewhat similar problem arose in a different context at the end of the 1990s. On 31 March 1995, the UN Security Council through Resolution 983 established the United Nations Preventive Deployment Force (UNPREDEP) to promote stability in the new state of Macedonia. It was widely judged a success, but came to an abrupt end in February 1999. The explanation was simple: China in the Security Council vetoed the extension of the mission, almost certainly in response to Macedonia's recognition of Taiwan. In theory the UN General Assembly, acting pursuant to the so-called 'Uniting for Peace' resolution of 1950, might have been able to extend the mission, but by the time the General Assembly next convened, events had moved on.[13]

How useful is peacekeeping? On the one hand, evaluating individual peace operations is a more complex undertaking than one might think,[14] and it is only relatively recently that a sophisticated framework has been developed with which to compare achievements in different theatres. This focuses on five steps: to '(1) identify primary goals relevant to the mission, generic and mandate-specific; (2) identify key questions required to achieve primary goals; (3) identify measures of progress to answer those questions; (4) identify benefits and limitations of those measures of progress; (5) ascertain extent to which primary goals have been accomplished'.[15] On the other hand, as a phenomenon, peacekeeping undoubtedly has had a broadly positive effect,[16] although just how effectively it works will depend on the circumstances of each case, as well as the capacity for organisational learning within a particular mission.[17] From a number of specific cases, it is also clear that in the absence of a neutral security force, it may be very difficult to implement the terms of peace agreements given ongoing distrust between the parties.[18] For refugees, however, the value of peace operations has typically been more at the point where repatriation becomes possible than as a tool for dealing with high levels of violence and mass atrocity crime where there is little or no 'peace' to 'keep'. To deal with the reality or the imminent threat of mass atrocity crimes, something else may be required.

The idea of humanitarian intervention

The solution that often surfaces at this point of the discussion is 'intervention'. The word 'intervention' can be used in a number of different senses. A central element of intervention is the use of armed force; the term is only occasionally used to refer to the application of economic pressure, or to describe communication strategies. It may be used to refer to actions that are undertaken by states with authorisation from the UN Security Council under Article 42 of the Charter. However, it can also be used to refer to deployments of force that lack such authorisation. The adjective 'humanitarian' is often attached at this point, as a way of distinguishing, at least rhetorically, between activities that are purely self-interested, and activities that the interveners would like others to think are driven by altruistic motives. Martha Finnemore has usefully defined 'humanitarian intervention' as 'deploying military force across borders for the purpose of protecting foreign nationals from man-made violence'.[19] Intervention can be undertaken to achieve this in a number of different ways. One might be the overthrow of the government, or some other kind of power holder, in order to open the door for new political arrangements. On the other hand, an intervention might be undertaken to create a 'safe haven' in a particular part of a country, without the overthrow of the government of the country being attempted. One kind of intervention that deserves particular note is the establishment through air power of a 'no-fly zone' in a state, such as was prescribed for Libya by the Security Council in March 2011; this can offer some protection to vulnerable people who might otherwise be exposed to bombing and strafing by the air force of the ruling authority, but involves only minimal intrusion of foreign actors into the country's airspace in order to shoot down any planes or helicopters that enter the 'no-fly zone'.

The addition of the word 'humanitarian' imports a range of other considerations. It is relatively easy to identify particular impulses in various historical contexts that one might readily deem 'humane': the activities of the Knights Hospitaller from the eleventh century AD onwards; the English Parliament's enactment of the *Statute of Charitable Uses* of 1601; anti-slavery activities of figures as diverse as William Wilberforce in England and John Brown in the US; and the establishment of the Red Cross movement in Switzerland in 1863, all come to mind as attempts to ameliorate suffering. In recent times, however, much more attention has been paid to paradoxical effects of humanitarian action,[20] some critics even seeing meliorist humanitarianism as adding to suffering by contributing to the prolongation of conflict.[21] But that said, the proponents of humanitarian intervention are typically focused not on ameliorating suffering directly, but on using force to change or constrain the power structures that allow suffering to occur.

Where an intervention occurs with express UN Security Council authority, there can be very little doubt as to its legal validity. It is well established that the Council can delegate the task of enforcement to one or more states.[22] Difficulty arises, however, where there is no such authority. Under such circumstances, two conflicting sets of principles come into play. One surrounds the notion of Westphalian sovereignty, in Krasner's sense of the term discussed in Chapter Four, based on 'the exclusion of external actors from authority structures within a given territory'. This particular idea finds expression legally in Article 2.7 of the *Charter*: 'Nothing contained in the present Charter shall authorize the United Nations to intervene in matters which are essentially within the domestic jurisdiction of any state or shall require the Members to submit such matters to settlement under the present Charter'. Many would see this as a core or foundational principle of the current international system, complementing the provision in Article 2.4 dealing with the threat or use of force. The other set of principles is both legal and moral, although predominantly the latter, and is embodied in instruments such as the *Genocide Convention* and various texts dealing with human rights. Tension arises because the instruments that provide the basis for condemning genocide and gross human rights violations do not specifically identify intervention as a legally-sanctioned response.

How this practically affects the prospects for intervention will then depend on the character of the states that may be disposed to intervene. If a state happens to be a permanent member of the Security Council, it can use the veto power to ensure that it encounters no condemnation of its actions in any resolution or presidential statement from the Council. It was for this reason that the Soviet invasions of Hungary in 1956, Czechoslovakia in 1968, and Afghanistan in 1979 were not condemned as violations of the *Charter*; similar points could be made about the US interventions in Grenada in 1983, Panama in 1989, and Iraq in 2003. Even if a state is not a permanent member, it may be able to rely on the protection of a state that is: Israel provides an obvious example. It is other kinds of states that need to think very carefully about what the consequences of intervention might be. Sometimes a state may intervene without serious problems because the intervention occurs in a part of the world in which few states beyond the immediate region have much interest; the Tanzanian invasion of Uganda, resulting in the overthrow of the Ugandan regime in April 1979, comes to mind. Nonetheless, it pays for states to be careful. When Iraq invaded Kuwait in August 1990, Iraqi leader Saddam Hussein may well have expected the protection in the Security Council of the Soviet Union. This did not materialise, which left Saddam exposed to the US-run Operation Desert Storm, authorised by Security Council resolution 678.[23]

It is fair to say that a great deal of skepticism over time came to surround the idea of humanitarian intervention. Several factors accounted for this. One was the danger that the language of humanitarianism could be used to disguise motivations that were anything but humane. Hitler, for example, used claims that ethnic Germans were suffering in Czechoslovakia and Poland as bases for moves against the territorial integrity of both those countries in 1938–1939. There is no evidence that this was anything other than a pretext to justify expansion on ideological and geopolitical grounds, and the consequences for both countries proved simply horrendous. Furthermore, even when one could credibly argue that some humanitarian good flowed from an intervention, as for example from the Vietnamese invasion of Cambodia in December 1978 to displace the Khmer Rouge regime, it was far from clear that the motivation for the intervention was humanitarian. Another factor related to the role of potential interveners as former colonial powers. A large numbers of contemporary states escaped from the colonial experience only in the period following the Second World War, and a consequence was that quite a number of postcolonial elites were extremely sensitive to the possibility of colonial control being reasserted in the name of humanitarian principles. This is not altogether surprising, for too often, policy settings that are blatantly self-interested have ended up being packaged in such a way as to suggest that they are being pursued only for the best of motives, for example when policy to keep refugees from entering Europe is defended as 'the only way to end "the human suffering" of migrants being exploited by smugglers'.[24] The overtones of the 'White Man's Burden' are hard to miss—as if refugees themselves are incapable of understanding what is in their interests, so that others are justified in doing their thinking for them.

Partly as a result of this history, an intervention that is undertaken without the support of the Security Council risks being seen as illegitimate. This is a distinct question from that of simple legality. An action can be legal and legitimate; or legal but not legitimate; or legitimate but not legal; or neither legal nor legitimate. In some ways legitimacy is the more significant factor, although legality may aid in making the case for some action as legitimate as well. Jean-Jacques Rousseau shrewdly observed that the 'strongest is never strong enough to be always master, unless he transforms strength into right, and obedience into duty'.[25] Legitimacy is concerned with the degrees to which actions, actors or institutions are appraised as rightful,[26] and legality may only be a part of this larger story. A compelling example of how states can encounter strife as a result of ignoring the importance of legitimacy came with the US invasion of Iraq in March 2003. In 1990, following Iraq's invasion of Kuwait, US President George H. W. Bush had showed great care in securing authorisation from the Security Council for the actions that he was disposed to take. With the Security Council behind him, he was able to build an inclusive coalition of states committed to the shared task of reversing the Iraqi occupation of Kuwait. By contrast, when US President George W. Bush embarked on the 2003 invasion, he did so without fresh authority from the Security Council, and entered the field with relatively few partners, supported only by a 'coalition of the obedient', as former British Foreign Secretary Douglas Hurd put it.[27] A consequence was that when the situation deteriorated severely in Iraq and the US stood to gain from securing the support of other actors, it was singularly poorly placed to obtain it, having earlier scorned or ignored a range of prescient doubters. The great value of legitimacy is that it provides one with a basis for socialising the costs of failure.[28] It therefore follows that *if* an intervention is undertaken with a view to protecting refugees faced with the threat of mass atrocity crime, it is extremely important to ensure the legitimacy of the undertaking.

That said, it would be a mistake to suggest that eager resort to humanitarian intervention has been a major problem in the period since the establishment of the United Nations. What is actually striking is how reluctant states have been to address issues of mass atrocity crime in a serious and direct fashion. There has been no shortage of cases of genocide and what some scholars have called 'politicide', namely the attempt to wipe out perceived political opponents;[29] but the extent of indifference to them is in fact rather shocking. The massacres of Bengalis by the Pakistan military in 1971 went mainly unaddressed in major Western capitals, and it was only Indian involvement that brought the Bangladesh crisis to the point of resolution. The Khmer Rouge regime was able to engage in industrial-scale atrocities between April 1975 and December 1978 while Washington licked its wounds in the post-Watergate, post-Vietnam era. The Rwandan genocide was not brought to a halt by a major international intervention; on the contrary, to the extent that major powers were involved, France's 'Opération Turquoise' was a deeply ambiguous undertaking that many observers saw as an attempt to maintain French influence in the Great Lakes region of Africa rather than confront the problem of mass atrocity crime. Unsurprisingly, when states have intervened, it has been much more obviously when their own interests have been at stake, or when the survival of a population has been threatened by natural disaster such as famine. The failure of the Clinton Administration to contribute to the halting of the Rwandan genocide, something largely driven by its earlier bitter experiences in Somalia, offers a reminder of how circumscribed Washington's conception of its role in the world can be.[30] Indeed, it was the failure to address mass atrocity crime in Rwanda that in part contributed to the most important attempt in the post-1945 era to reconceptualise intervention.

The Responsibility to Protect

At the dawn of the twenty-first century, something of a crisis of impotence seem to be haunting the established architecture for dealing with threats to the peace and mass atrocity crime. As just noted, states had proved ineffective in responding to some of the most serious affronts of the previous quarter of a century, and the Srebrenica massacre of July 1995 suggested that the United Nations system was not much better: this humiliating atrocity took place literally under the gaze of Dutch troops acting under a UN mandate,[31] and the massacre was subsequently held by the International Court of Justice to constitute genocide under international law.[32] In an attempt to confront this crisis of impotence, the Foreign Minister of Canada, Dr Lloyd Axworthy, on 14 September 2000 launched a new body, the International Commission on Intervention and State Sovereignty, tasked with offering fresh ideas on how the crisis could be overcome. The Commission had two Co-Chairs, namely Gareth Evans, President of the International Crisis Group and former Foreign Minister of Australia, and Mohamed Sahnoun, an eminent Algerian diplomat. The other members of the Commission were Gisèle Côté-Harper, Lee Hamilton, Michael Ignatieff, Vladimir Lukin, Klaus Naumann, Cyril Ramaphosa, Fidel V. Ramos, Cornelio Sommaruga, Eduardo Stein Barillas, and Ramesh Thakur.

The Commission pursued its task in a number of different ways.[33] Assisted by a dynamic international research team led by Professor Thomas Weiss, it generated a range of research papers and a substantial bibliography dealing with issues related to intervention. It also conducted eleven separate consultation roundtables in different parts of the world in order to access varying perspectives on the issues with which the commission was preoccupied. These meetings took place in Ottawa, Geneva, London, Maputo, Washington DC, Santiago, Cairo, Paris, New Delhi, Beijing, and Saint Petersburg. This writer took part in the consultation held in New Delhi, and can testify to the breadth and openness of the discussions that occurred. The 11 September 2001 terrorist attacks occurred less than three weeks before the final meeting of the Commission in Brussels on 30 September, but while they naturally captured virtually all the media attention in the weeks that followed, they did not derail the International Commission's project. In December 2001, the Report of the Commission was finally launched. It was entitled, simply, *The Responsibility to Protect*. The historian Sir Martin Gilbert subsequently described the idea of a responsibility to protect as 'the most significant adjustment to national sovereignty in 360 years'.[34]

The Commission's report defies terse summation, but a range of key points stood out. In probably the most famous observation in the report, the Commission argued that 'State sovereignty implies responsibility, and the primary responsibility for the protection of its people lies with the state itself ... Where a population is suffering serious harm, as a result of internal war, insurgency, repression or state failure, and the state in question is unwilling or unable to halt or avert it, the principle of non-intervention yields to the international responsibility to protect'.[35] As a foundation, it set out a reformulated conceptualisation of sovereignty:[36]

> The Charter of the UN is itself an example of an international obligation voluntarily accepted by member states. On the one hand, in granting membership of the UN, the international community welcomes the signatory state as a responsible member of the community of nations. On the other hand, the state itself, in signing the Charter, accepts the responsibilities of membership flowing from that signature. There is no transfer or dilution of state sovereignty. But there is a necessary re-characterization involved: from sovereignty as control to sovereignty as responsibility in both internal functions and external duties.

> Thinking of sovereignty as responsibility, in a way that is being increasingly recognized in state practice, has a threefold significance. First, it implies that the state authorities are responsible for the functions of protecting the safety and lives of citizens and promotion of their welfare. Secondly, it suggests that the national political authorities are respon-

sible to the citizens internally and to the international community through the UN. And thirdly, it means that the agents of state are responsible for their actions; that is to say, they are accountable for their acts of commission and omission.

In the view of the Commission, this led to three crucial changes in perspective:[37]

First, the responsibility to protect implies an evaluation of the issues from the point of view of those seeking or needing support, rather than those who may be considering intervention. Our preferred terminology refocuses the international searchlight back where it should always be: on the duty to protect communities from mass killing, women from systematic rape and children from starvation.

Secondly, the responsibility to protect acknowledges that the primary responsibility in this regard rests with the state concerned, and that it is only if the state is unable or unwilling to fulfill this responsibility, or is itself the perpetrator, that it becomes the responsibility of the international community to act in its place. In many cases, the state will seek to acquit its responsibility in full and active partnership with representatives of the international community. Thus the 'responsibility to protect' is more of a linking concept that bridges the divide between intervention and sovereignty; the language of the 'right or duty to intervene' is intrinsically more confrontational.

Thirdly, the responsibility to protect means not just the 'responsibility to react,' but the 'responsibility to prevent' and the 'responsibility to rebuild' as well. It directs our attention to the costs and results of action versus no action, and provides conceptual, normative and operational linkages between assistance, intervention and reconstruction.

The notion of a Responsibility to Protect is directly relevant to some refugee movements, namely those flowing from high-level threats.[38] Its preventive dimension, if given effect, could help abort the need for flight in the first place, and its primary focus on 'the point of view of those seeking or needing support' helps bring refugees, as one very important kind of victim, much more centrally to the attention of those seeking to plan responses to mass atrocity crimes.[39] Giving effect to the principle, however, has proved quite challenging.

The work of the International Commission was quintessentially an exercise in norm entrepreneurship, but norms have complicated lives and tend to develop in ways that might not have been fully anticipated by those who promoted them initially.[40] Ramesh Thakur, in a survey of the mountainous literature that has developed since 2001 on the Responsibility to Protect, notes 'distinctions between R2P as an analytic concept with a requirement for philosophical rigour and conceptual coherence; as a normative enterprise seeking to entrench the principle as the new norm; and as a political project operating in the messy and untidy real world of international politics'.[41] Gareth Evans has dated the birth of an 'actionable norm' from the UN's Sixtieth Anniversary World Summit in September 2005.[42] The key development to this end was the inclusion of two crucial paragraphs in the Summit's Outcome Document:[43]

138. Each individual State has the responsibility to protect its populations from genocide, war crimes, ethnic cleansing and crimes against humanity. This responsibility entails the prevention of such crimes, including their incitement, through appropriate and necessary means. We accept that responsibility and will act in accordance with it. The international community should, as appropriate, encourage and help States to exercise this responsibility and support the United Nations in establishing an early warning capability.

139. The international community, through the United Nations, also has the responsibility to use appropriate diplomatic, humanitarian and other peaceful means, in accordance with Chapters VI and VIII of the Charter, to help to protect populations from genocide, war crimes, ethnic cleansing and crimes against humanity. In this context, we are prepared to take collective action, in a timely and decisive manner, through the Security Council, in accordance with

the Charter, including Chapter VII, on a case-by-case basis and in cooperation with relevant regional organisations as appropriate, should peaceful means be inadequate and national authorities are manifestly failing to protect their populations from genocide, war crimes, ethnic cleansing and crimes against humanity. We stress the need for the General Assembly to continue consideration of the responsibility to protect populations from genocide, war crimes, ethnic cleansing and crimes against humanity and its implications, bearing in mind the principles of the Charter and international law. We also intend to commit ourselves, as necessary and appropriate, to helping States build capacity to protect their populations from genocide, war crimes, ethnic cleansing and crimes against humanity and to assisting those which are under stress before crises and conflicts break out.

There was a certain backlash from recalcitrant states, albeit ultimately short-lived, in response these paragraphs,[44] but the greater challenge to the Responsibility to Protect as a political project arose from Security Council Resolution 1973 of 17 March 2011, dealing with Libya. In paragraph 4 of the resolution, the Council authorised

Member States that have notified the Secretary-General, acting nationally or through regional organizations or arrangements, and acting in cooperation with the Secretary-General, to take all necessary measures ... to protect civilians and civilian populated areas under threat of attack in the Libyan Arab Jamahiriya, including Benghazi, while excluding a foreign occupation force of any form on any part of Libyan territory.

This was widely viewed as a practical application of the Responsibility to Protect, and to some extent it made the future trajectory of the doctrine hostage to the fidelity to its operational dimensions displayed by the Member States that the resolution empowered. One commentator has referred to a 'widespread view that the two leading interveners, Britain and France, clearly exceeded the mandate of the UN Security Council when they turned the original mandate of civilian protection into an explicit move for regime change'.[45] Michael W. Doyle has argued that as a result of the Libyan experience, the Responsibility to Protect is 'wounded'. As he puts it, 'To gain approval for the intervention in Libya, Western nations secured a resolution that passed with ten votes in favour, and no vetoes. But the legitimacy, in the sense of wide support, was not fulsome. There were abstentions from the not insignificant countries of Brazil, China, Germany, India, and Russia'.[46] He went on that 'The dissenters on the Security Council felt that they had been hoodwinked and sold a protection intervention that turned into a regime change intervention. The costs of this may now be visible in Syria, where, burned once, neither Russia nor China is prepared to abstain on resolutions presented by the US and the Europeans to sanction the Assad regime'.[47] This may simply prove that contact with live politicians is virtually guaranteed to take the gloss off any serious moral doctrine, but it does suggest that attempts to use the Responsibility to Protect doctrine for the benefit of refugees are likely to be beset with charges of inconsistency, with the risk that refugees' suffering may be manipulated to advance some other objectives. That is not, however, an argument against discharging such a responsibility when the circumstances are appropriate.

One warning, however, is in order.[48] In an environment increasingly rich with distinct but overlapping norms, there is a danger that states may attempt to shirk their responsibilities under one kind of normative framework by claiming that they are implicitly meeting those responsibilities by taking action mandated by some other framework. It is by no means beyond the bounds of possibility that a powerful state might argue that those with refugee claims should simply be held in limbo, since some kind of action legitimated by reference to the Responsibility to Protect will create the opportunity for them to repatriate. Unfortunately, one of the lessons of past attempts at intervention is that it is far from clear that intervention as an instrument is equal to the task of creating environments to which refugees can safely return. It is to these kind of problems of intervention that we now need to direct our attention.

'Intervention' as a solution

There are three twentieth-century examples of territorial occupations that had unambiguously positive outcomes: the Western occupations of Germany and Japan after the Second World War, and—a case that is usually overlooked—the occupation of Austria that concluded with the Austrian State Treaty of 1955.[49] In each of these cases, however, the occupation reflected a military victory on the part of the occupying powers, in circumstances where the vast bulk of the population of the occupied state accepted that it had been defeated, and that in key respects there was no going back to the past. The victorious allies as a consequence were able to deliver high levels of security for the day-to-day lives of ordinary people, and lay the foundations for pluralistic political processes that helped to generate high levels of political legitimacy for the new order. Furthermore, in Japan, the decision not to attempt to dethrone Emperor Hirohito but instead reduce him and his successors to a symbolic constitutional role hugely helped in smoothing the process of reshaping Japanese elite politics. There have been few interventions since then that have had such positive and clear-cut outcomes, although some small operations such as the INTERFET mission in East Timor proved effective.[50] On the contrary, in more recent times, the challenge for intervening powers has been to maintain a degree of momentum in a much messier political environment. This problem was neatly captured in David Halberstam's 1965 book about Vietnam entitled *The Making of a Quagmire*.[51] The US failure in Vietnam, ignominiously depicted in images of a helicopter lifting off from the roof of the US Embassy in Saigon in April 1975, had a searing effect on a generation of policymakers, but it also raised a host of serious questions about the utility of military power in fine-tuning political outcomes. The Vietnam case very powerfully demonstrated the dangers of losing domestic support for an intervention, and showed how sluggishly political leaders, in this case President Lyndon B. Johnson, could react to unwelcome suggestions that not all was going according to plan. It also highlighted the perils of relying on diplomatic cables as an exclusive source; in 1973, even before the end of the war, Bernard Brodie wrote that it 'was one of Johnson's great weaknesses that he had too much faith in the accuracy and reliability of these "cables"'.[52] (This warning could be applied equally to cables suggesting that it is safe for refugees to return to war-torn countries.) These issues remain potent to this day, and justify a degree of caution about suggestions that intervention is a key tool to address the root causes of refugee flows. It may be appropriate when one is dealing with forced migration caused by mass atrocity crime, but as we have seen, this can be the kind of situation in which potential interveners are least enthusiastic about becoming involved.

The more recent cases of Afghanistan and Iraq equally highlight the problems of intervention. The Afghanistan case is the more ambiguous of the two. While some analyses see the Afghan transition as blighted by contradictions more or less from the outset, others tend to emphasise failures of implementation rather than design flaws *per se*;[53] and it is still not clear that Afghanistan should be regarded as a failure in its entirety, although the current insecurity in much of the country is a major factor contributing to refugee outflows. It is harder to find much to celebrate in the March 2003 Iraq intervention, pursued with great zeal by President George W. Bush. Afghanistan was an immediate victim. 'As much as President Bush detested the notion', former Defense Secretary Robert M. Gates wrote in his memoirs, 'our later challenges in Afghanistan, especially the return of the Taliban in force by the time I became defense secretary, were, I believe, significantly compounded by the invasion of Iraq'.[54] But the problems of the Iraq intervention ran deeper than just this. There is no doubt that Saddam Hussein was a murderous tyrant,[55] and having invaded Kuwait in 1990, he was poorly placed to protest at the invasion of his own country. But many critics who had no time for Saddam were also unsettled by the idea that United States, without fresh authority from the Security Council, could intervene in another country's affairs simply because it had the capacity and the desire to do so. This left a cloud hanging over the legitimacy of the intervention from the outset. Even more seriously, the United States seemed bewilderingly unprepared for the hostile environment that it encountered following the overthrow of Saddam. The looting of the National Museum in Baghdad,[56] an institution which had not been included in a list of buildings requiring protection, sent a very clear signal that the US had not prepared properly for the tasks that lay ahead, and this emboldened former regime elements to engage in spoiling behaviour. Things spiralled downwards from this point, in ways that are by now well documented. And one did not have to be a specialist on Iraq to recognise the scale of potential problems. The most obvious—indeed, elementary—point was that overthrowing a tyrant such as Saddam was not the same as establishing a stable system to replace him. A free society is typically marked by a high degree of order, and usually emerges through a slow process of evolution;[57] by contrast, the displacement of a tyrant, except in circumstances of a complete conquest such as the defeat of Nazi Germany in 1945, risks creating an environment of *dis*order. Authority structures are in disarray; and those who control military force may have no idea how to use it in order to foster order and stability. In other words, it was astoundingly naïve to believe that anything other than chaos was likely to follow Saddam's removal.

The case of Iraq suggests that intervention in the form in which it is likely to be used in the twenty-first century is a crude tool for dealing with complex problems. Sometimes the case for using even a crude tool may be compelling, for example when it is necessary to protect a population from genocide, war crimes, ethnic cleansing and crimes against humanity, but where less dramatic forms of persecution are driving refugees to flight, it may well be the case that the cure in the form of intervention may prove to be even worse than the disease. It is easily forgotten that the worst period under Saddam Hussein in Iraq, at least in terms of direct regime persecution of the population, was not in the days, months or even years preceding the 2003 intervention, but in the 1980s, when in the context of the Iran-Iraq war and its aftermath, the regime did not hesitate to use the most brutal techniques imaginable in order to secure its position. Having done so, and having demonstrated its capacity to mobilise coercion, it thereafter did not need to do so on anything like as dramatic or overt a scale: the mere memory of what it had proved capable of doing in the past was enough to suppress opposition in the present. In the 1980s, however, Iraq was seen as a counterweight to Iran, and even received some intelligence assistance from the United States.[58] By 2003, many ordinary Iraqis had worked out ways of surviving in the environment that confronted them, and as long as they eschewed any kind of opposition to the regime, they could live tolerable lives despite the sanctions regime that hurt some of the more vulnerable.[59] The overthrow of Saddam, however, contributed directly to major security problems in the most important Iraqi cities—including car bombings, assassinations, and the formation of militias to defend the interests of various sectarian groups. The preponderance of evidence is that the intervening powers did not even fully understand what was going on around them, let alone have at their disposal any means for addressing the problem. With ISIS now controlling large tracts of Iraq, and Iran immeasurably strengthened as a regional power, it is difficult to enthuse about the consequences of the 2003 intervention.

As the Iraq case suggests, there are good reasons to be wary of unintended consequences that can flow from interventions. These are many and varied, but several stand out.[60] First, an intervention is likely to bring a range of new political forces to the political landscape, and exactly who these will be may be difficult to predict in advance. Traditional social figures may face young and charismatic challengers. In Iraq, no one in particular anticipated the emergence of Muqtada al-Sadr as a political force, but this was exactly what he proved to be, tapping into the fears of Shia coming under attack from Sunni spoilers and positioning himself as their defender through his militia known as the Mahdi Army. Second, an intervention may actually foster warlordism, since armed militias may seem useful partners for an international force struggling to maintain order after overthrowing the previous leaders. Warlords, however, are often (although not always) predatory and extractive,[61] and tend to have little interest in fostering the kind of state that could then put them out of business. In the long run, therefore, they may prove difficult allies. Third, an intervention may open up a wide range of fractious issues that might have been suppressed or bypassed under the previous dispensation. New groups may set out to settle old scores, and even if they do not do so in a violent fashion, they may end up provoking violence by those who feel that their interests are coming under threat, and that it is worth signalling that they have diverse ways of defending their interests. Fourth, an intervention can be under-resourced, and this can lead to a pervasive sense of disappointment on the part of those who may have entertained high hopes that they were about to be on the receiving end of a new Marshall Plan. Finally, if an intervention runs into problems, it can create serious strain amongst the various states that may have taken part in an initial coalition to overthrow a despised despot. Disputes can emerge not just over resourcing, but over tactics, military strategy, and ultimately the wider political objectives that a presence in a particular country might be serving.

At the end of the day, we are left in a somewhat paradoxical position. On the one hand, one would not wish to exclude the use of force as a means of providing protection to refugees in the direst circumstances. Armed coercion may be the only realistic tool for confronting certain kinds of threat that refugees face. To believe that one can bring a halt to genocide simply with words is innocent in the extreme. Yet at the same time, there is little to suggest that when dealing with lower-level threats of persecution, armed force is an effective tool to deploy. If anything, there is a risk that 'protection of refugees' will be used simply as a pretext for interventions designed to serve other ends. While the Responsibility to Protect doctrine has been a very important conceptual innovation, it is concerned only with high-level threats, and does not address the spectrum of concerns that may account for the bulk of refugee movements in the world. For this reason, intervention should not be seen as a 'magic bullet' to solve refugee problems, and certainly should not be used as an excuse for depriving refugees of rights to protection to which they are entitled under international law. Creative approaches to addressing refugee problems are more likely to result from a critical reappraisal of some of the rigidities in the international order that either drive refugees into the arms of people smugglers, or leave them trapped in misery at international borders.

8

'WHEN ADAM DELVED AND EVE SPAN ...'

SOME REFLECTIONS ON CLOSING
AND OPENING BORDERS

In 1381, during the Peasants' Revolt in England, the priest John Ball gave voice to a question which had great explosive power: 'When Adam delved and Eve Span, who was then the gentleman?' Like many people who ask explosive questions, Ball came to a sticky end, but the question's power resonates to this day. It reminds us that there is nothing natural about boundaries and borders, whether separating 'gentleman' from peasants, or citizens of one state from those of another. In the Garden of Eden they did not exist. They come about as a product of human action, even if not always of human design,[1] and they entrench particular relations of power, which may benefit some people and severely disadvantage others.

Running through this book has been the message that refugee problems are a reflection of the Westphalian system. There is a Persian proverb that says that if you do not like the image in the mirror, do not break the mirror; break your face.[2] In that spirit, this final chapter concludes not with a set of policy prescriptions, but rather with some thoughts on challenges which the discussions in earlier chapters have exposed. If the sufferings of refugees are to be ameliorated, it is not very likely that politics will show the way. Rather, it is through the recovery of moral sentiment that a path might be found. This writer is not optimistic, but there is little hope for a moderately decent world if it turns out that we have no sense of decency left. In the following pages, I discuss issues relating to the costs of border control, the implications of attempts to exclude refugees from seeking protection, and the morality of certain kinds of boundary.

The costs of controlled borders

In a famous work on the ethics of international relations, Stanley Hoffmann wrote that 'it remains the duty of each country to open its own borders as widely as possible, without looking for excuses or waiting for others to act'.[3] This is almost the exact opposite of what is happening. Haunted by the fear of terrorism in the aftermath of the November 2015 and March 2016 bombings in Paris and Brussels, political figures in Europe and beyond have moved to blame the refugee crisis. Words to this effect by the Australian Prime Minister, Malcolm Turnbull, prompted the Belgian Ambassador to Australia, Jean-Luc Bodson, to remark that 'My view is that the terrorists who committed the latest attacks and in Paris and in Belgium are European-raised and born. Maybe from foreign origins, but they are Europeans. So it has nothing to do with the refugee crisis'.[4] Nonetheless, if moral arguments such as Hoffmann's cut little ice just at present, arguments based on the costs flowing from controlled borders might carry more weight, at least for some listeners. To start with, there are economic costs that flow from limiting the flow of people across borders. The important costs are not those associated with bureaucratic agencies for border control, although these may be considerable. The more substantial costs are those that result from the inefficiencies generated by interference with free trade in labour as a factor of production. Clemens has argued that the

> gains from eliminating migration barriers dwarf—by an order of magnitude or two—the gains from eliminating other types of barriers. For the elimination of trade policy barriers and capital flow barriers, the estimated gains amount to less than a few percent of world GDP. For labor mobility barriers, the estimated gains are often in the range of 50–150 per cent of world GDP.[5]

The intellectual battle in favour of free trade in goods, services and capital has now been won; amongst serious economists it is very difficult to find supporters of trade protection, simply because the dead-weight losses from protection are so easy to establish both theoretically and empirically.[6] Where people are concerned, the battle is yet to be taken up. Money can move much more easily than people.[7]

An irony here is that many countries because of their demographic attributes are facing the looming problem of an ageing, and shrinking, population with too few younger people available to look after the old, either directly as care givers or through the payment of taxation. A UN report in October 2015 concluded that 'Several countries are expected to see their populations decline by more than 15 per cent by 2050, including Bosnia and Herzegovina, Bulgaria, Croatia, Hungary, Japan, Latvia, Lithuania, Republic of Moldova, Romania, Serbia, and Ukraine. Fertility in all European countries is now below the level required for full replacement of the population in the long run (around 2.1 children per woman, on average), and in the majority of cases, fertility has been below the replacement level for several decades'.[8] There is therefore a sense in which Europe might be well advised to welcome an influx of young refugees, rather than engage in costly and morally-questionable efforts to repel them.

A further problem with the border control mechanisms used to exclude refugees is that they almost inevitably end up giving sweeping powers to bureaucracies, potentially creating major problems of accountability. The risks of untrammelled administrative discretion were identified by the Lord Chief Justice of England and Wales, Lord Hewart of Bury, in his famous 1929 book *The New Despotism*.[9] Immigration bureaucracies have provided powerful examples of the problems that Hewart highlighted. They have also proved keen to insulate themselves from oversight. Thus in Australia, the Howard Government sought through section 474 of the *Migration Act* 1958 to ensure that a wide range of administrative decisions made by immigration officials could not, in the words of section 474(1)(b), 'be challenged, appealed against, reviewed, quashed or called in question in any court'. This approach proved less than successful, as the High Court of Australia held that the provision could not save a 'decision' that was vitiated by 'jurisdictional error': in such a case there would be no decision at all to save.[10] The deeper problem this exposed, however, was indifference to the basic principle of the rule of law. Autocrats sometimes argue that the rule of law exists because legislation has been adopted which authorises the actions they wish to take. This was certainly the case at various times in Nazi Germany and Stalinist Russia, but it actually reflects a fundamental misunderstanding (or misrepresentation) of the rule of law. The 'rule of law' is strictly a meta-legal principle—a principle about law. It requires that the requirements of law bind both the ruled and their rulers. This was captured in a thunderous pronouncement of the seventeenth century English essayist Thomas Fuller: 'Be you never so high, the law is above you'.[11] The legal theorist Joseph Raz has identified a number of critical elements of the rule of law, most significantly that the independence of the judiciary must be guaranteed, the principles of natural justice must be observed, and courts should have review powers over the implementation of the principles of the rule of law.[12] Above all, it is necessary that both polity and society be infused with a spirit and culture of legality. The rule of law is a principle of great value, protecting individual liberties and fostering prosperity.[13] It is not something to be sacrificed lightly. Without the rule of law, abuse of arbitrary power is left free to flourish. Refugees will be losers from such a development—but they will not be the only losers.

As Chandran Kukathas has argued, the techniques that states adopt to control their borders almost inevitably imperil the liberties of their own citizens at the same time.[14] This was strikingly illustrated in an episode in August 2015 involving the 'Australian Border Force'. Staff of this new agency had been given a broad range of powers to give effect to its border control objectives, as well as ominous uniforms which added to the alarming image of the agency's officers. On 28 August, a press release announced the beginning of 'Operation Fortitude'. The key section reads as follows:[15]

> ABF Regional Commander Victoria and Tasmania, Don Smith, is proud the ABF will be participating in the operation.
>
> 'While the ABF regularly conducts a range of compliance field-work, this is the first time we've been involved in an inter-agency operation of this nature and we're very proud be able to support each of our organisations to achieve our common mission of promoting a secure and cohesive society here in Melbourne.'
>
> 'ABF officers will be positioned at various locations around the CBD speaking with any individual we cross paths with,' Mr Smith said.
>
> 'You need to be aware of the conditions of your visa; if you commit visa fraud you should know it's only a matter of time before you're caught out.'

The effect of the press release was to spark widespread outrage. Australia has no national identity card system. Most Australians do not carry evidence to establish their citizenship, and nor are they legally obliged to do so. The suspicion immediately surfaced that racial profiling would be employed to select those individuals with whom the Border Force would 'cross paths', and since Australia in the twenty-first century is a decidedly multicultural society, at any given moment in the centre of a city such as Melbourne, there are likely to be large numbers of Australian citizens of non-European ancestry. By the time the Border Force issued a further statement to try to dispel the impression that people might be targeted for attention on the basis of their physical appearance, a major protest demonstration was underway that created traffic snarls in central Melbourne. 'Operation Fortitude' was cancelled, and recriminations rapidly began, with the expression 'Border Farce' figuring prominently on social media. In October 2015, the Secretary of the Department of Immigration and Border Protection, Michael Pezzullo, and the Commissioner of the Border Force, Roman Quaedvlieg, were forced to offer grovelling apologies to a Senate Committee over the exercise.[16] The episode was instructive not so much because of its scale—since it was aborted before it could even get off the ground—but because of the mindset and culture that it exposed.[17] The offending press release passed in draft form through numerous hands in the relevant agencies before it was released, and no one seemed to grasp what kind of backlash it would most likely produce.

This brings us back to fundamental points about freedom and the state. One of the most important warnings about the propensities of the state was Lord Acton's observation in 1887 that power tends to corrupt and absolute power corrupts absolutely.[18] In the post-September 11, 2001 period, important inroads have been made in a number of different countries into personal freedoms in the name of action to prevent terrorism,[19] and border control routinely figures in such discussions, with refugees depicted as sources of danger. Implicit in this is the proposition that border control bureaucracies are effective devices for preventing the inflow of threatening persons. Arguably, it is only on such a basis that one could justify the increasingly intrusive powers that have been given to such bureaucracies, as illustrated in the case of 'Operation Fortitude'. Yet there may be good reasons for viewing such justifications with considerable caution. The capacity of bureaucracies to identify people who will pose threats in the future is highly questionable. In the words of the FBI Director, every one of the 11 September attackers 'came easily and lawfully from abroad'.[20] Subsequent analysis identified many warning signs that should have been detected, but the fact that they were not serves to highlight that it is a mistake to have unrealistically high expectations of human systems with human failings. A similar point could be made about Man Haron Monis, who, in what was widely reported as a terrorist attack, took hostages at a Lindt Chocolate shop in Martin Place in Sydney in December 2014 and was shot dead after having murdered the young manager of the shop. Monis had not made his way illicitly to Australia; he had entered the country legally with a business visa issued by the Australian government in October 1996.[21] Again, there were warning signs aplenty that went largely unremarked. When this can happen, it may be appropriate to reconsider the scale of the powers granted to border control agencies in the name of counterterrorism, and particularly the disposition to see refugees who arrive by boat or on foot as threatening, and to treat them badly simply because they arrive without being subject to prior bureaucratic scrutiny. Such scrutiny is not the magician's wand it is sometimes depicted as being.

One other passing comment about borders is in order. The world is actually full of borders that are *not* policed or controlled to ensure that refugees and asylum seekers cannot traverse them. These are the borders that exist between different states, provinces, or Länder in federal systems such as the United States, Australia, Canada or Germany. Many of these units are geographically larger and have bigger populations than some of the 'nation-states' that make up Europe. Not only are the boundaries within the United States, Australia, Canada or Germany free of intrusive control mechanisms, but it would be unthinkable if any attempt to establish such controls were to be made. The reason is that the benefits of free movement of people at this level have been widely recognised and accepted. Those who seek to defend rigorous control of movement between territorial states are almost never heard defending controls at lower levels. It might be useful if they were obliged to explain why.

The moral costs of refugee exclusion

At a conference attended by this writer in December 2012, Roman Catholic Bishop Eugene Hurley of Darwin quoted a most insightful observation made to him by an asylum seeker held in a detention centre he was visiting: 'If freedom is all you have ever known, then you've never known freedom'. In a number of countries in recent years, the freedom of refugees and asylum-seekers has been a major casualty of policies designed either to isolate such people from communities that might support them, or to deter them from seeking protection in those countries in the first place. This has sometimes been justified on the Orwellian basis that the detention involved is 'administrative' rather than 'punitive', but if freedom is something of value, depriving people of their freedom is intrinsically punitive.

There are good reasons to be extremely cautious about detention at the behest of the executive. In the Supreme Court of the United States, Mr Justice Jackson warned that 'Executive imprisonment has been considered oppressive and lawless since John, at Runnymede, pledged that no free man should be imprisoned, dispossessed, outlawed, or exiled save by the judgment of his peers or by the law of the land'.[22] Indeed, the famous writ of

Habeas Corpus emerged as a device to prevent arbitrary detention by the Crown or Executive.[23] Immigration detention comes in a number of different forms and serves a number of different purposes.[24] One such form is limited short-term detention of undocumented or unauthorised entrants, simply for the purpose of ensuring that such persons are not carrying communicable diseases that could be a threat to members of the community they are seeking to enter. This approach can also be used to ensure that those seeking to enter are not known criminals or persons otherwise likely to pose a real threat to existing members of the community. Countries such as France and Spain have limits on the duration of immigration detention. The issue has become increasingly controversial in the United Kingdom, however, as it does not have comparable limits.[25] In March 2015, the *Report of the Inquiry into the Use of Immigration Detention in the United Kingdom* recommended that 'There should be a time limit of 28 days on the length of time that anyone can be held in immigration detention';[26] and in March 2016, the House of Lords, on the motion of the former Chief Inspector of Prisons, Lord Ramsbotham, voted by 187 to 170 to insert such a limit in the *Immigration Bill* that the House was debating. Lord Ramsbotham did not mince his words, stating that 'The culture of disbelief that pervades the Home Office, allied to the appalling standard of its casework over the years—witnessed by the staggeringly high number of successful appeals against its decisions—and the appalling quality of its communication with applicants, gives me no confidence that it is capable of carrying out what the Government apparently wish. Nothing has been done to improve the situation for years'.[27]

In Australia, the other main state to practise indefinite immigration detention, the situation is arguably even worse. In March 2015, the United Nations Special Rapporteur on Torture and other Cruel, Inhuman or Degrading Treatment or Punishment, investigating potential violations of the Convention against Torture (CAT), reported that the

> Government of Australia, by failing to provide adequate detention conditions; end the practice of detention of children; and put a stop to the escalating violence and tension at the Regional Processing Centre, has violated the right of the asylum seekers, including children, to be free from torture or cruel, inhuman or degrading treatment, as provided by articles 1 and 16 of the CAT.[28]

In two respects, Australia's practice of detention is distinctive. First, it involves the use both of facilities in mainland Australia and the Australian Indian Ocean territory of Christmas Island, and 'offshore' establishments in Nauru and Papua New Guinea, funded by Australia but subject to the legal fiction that it is the governments of those states that are responsible for the asylum seekers sent there. Second, detention is defended as a deterrent to unauthorised entrants, with any amelioration of the detention regime depicted as a potential marketing tool for people smugglers. The logic of deterrence has a devastating implication: to be effective as a deterrent, it is necessary that those who are detained suffer in the process.

That this is a consequence of detention is by now very thoroughly documented. Dehumanisation is a central element of the policy of deterrence, both in terms of how the public see refugees,[29] and how refugees are treated. Not long after the Tampa Affair in 2001, the Defence Minister's office instructed that 'personalising or humanising images' of asylum seekers were not to be released.[30] For a time, detainees were identified not by name but by number.[31] In 1999, in a case before the Federal Court of Australia, the Government did not contest the claim that the plaintiff's psychiatric illness, marked by 'severe paranoid delusions', was a result of his prolonged detention.[32] The effects of detention on the mental health of children were especially grave, as two searing reports made clear.[33] The adverse mental health effects of detention have been further recorded in a number of meticulous studies,[34] to the point where the morality of involvement with the detention system has been raised for serious ethical debate within the medical profession.[35] The importance of bearing witness to such abuses is not to be discounted. Rabbi Joachim Prinz made this point in a speech to the famous March on Washington in August 1963:

> When I was the rabbi of the Jewish community in Berlin under the Hitler regime, I learned many things. The most important thing that I learned ... under those tragic circumstances was that bigotry and hatred are not the most urgent problem. The most urgent, the most disgraceful, the most shameful and the most tragic problem is silence.[36]

And some have been prepared to break the silence. No less a figure than the Internal Affairs Minister of New Zealand, Peter Dunne, struck out in November 2015: 'The modern concentration camp approach Australia has taken is simply wrong ... Australia is a sovereign state. We cannot require it to change its laws, just because they affront us ... But we can, and should, be speaking out as loudly and as frequently as we can against abhorrent practices, especially given the mantle of family Australians like to drape upon us'.[37]

Some architects of the system of detention will most likely never appreciate just what they have wrought, or at least they will contrive not to do so. On Christmas Day 1891, Anatole France published a short story in *Le Temps* entitled 'Le procurateur de Judée', setting out a rambling conversation between two Roman administrators, L. Aelius Lamia and Pontius Pilate. At the end, Lamia recalls a Jewish girl of his acquaintance who took up with a young Galilean preacher called Jesus the Nazarene. 'Pontius', he asks, 'do you remember that man?' 'Jesus', responds Pontius, 'Jesus the Nazarene. I don't recall'.[38] Perhaps those who wash their hands of responsibility are wont to respond in this way. But not everyone escapes unscathed, and a recent reflection on immigration detention captures this.[39] The author, Dr Howard Goldenberg, noted that

> Male patients—and the great majority in my care happened to be adult and male—in immigration detention suffered from a spiritual malaise, an affliction I have not seen described and which I struggle to categorise. Its features include an inversion of belief such that the detained person replaces trust in fellow humans with mistrust, with an expectation of mendacity and malignity of purpose.

He went on to offer the following observations:

> This inversion of the spiritual substrata of life reminded me of Primo Levi's descriptions of that distinctive moral universe, the Nazi concentration camp, where the SS intentionally destroyed a world of hope and faith and kindness. In Levi's analysis each of these three elements—which are socially virtuous and utile in the world outside the camp—become dangerous and harmful within the camp. I do not suspect any such intent on my island. But the outcomes here are just as certain even if unintended.

> An unanticipated hazard was experienced by carers, both among the guards and the clinicians. The hazard was moral in nature. Quickly many came to sense wrongs in the system. The wrongs included treating as criminals persons who had broken no law; imprisoning persons who had shown every desperation to be free; humiliating our patients with a dehumanising system of identification by boat number rather than by name. All who worked in the Centre understood we were functioning parts of an unkind system: while we were to do no harm, we were to delimit our own capacity to do good.

> Evidence of the moral hazard, the sense of our violence against our own values, emerged in the behaviour of the captors. Doctors drank every night, smoked heavily and suffered nightmares. More than one guard attempted suicide, one successfully.

What Goldenberg describes here is a paradigmatic example of a system grounded in moral cruelty, which the late Judith Shklar defined as 'deliberate and persistent humiliation, so that the victim can eventually trust neither himself nor anyone else'.[40] What sometimes goes unnoticed, but Goldenberg captures with great perspicacity, is that moral cruelty has many victims. As Nietzsche put it, 'When you gaze long into an abyss the abyss also gazes into you'.[41]

Confronting the 'Birthright Lottery'

One of the great obstacles in securing more humane approaches to refugee issues is the perception on the part of politicians that harsh treatment of refugees is a vote-winner with at least some of their constituents. This way of thinking hardly points to great skills of leadership—'I must follow the crowd, as I am their leader', Napoleon III once remarked—but it constitutes a problem for the policy process. There is, however, a way of addressing this, and it lies in the idea of framing. Framing 'refers to the process by which people develop a particular conceptualization of an issue or reorient their thinking about an issue'.[42] Issues can be framed for the consumption of the general public in a number of different ways. One way of framing the refugee issue is as a threat. But another is to frame it as an opportunity to do good, to reveal what Abraham Lincoln in his First Inaugural Address described as 'the better angels of our nature'. Too often, the system of states is framed as somehow a reflection of the essences of the world, rather than as a contingent set of arrangements that in their current form are relatively novel, with specific details that demand occasional reappraisal. Ayelet Shachar has provocatively captured one aspect of this challenge in her conception of the 'Birthright Lottery': in the wider scale of things, people's chances in life to a very large extent depend on where and to whom they were born. She argues that 'Given that the vast majority of the world's population remain excluded from well-off polities under the current birthright regime, it quickly becomes clear that neglecting their needs and interests simply because extant laws define them as nonmembers is not only morally wrong; it is also politically unwise'.[43] Her proposed response is a birthright privilege levy, but another would be to use the idea of the birthright lottery to reframe debate around the issue of responsibilities towards refugees. The crucial point is that through the reframing of issues, strong leaders can adopt and promote strongly-humanitarian policies, as Angela Merkel has arguably succeeded in doing in Germany. An unwillingness to make the effort is often the mark of a weak politician, happy to follow the nastier or meaner parts of the crowd.

The idea of territory, of course, has a venerable history,[44] and there are arguments regularly advanced to defend the moral status of the territorial state, ranging from the claim that good fences make good neighbours,[45] to claims based on self-determination as a basis for protecting vulnerable groups from assaults by others, to claims based on the territorial state as a source of nurture for communities and social capital. Most proponents of such arguments, however, tend to make special cases for refugees. For example, Margaret Moore has recently argued that

> Even if the interest that political communities have in collective self-determination means that they are not required to accept individual people seeking to improve their lot, they must still accept refugees. Since it is likely that countries adjacent to oppressive regimes do more than other countries to meet this obligation, other countries should strive to fulfil that duty too, by bearing some of the costs and by accepting their fair share of refugees.[46]

Furthermore, there are some important potential downsides to the nurturing of communities. Closed communities can become hothouses for the cultivation of very negative sentiments such as fear and hatred of strangers;[47] even the most casual users of social media would be aware of the deep hostilities towards refugees that are routinely articulated where norms of face-to-face courtesy do not apply and the attackers can shield their ugly views behind a veil of anonymity.

In a globalised world, the credibility of the birthright lottery as grounds for excluding people from protection may be diminishing, and although states may still have the capacity to drive away those in need, the legitimacy of their claimed right to do so may be subject to more and more questioning.[48] One way of ameliorating this might be to explore whether creating regular migration opportunities for refugees could offer a wealth-creating solution, by allowing refugees access to states with labour shortages. The Nansen passport in the 1920s was designed to facilitate such movements. Because of the potential for exploitation of vulnerable refugees, such approaches might need to be pursued with some care, but the economic case is a strong one, even if such a model falls short of providing the gains that genuine freedom of movement could offer. The challenge, as always, is political. In Katy Long's words, it lies in 'persuading states that the costs of protracted displacement—of failing to solve refugee crises for generations—are not an acceptable price to pay for the illusion of migration control'.[49]

A final word

We began this book with some stories of individual refugees, and it is therefore fitting to conclude in the same way. The principal message of the book, standing above all others, is that refugees are human, just like us. The problem is that all too often, we fail to treat them as human, something that says more about us than about them. State agencies are often the worst offenders, and the story of Fazel Chegeni illustrates this in the most poignant of fashions.[50]

Fazel Chegeni was a Faili Kurd, born in Iran in 1981. Consigned to the margins of society by his family background, he was arrested and tortured in 2006, and although he was ultimately released, he experienced years of harassment thereafter. Finally he borrowed enough money to leave, and with the services of a people smuggler, arrived in Australia on 23 October 2011, and was subjected to mandatory detention. In March 2012, he was found to be a refugee, but given the elaborate clearances required under Australian bureaucratic procedures, he was not released from detention until 8 April 2013.

His freedom was to be short-lived. On 22 December 2011, he had been involved in an altercation with other detainees.[51] Some two years later, he appeared in the Magistrate's Court of Western Australia charged with assault. On legal advice, he pleaded guilty. The magistrate, one Barbara Lane, convicted him and sentenced him to six months and one day's imprisonment. On appeal, the sentence was found to be 'manifestly excessive', and a non-custodial penalty known as a 'good behaviour bond' was substituted. In response to the appeal, the Court held that 'The attack lasted for a very short time, about one minute ... The victim was not seriously injured and made a full recovery from his injuries. No property was damaged. No staff were attacked. Order was quickly restored. Each of the appellants has no prior convictions and is of good character'.[52] The magistrate subsequently resigned after a Supreme Court finding that she had acted in another case in a way that amounted to a breach of procedural fairness.[53] But this was no use to Fazel Chegeni. Despite being a refugee, he had been re-detained from 18 December 2013 at the behest of the Minister for Immigration and Border Protection. Since the appeal had overturned his penalty but not his conviction, he was caught by section 501 (6)(aa)(i) of the *Migration Act* 1958, which provided that 'a person does not pass the character test if ... the person has been convicted of an offence that was committed ... while the person was in immigration detention'.[54] This provision enabled the Minister to re-detain him. Professor Gillian Triggs, President of the Australian Human Rights Commission, described the response as 'draconian', and remarked 'What we have here is people being warehoused, for years and years on end, as some sort of gesture to a political objective, which is very ill-informed and politically ideological'.[55]

Fazel Chegeni faced the possibility of spending the rest of his life in detention. Despite increasingly dire warnings about his deteriorating mental health from those he encountered, the Minister remained obdurate in the face of requests that something be done to help him. On 6 November 2015, completely worn down by his experiences, Fazel Chegeni went missing from the Christmas Island detention centre. His body was found two days later. A few days after his death, a memorial vigil was held for him in Melbourne by some of his surviving friends. "Fazel is free now," one wrote. "God gave him a visa."[56]

NOTES

1. INTRODUCTION

1. See http://data.unhcr.org/mediterranean/regional.php (accessed 6 January 2016).

2. Dan Bilefsky, 'Denmark Moves to Make Refugees Hand Over Valuables', *The New York Times*, 14 January 2016.

3. See, for example, Melanie Phillips, 'Osborne is hoodwinking us on immigration', *The Times*, 4 December 2015.

4. Shehab Khan, 'Refugees coming to Europe an "organised invasion", says Czech President Milos Zeman', *The Independent*, 28 December 2015.

5. See Florian Flade, Marcel Paul and Kristian Frigelj, '1054 Strafanzeigen nach Übergriffen von Köln', *Die Welt*, 10 February 2016.

6. Boris Pasternak, *Doktor Zhivago* (Moscow: Sovetskaia Rossiia, 1989) pp. 585–586.

7. *Exodus*, 13: 3.

8. *Matthew*, 2: 13–15.

9. See Muhammad Khalid Masud, 'The obligation to migrate: the doctrine of *hijra* in Islamic law', in Dale F. Eickelman and James Piscatori (eds), *Muslim Travellers: Pilgrimage, Migration, and the Religious Imagination* (London: Routledge, 1990) pp. 29–49.

10. See Arafat Madi Shoukri, *Refugee Status in Islam: Concepts of Protection in Islamic Tradition and International Law* (London: I.B. Tauris, 2011) pp. 34–38.

11. On the harshness of life for wartime refugees in Switzerland, see Marc Vuilleumier, *Immigrés et réfugiés en Suisse: Aperçu historique* (Zurich: Pro Helvetia, 1992) pp. 82–83.

12. See Peter Jelavich, *Berlin Cabaret* (Cambridge: Harvard University Press, 1993) pp. 275, 280–282.

13. Anka Muhlstein, 'His Exile Was Intolerable', *The New York Review of Books*, vol. 61, no. 8, 8 May 2014.

14. Richard and Clara Winston (eds), *The Letters of Thomas Mann* (Harmondsworth: Penguin, 1975) p. 311. Mann's younger sister had committed suicide in 1910, an experience that may also have coloured his approach to Zweig's death: see Manfred Flügge, *Das Jahrhundert der Manns* (Berlin: Aufbau, 2015) pp. 50–56.

15. See Donald Prater, *Thomas Mann: A Life* (Oxford: Oxford University Press, 1995).

16. See Frederic Spotts, *Cursed Legacy: The Tragic Life of Klaus Mann* (New Haven: Yale University Press, 2016). Spotts, however, argues in favour of death by accidental overdose rather than suicide.

17. Ahmed Rashid, *Taliban: Militant Islam, Oil and Fundamentalism in Central Asia* (New Haven: Yale University Press, 2000) p. 73.

18. See Michel Lawrence, *All of Us: Multiculturalism—Australian style* (Melbourne: Scribe Publications, 2008) p. 66.

19. See Michael Gordon, *Freeing Ali: The Human Face of the Pacific Solution* (Sydney: University of New South Wales Press, 2005).

20. Michael Gordon, 'A refugee reconnects', *The Saturday Age*, 2 July 2011.

21. See Malala Yousafzai and Christina Lamb, *I Am Malala: The Girl Who Stood Up for Education and was Shot by the Taliban* (London: Weidenfeld & Nicolson, 2014).

22. See Justin Wm. Moyer, 'Aylan's story: 'How desperation left a 3-year-old boy washed up on a Turkish beach', *The Washington Post*, 3 September 2015.

23. See Joe Friesen, 'Prime Minister's Office ordered halt to refugee processing', *The Globe and Mail*, 8 October 2015.

24. E. F. Kunz, 'The Refugee in Flight: Kinetic Models and Forms of Displacement', *International Migration Review*, vol. 7, no. 2, Summer 1973, pp. 125–146 at pp. 131–132.

25. See Eugene Kamenka, 'On Being a Refugee', in Amin Saikal (ed.), *Refugees in the Modern World* (Canberra: Canberra Studies in World Affairs no. 25, Department of International Relations, Research School of Pacific Studies, The Australian National University, 1989) pp. 11–15.

26. Kunz, 'The Refugee in Flight'.

27. Gil Loescher, *Beyond Charity: International Cooperation and the Global Refugee Crisis* (New York: Oxford University Press, 1993) p. 17.

28. Winston S. Churchill, *The Second World War* (London: Chartwell Edition, Educational Book Company, 1954) Vol. VI, p. 519.

29. Tom McCarthy and Patrick Wintour, 'Obama savages Republican calls to give priority to Christians from Syria', *The Guardian*, 16 November 2015; David M. Herszenhorn and Michael D. Shear, 'Republicans Want to Suspend Program Accepting Syrian Refugees', *The New York Times*, 18 November 2015.

30. *A Survey of the Afghan People: Afghanistan in 2015* (Kabul: The Asia Foundation, 2015) p. 90, question D-16.

31. Wayne Errington and Peter Van Onselen, *John Winston Howard: The Biography* (Melbourne: Melbourne University Press, 2007) pp. 300–301. Prime Minister Howard, unsurprisingly, sought to justify his policies by reference to ideas of sovereignty and humanitarianism rather than in terms of domestic politics. See William Maley, 'Asylum-seekers in Australia's international relations', *Australian Journal of International Affairs*, vol. 57, no. 1, 2003, pp. 187–202; Danielle Every, 'A Reasonable, Practical and Moderate Humanitarianism: The Co-option of Humanitarianism in the Australian Asylum-Seeker Debates', *Journal of Refugee Studies*, vol. 21, no. 2, June 2008, pp. 210–229.

32. See Liza Schuster, *The Use and Abuse of Political Asylum in Britain and Germany* (London: Frank Cass, 2003) p. 5.

33. See Christian Reus–Smit, *Individual Rights and the Making of the International System* (Cambridge: Cambridge University Press, 2013).

34. See Robert E. Goodin, 'What is So Special About our Fellow Countrymen', *Ethics*, vol. 98, no. 4, July 1988, pp. 663–686.

35. See Samantha Power, *"A Problem from Hell": America and the Age of Genocide* (New York: Basic Books, 2002).

36. Norman Angell and Dorothy Frances Buxton, *You and the Refugee* (London: Penguin, 1939).

2. DEFINING 'REFUGEES'

1. Richard Robinson, *Definition* (Oxford: Oxford University Press, 1950).
2. See the discussion in Jens David Ohlin, *The Assault on International Law* (New York: Oxford University Press, 2015).
3. William Shakespeare, *Measure for Measure*, Act II, Scene II.
4. Other sources, less directly relevant to defining refugees, are peremptory norms of international law (*jus cogens*), such as the prohibitions on genocide and apartheid, and 'decisions' of the United Nations Security Council that are binding upon states under Article 25 of the *Charter of the United Nations*.
5. Ian Brownlie (ed.), *Basic Documents in International Law* (Oxford: Oxford University Press, 2009) pp. 270–297.
6. Robert O. Keohane, 'Reciprocity in international relations', *International Organization*, vol. 40, no. 1, Winter 1986, pp. 1–27.
7. On the nature of customary international law, see James Crawford, *Brownlie's Principles of Public International Law* (Oxford: Oxford University Press, 2012) pp. 23–30.
8. James C. Hathaway, 'The Evolution of Refugee Status in International Law, 1920–1950', *International and Comparative Law Quarterly*, vol. 33, no. 2, April 1984, pp. 348–380.
9. Guy S. Goodwin Gill and Jane McAdam, *The Refugee in International Law* (Oxford: Oxford University Press, 2007) pp. 16–20.
10. Jane McAdam, 'Rethinking the Origins of "Persecution" in Refugee Law', *International Journal of Refugee Law*, vol. 25, no. 4, December 2013, pp. 667–692.
11. See John G. Stoessinger, *The Refugee and the World Community* (Minneapolis: University of Minnesota Press, 1956) pp. 85–155.
12. Louise W. Holborn, *The International Refugee Organization. A Specialized Agency of the United Nations: Its History and Work 1946–1952* (London: Oxford University Press, 1956) p. 433.
13. For an overview, see Alexander Betts, Gil Loescher and James Milner, *UNHCR: The Politics and Practice of Refugee Protection* (London: Routledge, 2012).
14. See *Statute of the Office of the United Nations High Commissioner for Refugees* (Geneva: Public Information Section, UNHCR, 1996).

15. Gil Loescher, *The UNHCR and World Politics: A Perilous Path* (Oxford: Oxford University Press, 2001).

16. See, generally, William Maley, 'A New Tower of Babel? Reappraising the Architecture of Refugee Protection', in Edward Newman and Joanne Van Selm (eds), *Refugees and Forced Displacement: International Security, Human Vulnerability, and the State* (Tokyo: United Nations University Press, 2003) pp. 306–329.

17. See S. Alex Cunliffe and Michael Pugh, 'UNHCR as leader in humanitarian assistance: a triumph of politics over law?', in Frances Nicholson and Patrick Twomey (eds), *Refugee Rights and Realities: Evolving International Concepts and Regimes* (Cambridge: Cambridge University Press, 1999) pp. 175–199.

18. *Reuters*, 20 September 1999.

19. See Raimo Väyrynen, 'Funding Dilemmas in Refugee Assistance: Political Interests and Institutional Reforms in the UNHCR', *International Migration Review*, vol. 35, no. 1, Spring 2001, pp. 143–167.

20. *UNHCR Global Report 2014* (Geneva: United Nations High Commissioner for Refugees, 2015) p. 143.

21. For details of the drafting process, see *The Refugee Convention, 1951: The Travaux Preparatoires analysed, with a Commentary by the late Dr Paul Weis* (Cambridge: Cambridge International Documents Series, Volume 7, Cambridge University Press, 1995). On the operation of the *Convention*, see Andreas Zimmermann (ed.), *The 1951 Convention Relating to the Status of Refugees and its 1967 Protocol* (Oxford: Oxford University Press, 2011).

22. Article 1.A (1) provided for the continuation of refugee status for so-called 'statutory refugees' recognised under earlier instruments. Important at the time, this provision is now of minimal relevance.

23. See James C. Hathaway and Michelle Foster, *The Law of Refugee Status* (Cambridge: Cambridge University Press, 2014) pp. 182–287.

24. In December 2014, the Australian Government secured parliamentary approval for legislation that expunged from the *Migration Act* 1958 the specific references to the 1951 *Convention* that it had previously contained, and inserted a new section 197C(2) which provided that 'An

officer's duty to remove as soon as reasonably practicable an unlawful non-citizen under section 198 arises irrespective of whether there has been an assessment, according to law, of Australia's non-refoulement obligations in respect of the non-citizen'.

25. James Crawford and Patricia Hyndman, 'Three Heresies in the Application of the Refugee Convention', *International Journal of Refugee Law*, vol. 1, no. 2, 1989, pp. 155–179 at p. 166.

26. See Vanessa Holder, *Refugees from Armed Conflict: The 1951 Refugee Convention and International Humanitarian Law* (Cambridge: Intersentia, 2015).

27. Stephen H. Legomsky, 'Refugees, Asylum and the Rule of Law in the USA', in Susan Kneebone (ed.), *Refugees, Asylum Seekers and the Rule of Law: Comparative Perspectives* (Cambridge: Cambridge University Press, 2009) pp. 122–170 at p. 163. See also Azadeh Dastyari, *United States Migrant Interdiction and the Detention of Refugees in Guantánamo Bay* (Cambridge: Cambridge University Press, 2015) pp. 28–30.

28. For a comprehensive discussion of these rights, see James C. Hathaway, *The Rights of Refugees under International Law* (Cambridge: Cambridge University Press, 2005).

29. See William Maley, 'Political Transitions and the Cessation of Refugee Status: Some Lessons from Afghanistan and Iraq', *Law in Context*, vol. 22, no. 2, April 2005, pp. 156–186.

30. See Marina Sharpe, *The 1969 OAU Refugee Convention and the Protection of People fleeing Armed Conflict and Other Situations of Violence in the Context of Individual Refugee Status Determination* (Geneva: Legal and Protection Policy Research Series, PPLA/2013/01, Division of International Protection, UNHCR, January 2013) pp. 14–18.

31. On human movement as a manifestation of vulnerability, see Ian Clark, *The Vulnerable in International Society* (Oxford: Oxford University Press, 2013) pp. 84–105.

32. See Paul Hollander, *The Many Faces of Socialism: Comparative Sociology and Politics* (New Brunswick: Transaction Books, 1983) pp. 79–103; Andrea Chandler, *Institutions of Isolation: Border Controls in the Soviet Union and its Successor States 1917–1993* (Montreal and Kingston: McGill-Queen's University Press, 1998).

33. For a sample of such reasoning, see Adrienne Millbank, 'The Elephant on the Boat: The Problem that is the Refugee Convention', *People and Place*, vol. 18, no. 4, 2010, pp. 41–49.

34. Matthew E. Price, *Rethinking Asylum: History, Purpose, and Limits* (Cambridge: Cambridge University Press, 2009).

35. See Jane McAdam, 'Australia and Asylum Seekers', *International Journal of Refugee Law*, vol. 25, no. 3, September 2013, pp. 435–448; Jane McAdam and Fiona Chong, *Refugees: Why Seeking Asylum is Legal and Australia's Policies Are Not* (Sydney: UNSW Press, 2014).

36. On this episode, see Tony Kevin, *A Certain Maritime Incident: The Sinking of SIEV X* (Melbourne: Scribe Publications, 2004).

37. *Migration Regulations* 1994, Condition 8570, Schedule 8, inserted by the *Migration and Maritime Powers Legislation Amendment (Resolving the Asylum Legacy Caseload) Act* 2014, Schedule 2.

38. Jane McAdam, *Complementary Protection in International Refugee Law* (Oxford: Oxford University Press, 2007) p. 21.

39. See Frits Kalshoven and Liesbeth Zegveld, *Constraints on the Waging of War: An Introduction to International Humanitarian Law* (Cambridge: Cambridge University Press, 2011).

40. See the cases discussed in Fiona Terry, *Condemned to Repeat? The Paradox of Humanitarian Action* (Ithaca: Cornell University Press, 2002) and Sarah Kenyon Lister, *Dangerous Sanctuaries: Refugee Camps, Civil War, and the Dilemmas of Humanitarian Aid* (Ithaca: Cornell University Press, 2005).

41. See Stephen John Stedman and Fred Tanner (eds), *Refugee Manipulation: War, Politics, and the Abuse of Human Suffering* (Washington DC: Brookings Institution Press, 2003).

42. See *F.K.A.G. et al. v. Australia* (United Nations: CCPR/C/108/D/2094/2011, 20 August 2013).

43. McAdam, *Complementary Protection in International Refugee Law*, p. 126.

44. See Darius Rejali, *Torture and Democracy* (Princeton: Princeton University Press, 2007).

45. Senate Select Committee on Intelligence, *The Senate Intelligence Committee Report on Torture: Committee Study of the Central Intelligence*

Agency's Detention and Interrogation Program (New York: Melville House, 2014) p. 22.

46. On genocide more broadly, see Leo Kuper, *The Prevention of Genocide* (New Haven: Yale University Press, 1985); Daniel Chirot and Clark McCauley, *Why Not Kill Them All? The Logic and Prevention of Mass Political Murder* (Princeton: Princeton University Press, 2006).

47. Joint Media Release, *Changes to Australia's immigration processing system* (Canberra: Commonwealth of Australia, 9 April 2010).

48. *Asylum Trends—Australia: 2010–2011 Annual Publication* (Canberra: Department of Immigration and Citizenship, 2011) pp. 31, 33–4.

49. See Diana Eades, Helen Fraser, Jeff Siegel, Tim McNamara and Brett Baker, 'Linguistic Identification in the Determination of Nationality: A Preliminary Report', *Language Policy*, vol. 2, no. 2, 2003, pp. 179–199; Diana Eades, 'Testing the Claims of Asylum Seekers: The Role of Language Analysis', *Language Assessment Quarterly*, vol. 6, no. 1, 2009, pp. 30–40; Jan Blommaert, 'Language, Asylum, and the National Order', *Current Anthropology*, vol. 50, no. 4, August 2009, pp. 415–425, 436–441; Tim McNamara, 'The Promise and Threat of the Shibboleth: Linguistic Representations of Asylum Seekers', in Daniel H. Rellstab and Christiane Schlote (eds), *Representations of War, Migration and Refugeehood: Interdisciplinary Perspectives* (New York: Routledge, 2014) pp. 93–108.

50. Maaike Verrips, 'Language Analysis and Contra-Expertise in the Dutch Asylum Procedure', *International Journal of Speech, Language and the Law*, vol. 17, no. 2, 2010, pp. 279–294 at p. 291. For further discussion of European practice, see Karin Zwaan, Peter Muysken and Maaike Verrips (eds), *Language and Origin. The Role of Language in European Asylum Procedures: A Linguistic and Legal Survey* (Nijmegen: Wolf Legal Publishers, 2010).

51. For a skeptical Australian assessment, see *SBAQ* v. *Minister for Immigration & Multicultural & Indigenous Affairs* [2002] FCA 985, per Mansfield J.

52. See Meghana Nayak, *Who is Worthy of Protection? Gender-Based Asylum and US Immigration Policies* (New York: Oxford University Press, 2015).

53. See Elizabeth Rubin, 'Locked Up for Seeking Asylum', *The New York Times*, 3 April 2016.

54. Cécile Rousseau, François Crépeau, Patricia Foxen and France Houle, 'The Complexity of Determining Refugeehood: A Multidisciplinary Analysis of the Decision-making Process of the Canadian Immigration and Refugee Board', *Journal of Refugee Studies*, vol. 15, no. 1, March 2002, pp. 43–70; For studies of decision-making in the United States, see Jaya Ramji-Nogales, Andrew I. Schoenholtz and Philip G. Schrag, *Refugee Roulette: Disparities in Asylum Adjudication and Proposals for Reform* (New York: New York University Press, 2009); Banks Miller, Linda Camp Keith and Jennifer S. Holmes, *Immigration Judges and U.S. Asylum Policy* (Philadelphia: University of Pennsylvania Press, 2015).

55. For further discussion of these issues, see Michael Herzfeld, *The Social Production of Indifference: Exploring the Symbolic Roots of Western Bureaucracy* (Chicago: University of Chicago Press, 1992); Stanley Cohen, *States of Denial: Knowing about Atrocities and Suffering* (Cambridge: Polity Press, 2001).

56. See *1211917 [2012] RRTA 1116* (17 December 2012) para.93.

57. See Jane McAdam and Fiona Chong, *Complementary Protection in Australia: A Review of the Jurisprudence* (Sydney: Andrew and Renate Kaldor Centre for International Refugee Law, University of New South Wales, 6 December 2013) p. 10. fn.41.

58. See Abdul Karim Hekmat, 'Taliban tortures Abbott government deportee', *The Saturday Paper*, 4 October 2014.

59. See 'Sayed Habib Musawi "tortured, killed by Taliban because he was Australian"', *The Guardian*, 30 September 2014.

60. Henry S. Bradsher, *Afghan Communism and Soviet Intervention* (Karachi: Oxford University Press, 1989) p. 211.

61. More detailed discussion of these calendars can be found in Klaus Ferdinand, *Preliminary Notes on Hazara Culture (The Danish Scientific Mission to Afghanistan 1952–55)* (Copenhagen: Enjar Munksgaard, 1959) pp. 40–46; Hassan Poladi, *The Hazaras* (Stockton: Mughal Publishing, 1989) pp. 153–155.

62. See *Hussain v. Minister for Immigration and Multicultural Affairs* [2001] FCA 523, per Carr J.

63. *Inquiry into the Circumstances of the Vivian Alvarez Matter: Report under the Ombudsman Act 1976 by the Commonwealth Ombudsman, Professor John McMillan, of an inquiry undertaken by Mr Neil Comrie AO APM* (Canberra: Report no.081, Commonwealth Ombudsman, September 2005).

64. See Anna Wierzbicka, *Imprisoned in English: The Hazards of English as a Default Language* (New York: Oxford University Press, 2014).

65. I would like to thank Professor Anna Wierzbicka for sharing her thoughts on this point.

66. For an interesting recent discussion, see Benjamin Meiches, 'A Political Ecology of the Camp', *Security Dialogue*, vol. 46, no. 5, October 2015, pp. 476–492.

67. See Susan Martin, 'Climate Change, Migration, and Governance' *Global Governance*, vol. 16, no. 3, July–September 2010, pp. 397–414; Jane McAdam, *Climate Change, Forced Migration, and International Law* (Oxford: Oxford University Press, 2012).

68. *Teitiota* v. *Ministry of Business Innovation and Employment* [2015] NZSC 107 (20 July 2015) para.5.

69. *Teitiota* v. *Ministry of Business Innovation and Employment*, para.13.

70. Alexander Betts, *Survival Migration: Failed Governance and the Crisis of Displacement* (Ithaca: Cornell University Press, 2013) pp. 4–5.

71. Andrew E. Shacknove, 'Who Is a Refugee?', *Ethics*, vol. 95, no. 2, January 1985, pp. 274–284 at p. 282.

72. See William Maley, 'Peace, Needs and Utopia', *Political Studies*, vol. 33, no. 4, December 1985, pp. 578–591.

73. See Matthew J. Gibney, *The Ethics and Politics of Asylum: Liberal Democracy and the Response to Refugees* (Cambridge: Cambridge University Press, 2004) p. 9.

3. EXILE AND REFUGE: A BRIEF OVERVIEW

1. Thomas Hobbes, *Leviathan* (Cambridge: Cambridge University Press, 1996) pp. 88–89.

2. Aristide R. Zolberg, Astri Suhrke and Sergio Aguayo, *Escape from Violence: Conflict and the Refugee Crisis in the Developing World* (New York: Oxford University Press, 1989) p. 33.

3. See Susanne Schmeidl, 'The early warning of forced migration: State or human security', in Edward Newman and Joanne van Selm (eds), *Refugees and Forced Displacement: International Security, Human Vulnerability, and the State* (Tokyo: United Nations University Press, 2003) pp. 130–155 at p. 137.

4. Charles Tilly, 'War Making and State Making as Organized Crime', in Peter Evans, Dietrich Rueschemeyer and Theda Skocpol (eds). *Bringing the State Back In* (Cambridge: Cambridge University Press, 1985) pp. 169–191 at p. 170. For further elaboration of these ideas, see Charles Tilly, *Coercion, Capital and European States, AD 990–1992* (Oxford: Blackwell, 1992) pp. 67–95.

5. See David Cannadine, *The Undivided Past: Humanity Beyond Our Differences* (New York: Alfred A. Knopf, 2013).

6. Emma Graham-Harrison, Patrick Kingsley and Tracy McVeigh, 'Cheering German crowds greet refugees after long trek from Budapest to Munich', *The Observer*, 6 September 2015

7. Heather Rae, *State Identities and the Homogenisation of Peoples* (Cambridge: Cambridge University Press, 2002) p. 5.

8. Ibid., pp. 117–118.

9. See Zolberg, Suhrke and Aguayo, *Escape from Violence*, p. 5.

10. Rae, *State Identities and the Homogenisation of Peoples*, pp. 124–211. For more detail on these cases, see Taner Akçam, *The Young Turks' Crime Against Humanity: The Armenian Genocide and Ethnic Cleansing in the Ottoman Empire* (Princeton: Princeton University Press, 2012); Norman Cigar, *Genocide in Bosnia: The Policy of 'Ethnic Cleansing'* (College Station: Texas A&M University Press, 1995).

11. See Gertrude Himmelfarb, *On Looking into the Abyss: Untimely Thoughts on Culture and Society* (New York: Vintage Books, 1994) pp. 107–121.

12. Isaiah Berlin, *The Sense of Reality: Studies in Ideas and Their History* (New York: Farrar, Straus & Giroux, 1996) p. 251.

13. See Russell Hardin, *One for All: The Logic of Group Conflict* (Princeton: Princeton University Press, 1995).

14. Ernest Gellner, *Nations and Nationalism* (Oxford: Basil Blackwell, 1983) p. 2.

15. Quoted in Warren Zimmermann, *Origins of a Catastrophe* (New York: Times Books, 1996) p. 212.

16. See Charles Kimball, *When Religion Becomes Evil* (New York: HarperCollins, 2002).

17. See Leszek Kolakowski, *Religion* (Glasgow: Fontana, 1982).

18. An account that illustrates this can be found in David Edmonds and John Eidinow, *Wittgenstein's Poker* (New York: HarperCollins, 2001) pp. 124–134.

19. Steven Seidman, 'Defilement and disgust: Theorizing the other', *American Journal of Cultural Sociology*, vol. 1, no. 1, 2013, pp. 3–25 at p. 6. The tendency to see individuals or groups as 'the other' is by no means an exclusively Western one: see Naser Ghobadzdeh and Shahram Akbarzadeh, 'Sectarianism and the prevalence of "othering" in Islamic thought', *Third World Quarterly*, vol. 36, no. 4, 2015, pp. 691–704.

20. For a recent discussion by a former Ambassador to Israel, see Peter Rodgers, *Herzl's Nightmare: One Land, Two People* (Melbourne: Scribe Publications, 2004).

21. John F. Kennedy, *A Nation of Immigrants* (London: Hamish Hamilton, 1964) p. 7.

22. Lawrence Stone, 'The Results of the English Revolutions of the Seventeenth Century', in J.G.A. Pocock (ed.), *Three British Revolutions: 1641, 1688, 1776* (Princeton: Princeton University Press, 1980) pp. 23–108 at p. 23.

23. Zolberg, Suhrke and Aguayo, *Escape from Violence*, p. 9.

24. See Michael W. Fitzgerald, '"We Have Found a Moses": Theodore Bilbo, Black Nationalism, and the Greater Liberia Bill of 1939', *Journal of Southern History*, vol. 63, no. 2, May 1997, pp. 293–320 at p. 297.

25. See Magnus Brechtken, „*Madagaskar für die Juden": Antisemitische Idee und politische Praxis 1885–1945* (Munich: Oldenbourg Verlag, 1997) pp. 221–284.

26. See Kenneth Minogue, *Alien Powers: The Pure Theory of Ideology* (London: Weidenfeld & Nicolson, 1985) pp. 37–38.

27. Vincenzo Ferrone, *The Enlightenment: History of an Idea* (Princeton: Princeton University Press, 2015). For a broadly representative selection of Enlightenment writings, see David Williams (ed.), *The Enlightenment* (Cambridge: Cambridge University Press, 1999).

28. See Isaiah Berlin, *The Roots of Romanticism* (Princeton: Princeton

University Press, 1999); Isaiah Berlin, *Three Critics of the Enlightenment: Vico, Hamann, Herder* (London: Pimlico, 2000).

29. See Vicki A. Spencer, *Herder's Political Thought: A Study of Language, Culture, and Community* (Toronto: University of Toronto Press, 2012).

30. See Isaiah Berlin, *The Crooked Timber of Humanity: Chapters in the History of Ideas* (London: John Murray, 1990) pp. 91–174.

31. For an overview, see A. James Gregor, *Totalitarianism and Political Religion: An Intellectual History* (Stanford: Stanford University Press, 2012).

32. Isaiah Berlin, *Karl Marx* (Oxford: Oxford University Press, 1963) p. 180.

33. The best overview can be found in Leszek Kolakowski, *Main Currents of Marxism* (Oxford: Oxford University Press, 1978) Vols I-III.

34. See Eugene Kamenka, *The Ethical Foundations of Marxism* (London: Routledge & Kegan Paul, 1962).

35. See David W. Lovell, *From Marx to Lenin: An Evaluation of Marx's Responsibility for Soviet Authoritarianism* (Cambridge: Cambridge University Press, 1985).

36. See James Joll, *The Anarchists* (London: Methuen, 1979) pp. 99–129.

37. Ibid., p. 126.

38. See Frank E. Manuel and Fritzie P. Manuel, *Utopian Thought in the Western World* (Cambridge: Harvard University Press, 1979).

39. Leszek Kolakowski, *Modernity on Endless Trial* (Chicago: University of Chicago Press, 1990) p. 132.

40. See Gavin Souter, *A Peculiar People: The Australians in Paraguay* (Sydney: Angus & Robertson, 1968).

41. A. J. Polan, *Lenin and the End of Politics* (London: Methuen, 1984) p. 208. Marxists, and for that matter some anarchists, tended to be deeply scornful of utopian socialism, but were not immune to utopianism themselves. See David W. Lovell, 'Socialism, Utopianism and the "Utopian Socialists"', *History of European Ideas*, vol. 14, no. 2, 1992, pp. 185–201. See also John Passmore, *The Perfectibility of Man* (London: Duckworth, 1970) p. 184.

42. Robert Nozick, *Anarchy, State and Utopia* (Oxford: Basil Blackwell, 1974) pp. 319–320.

43. Quoted in Andrzej Walicki, *Marxism and the Leap to the Kingdom of Freedom: The Rise and Fall of the Communist Utopia* (Stanford: Stanford University Press, 1995) p. 307.

44. Richard Pipes (ed.), *The Unknown Lenin: From the Secret Archive* (New Haven: Yale University Press, 1996) pp. 152–153.

45. 'Prikaz o zalozhnikakh', *Izvestiia*, 4 September 1918, p. 5.

46. Sheila Fitzpatrick, 'The Civil War as a Formative Experience', in Abbott Gleason, Peter Kenez and Richard Stites (eds), *Bolshevik Culture* (Bloomington: Indiana University Press, 1985) pp. 57–76 at pp. 66–67.

47. George Leggatt, *The Cheka: Lenin's Political Police* (Oxford: Oxford University Press, 1981) pp. 359–360.

48. Claudena M. Skran, *Refugees in Inter-War Europe: The Emergence of a Regime* (Oxford: Oxford University Press, 1995) p. 33.

49. Hannah Arendt, *The Origins of Totalitarianism* (New York: Harcourt Brace Jovanovich, 1973) p. 267.

50. F.S. Northedge, *The League of Nations: Its Life and Times 1920–1946* (Leicester: Leicester University Press, 1988) p. 77.

51. See Peter Gatrell, *The Making of the Modern Refugee* (Oxford: Oxford University Press, 2013) p. 56.

52. See Gerhard L. Weinberg, *Germany, Hitler and World War II* (Cambridge: Cambridge University Press, 1995) p. 60.

53. See Mark Roseman, *The Wannsee Conference and the Final Solution: A Reconsideration* (London: Folio Society, 2012). Mass killings of Jews had of course begun before the Wannsee Conference, notably at the hands of the mobile *Einsatzgruppen* in Poland from 1939 and in the USSR following the German invasion of the Soviet Union on 22 June 1941. See Lucy Dawidowicz, *The War against the Jews 1933–1945* (New York: Penguin, 1975) pp. 152–157, 164–168.

54. Skran, *Refugees in Inter-War Europe*, p. 50.

55. Quoted in Richard J. Evans, *The Third Reich in Power: 1933–1939* (London: Penguin, 2006) pp. 598–599.

56. Quoted in Skran, *Refugees in Inter-War Europe*, p. 235. For McDonald's own perspectives, see Richard Breitman, Barbara McDonald Stewart and Severin Hochberg (eds), *Advocate for the Doomed: The Diaries and Papers of James G. McDonald, 1932–1935* (Bloomington: Indiana

University Press, 2007); and Richard Breitman, Barbara McDonald Stewart and Severin Hochberg (eds), *Refugees and Rescue: The Diaries and Papers of James G. McDonald, 1935–1945* (Bloomington: Indiana University Press, 2009).

57. Skran, *Refugees in Inter-War Europe*, p. 230.

58. On the diplomacy of this period, see Telford Taylor, *Munich: The Price of Peace* (New York: Doubleday, 1979); Donald Cameron Watt, *How War Came: The Immediate Origins of the Second World War 1938–1939* (New York: Pantheon Books, 1989); Zara Steiner, *The Triumph of the Dark: European International History 1933–1939* (Oxford: Oxford University Press, 2011). On refugee experiences at this time, see Tony Kushner and Katharine Knox, *Refugees in an Age of Genocide* (London: Frank Cass, 1999) pp. 126–171.

59. Gatrell, *The Making of the Modern Refugee*, p. 77.

60. Quoted in Martin Gilbert, *The Holocaust: The Jewish Tragedy* (London: Fontana-Collins, 1986) p. 64.

61. Ishaan Tharoor, 'Europe's fear of Muslim refugees echoes rhetoric of 1930s anti-Semitism', *The Washington Post*, 2 September 2015.

62. Ibid.

63. For more detail on British policy at this time, see Louise London, *Whitehall and the Jews, 1933–1948: British immigration policy, Jewish refugees and the Holocaust* (Cambridge: Cambridge University Press, 2008) pp. 58–168.

64. See Bernard Wasserstein, *The Ambiguity of Virtue: Gertrude van Tijn and the Fate of the Dutch Jews* (Cambridge: Harvard University Press, 2014) p. 62.

65. See Douglas Frantz and Catherine Collins, *Death on the Black Sea: The Untold Story of the Struma and World War II's Holocaust at Sea* (New York: Harper Books, 2003).

66. Quoted in Martin Gilbert, *Auschwitz and the Allies* (London: Michael Joseph, 1981) p. 312.

67. Stephen Castles and Mark J. Miller, *The Age of Migration: International Population Movements in the Modern World* (Basingstoke: Palgrave Macmillan, 2003) p. 105.

68. See Robert Conquest, *The Nation Killers: The Soviet Deportation of*

Nationalities (London: Macmillan, 1970); Aleksandr Nekrich, *The Punished Peoples: The deportation and fate of Soviet minorities at the end of the Second World War* (New York: W.W. Norton, 1978); Isabelle Kreindler, 'The Soviet Deported Nationalities: A Summary and an Update', *Soviet Studies*, vol. 38, no. 3, July 1986, pp. 387–405.

69. See John B. Dunlop, *Russia Confronts Chechnya: Roots of a Separatist Conflict* (Cambridge: Cambridge University Press, 1998) pp. 58–74.

70. Ian Talbot and Gurharpal Singh, *The Partition of India* (Cambridge: Cambridge University Press, 2009) p. 90.

71. Gatrell, *The Making of the Modern Refugee*, p. 151.

72. See Gyanendra Pandey, *Remembering Partition: Violence, Nationalism and History in India* (Cambridge: Cambridge University Press, 2001) pp. 88–91.

73. Talbot and Singh, *The Partition of India*, p. 62.

74. See Elizabeth Becker, *When the War Was Over: Cambodia and the Khmer Rouge Revolution* (New York: Public Affairs, 1998).

75. See William Shawcross, *The Quality of Mercy: Cambodia, Holocaust and Modern Conscience* (New York: Simon & Schuster, 1984).

76. See Zolberg, Suhrke and Aguayo, *Escape from Violence*, pp. 170–173; Gatrell, *The Making of the Modern Refugee*, pp. 213–216.

77. See William Maley, 'Regional Conflicts: Afghanistan and Cambodia', in Ramesh Thakur and Carlyle A. Thayer (eds.), *Rethinking Regional Relations: Asia Pacific and the Former Soviet Union* (Boulder: Westview Press, 1993) pp. 183–200.

78. For the most penetrating explorations of this topic, see Townsend Hoopes, *The Limits of Intervention: An inside account of how the Johnson policy on escalation in Vietnam was reversed* (New York: McKay, 1969); Guenter Lewy, *America in Vietnam* (New York: Oxford University Press, 1978).

79. Henry Kissinger, *Crisis: The Anatomy Of Two Major Foreign Policy Crises* (New York: Simon & Schuster, 2003) p. 544.

80. Zolberg, Suhrke and Aguayo, *Escape from Violence*, p. 164.

81. Dennis McNamara, 'The Origins and Effects of "Humane Deterrence" Policies in Southeast Asia', in Gil Loescher and Laila Monahan (eds), *Refugees and International Relations* (New York: Oxford University Press, 1989) pp. 123–133 at p. 125.

82. See W. Courtland Robinson, *Terms of Refuge: The Indochinese Exodus and the International Response* (London: Zed Books, 1998) pp. 50–58.

83. Astri Suhrke, 'Burden-sharing during Refugee Emergencies: The Logic of Collective versus National Action', *Journal of Refugee Studies*, vol. 11, no. 4, December 1998, pp. 396–415 at p. 413.

84. Arthur C. Helton, 'Refugee Determination under the Comprehensive Plan of Action: Overview and Assessment', *International Journal of Refugee Law*, vol. 5 no. 4, December 1993, pp. 544–558.

85. Gil Loescher, *The UNHCR and World Politics: A Perilous Path* (Oxford: Oxford University Press, 2001) p. 208.

86. See Hiram A. Ruiz, *Left Out in the Cold: The Perilous Homecoming of Afghan Refugees* (Washington DC: US Committee for Refugees, 1992).

87. For an overview, see Joanna van Selm, 'Refugee Resettlement', in Elena Fiddian-Qasmiyeh, Gil Loescher, Katy Long and Nando Sigona (eds), *The Oxford Handbook of Refugee and Forced Migration Studies* (Oxford: Oxford University Press, 2014) pp. 512–524.

88. Quoted in Barry N. Stein, 'Durable Solutions for Developing Country Refugees', *International Migration Review*, vol. 20, no. 2, Summer 1986, pp. 264–282 at p. 264.

89. See Gil Loescher, James Milner, Edward Newman and Gary Troeller (eds), *Protracted Refugee Situations: Political, Human Rights and Security Implications* (Tokyo: United Nations University Press, 2008).

90. See William Maley, 'Introduction: Interpreting the Taliban', in William Maley (ed.), *Fundamentalism Reborn? Afghanistan and the Taliban* (London: Hurst & Co., 1998) pp. 1–28.

91. See William Maley, *The Afghanistan Wars* (Basingstoke: Palgrave Macmillan, 2009).

92. See Nancy Hatch Dupree, 'The Demography of Afghan Refugees in Pakistan', in Hafeez Malik (ed.), *Soviet-American Relations with Pakistan, Iran and Afghanistan* (Basingstoke: Macmillan, 1987) pp. 366–395; Nancy Hatch Dupree, 'Demographic Reporting on Afghan Refugees in Pakistan', *Modern Asian Studies*, vol. 22, no. 4, October 1988, pp. 845–865.

93. See Rupert Colville, 'The Biggest Case Load in the World', *Refugees*, no. 108, 1997, pp. 3–9; Daniel A. Kronenfeld, 'Afghan Refugees in

Pakistan: Not All Refugees, Not Always in Pakistan, Not Necessarily Afghan?', *Journal of Refugee Studies*, vol. 21, no. 11, March 2008, pp. 43–63.

94. See Susanne Schmeidl, '(Human) Security Dilemmas: Long-term Implications of the Afghan Refugee Crisis', *Third World Quarterly*, vol. 23, no. 1, 2002, pp. 7–29.

95. See Pierre Centlivres and Micheline Centlivres-Demont, 'Hommes d'influence et hommes de partis: L'organisation politique dans les villages de réfugiés afghans au Pakistan', in Erwin Grötzbach (ed.), *Neue Beiträge zur Afghanistanforschung* (Liestal: Stiftung Bibliotheca Afghanica, 1988) pp. 29–43.

96. For more detail, see Sana Haroon, *Frontiers of Faith: Islam in the Indo-Afghan Borderland* (London: Hurst & Co., 2007) pp. 13–21.

97. See Rizwan Hussain, *Pakistan and the Emergence of Islamic Militancy in Afghanistan* (Aldershot: Ashgate, 2005).

98. See Susanne Schmeidl and William Maley, 'The Case of the Afghan Refugee Population: Finding Durable Solutions in Contested Transitions', in Howard Adelman (ed.), *Protracted Displacement in Asia: No Place to Call Home* (Aldershot: Ashgate, 2008) pp. 131–179.

99. S. Iftikhar Murshed, *Afghanistan: The Taliban Years* (London: Bennett & Bloom, 2006) p. 45.

100. *UNHCR Mid-Year Trends 2015* (Geneva: UNHCR, 2015) p. 6.

101. See Dennison Rusinow, *The Yugoslav Experiment 1948–1974* (London: Hurst & Co., 1977).

102. For details, see Robert J. Donia and John V.A. Fine, *Bosnia and Hercegovina: A Tradition Betrayed* (London: Hurst & Co., 1994); Noel Malcolm, *Bosnia: A Short History* (London: Macmillan, 1994); David Rieff, *Slaughterhouse: Bosnia and the Failure of the West* (New York: Vintage, 1995); Susan L. Woodward, *Balkan Tragedy: Chaos and Dissolution after the Cold War* (Washington DC: The Brookings Institution, 1995); Laura Silber and Allan Little, *The Death of Yugoslavia* (Harmondsworth: Penguin, 1995).

103. See William Maley, 'The United Nations and Ethnic Conflict Management: Lessons from the Disintegration of Yugoslavia', *Nationalities Papers*, vol. 25, no. 3, September 1997, pp. 559–573.

104. For the lower figure, see Mark Cutts, *The humanitarian operation in Bosnia, 1992–95: dilemmas of negotiating humanitarian access* (Geneva: Working Paper no. 8, New Issues in Refugee Research, Policy Research Unit, UNHCR, May 1999) p. 1; for the higher figure, see *Going Nowhere Fast: Refugees and Internally Displaced Persons in Bosnia and Herzegovina* (Brussels: ICG Bosnia Report no. 23, International Crisis Group, 1 May 1997) p. i.

105. *UNHCR Mid-Year Trends 2015*, p. 21.

106. See Richard Black, 'Conceptions of "home" and the political geography of refugee repatriation: between assumption and contested reality in Bosnia-Herzegovina', *Applied Geography*, vol. 22, no. 2, April 2002, pp. 123–138 at pp. 126–128.

107. See Megan Bradley, *Refugee Repatriation: Justice, Responsibility and Redress* (Cambridge: Cambridge University Press, 2013) pp. 122–148.

108. See Ali A. Allawi, *The Occupation of Iraq: Winning the War, Losing the Peace* (New Haven: Yale University Press, 2007).

109. *UNHCR Mid-Year Trends 2015*, p. 6.

110. See Marie-Eve Loiselle, 'The Normative Status of the Responsibility to Protect after Libya', *Global Responsibility to Protect*, vol. 5, no. 3, 2013, pp. 317–341.

111. See Christopher S. Chivvis, *The French War on Al Qa'ida in Africa* (Cambridge: Cambridge University Press, 2016).

112. See Megan Bradley, Ibrahim Fraihat and Houda Mzioudet, *Libya's Displacement Crisis: Uprooted by Revolution and Civil War* (Washington DC: Georgetown University Press, 2016) pp. 16–51.

113. *UNHCR Mid-Year Trends 2015*, p. 22.

114. Ibid., p. 23.

115. Ibid., pp. 17,18.

116. Ibid., p. 19.

117. Ibid., p. 19.

118. See *World Population Prospects: The 2015 Revision. Key Findings and Advance Tables* (New York: United Nations, Working Paper no. ESA/P/WP241, Population Division, Department of Economic and Social Affairs, October 2015) p. 2.

119. '"We need more from everywhere" to help migrants, U.N. refugee commissioner says', *The Washington Post*, 29 October 2015.

120. For an incisive discussion, see Maurizio Albahari, *Crimes of Peace: Mediterranean Migrations at the World's Deadliest Border* (Philadelphia: University of Pennsylvania Press, 2015).

121. See Todd Sandler, *Global Collective Action* (Cambridge: Cambridge University Press, 2004).

4. STATES AND REFUGEES

1. Emma Haddad, *The Refugee in International Society: Between Sovereigns* (Cambridge: Cambridge University Press, 2008) p. 7.

2. See Bertrand de Jouvenel, *The Pure Theory of Politics* (Cambridge: Cambridge University Press, 1963) pp. 204–212.

3. See Peter H. Wilson, *Europe's Tragedy: A History of the Thirty Years War* (London: Allen Lane, 2009) pp. 3–4, 269–275.

4. Quoted in Norman Davis, *Europe: A History* (Oxford: Oxford University Press, 1996) p. 568.

5. Derek Croxton, 'The Peace of Westphalia of 1648 and the Origins of Sovereignty', *International History Review*, vol. 21, no. 3, September 1999, pp. 569–591 at p. 577.

6. Christian Reus-Smit, *The Moral Purpose of the State: Culture, Social Identity, and Institutional Rationality in International Relations* (Princeton: Princeton University Press, 1999) p. 113.

7. See Jean Bodin, *On Sovereignty* (Cambridge: Cambridge University Press, 1992).

8. For further discussion, see Daniel Philpott, *Revolutions in Sovereignty: How Ideas Shaped Modern International Relations* (Princeton: Princeton University Press, 2001) pp. 46–72.

9. See Stephen D. Krasner, *Sovereignty: Organized Hypocrisy* (Princeton: Princeton University Press, 1999) pp. 3–4. Krasner has since opted to refer to 'Vattelian' rather than 'Westphalian' sovereignty: see Stephen D. Krasner, 'Rethinking the sovereign state model', *Review of International Studies*, vol. 27, no. 5, December 2001, pp. 17–42 at p. 20.

10. Ruben Zaiotti, *Cultures of Border Control: Schengen and the Evolution of European Frontiers* (Chicago: University of Chicago Press, 2011) p. 47. See also George Gavrilis, *The Dynamics of Interstate Boundaries* (Cambridge: Cambridge University Press, 2008).

11. See Croxton, 'The Peace of Westphalia of 1648 and the Origins of Sovereignty', p. 575, fn. 2; Christian Reus-Smit, *Individual Rights and the Making of the International System* (Cambridge: Cambridge University Press, 2013) p. 102; Phil Orchard, *A Right to Flee: Refugees, States, and the Construction of International Cooperation* (Cambridge: Cambridge University Press, 2014) p. 58.

12. See Kamal Sadiq, *Paper Citizens: How Illegal Immigrants acquire Citizenship in Developing Countries* (New York: Oxford University Press 2009); Mark B. Salter, 'International Cooperation on Travel Document Security in the Developed World', in Rey Koslowski (ed.), *Global Mobility Regimes* (New York: Palgrave Macmillan, 2011) pp. 115–129.

13. On these dimensions, see Francis Fukuyama, *State-Building: Governance and World Order in the 21st Century* (Ithaca: Cornell University Press, 2004).

14. Joel S. Migdal, *Strong Societies and Weak States: State-Society Relations and State Capabilities in the Third World* (Princeton: Princeton University Press, 1988) p. 4.

15. See Martin van Creveld, *The Rise and Decline of the State* (Cambridge: Cambridge University Press, 1999) pp. 126–188.

16. See Henry Parris, *Constitutional Bureaucracy: The Development of British Central Administration since the Eighteenth Century* (London: George Allen & Unwin, 1969).

17. See Max Weber, *Economy and Society: An Outline of Interpretive Sociology* (Berkeley & Los Angeles: University of California Press, 1978) Vol. II, pp. 956–1005.

18. John Torpey, *The Invention of the Passport: Surveillance, Citizenship and the State* (Cambridge: Cambridge University Press, 2000) p. 3.

19. Ibid., p. 136.

20. See Gerrit W. Gong, *The Standard of 'Civilization' in International Society* (Oxford: Oxford University Press, 1984); Brett Bowden, *The Empire of Civilization: The Evolution of an Imperial Idea* (Chicago: University of Chicago Press, 2009).

21. James C. Hathaway, 'Foreword', in Thomas Gammeltoft-Hansen, *Access to Asylum: International Refugee Law and the Globalisation of Migration Control* (Cambridge: Cambridge University Press, 2011) pp. ix–x at

p. ix. For further discussion of methods of restriction, see Matthew J. Gibney, "'A Thousand Little Guantanamos'': Western States and Measures to Prevent the Arrival of Refugees', in Kate E. Tunstall (ed.), *Displacement, Asylum, Migration: The Oxford Amnesty Lectures 2004* (Oxford: Oxford University Press, 2006) pp. 139–169; Matthew E. Price, *Rethinking Asylum: History, Purpose, and Limits* (Cambridge: Cambridge University Press, 2009) pp. 207–231. For a study setting such methods in a wider context, see Vicki Squire, *The Exclusionary Politics of Asylum* (Basingstoke: Palgrave Macmillan, 2009).

22. Gibney, "'A Thousand Little Guantanamos'", p. 143.

23. See Sharon Pickering, *Refugees and State Crime* (Sydney: The Federation Press, 2005); Catherine Dauvergne, *Making People Illegal: What Globalization Means for Migration and Law* (Cambridge: Cambridge University Press, 2008); Anne McNevin, *Contesting Citizenship: Irregular Migrants and New Frontiers of the Political* (New York: Columbia University Press, 2011).

24. See Rod Nordland, *The Lovers: Afghanistan's Romeo and Juliet* (New York: HarperCollins, 2016).

25. Rod Nordland, 'In Danger in Afghanistan, Unable to Flee', *The New York Times*, 6 December 2015.

26. Joel S. Migdal, 'The State in Society: An Approach to Struggles for Domination', in Joel S. Migdal, Atul Kohli, and Vivienne Shue (eds), *State Power and Social Forces: Domination and Transformation in the Third World* (Cambridge: Cambridge University Press, 1994) pp. 7–34 at p. 16.

27. See Weber, *Economy and Society: An Outline of Interpretive Sociology*, Vol. II, pp. 973–975.

28. See Peter Self, *Administrative Theories and Politics* (London: George Allen & Unwin, 1977) pp. 55–86.

29. See William A. Niskanen, *Bureaucracy and Representative Government* (Chicago: Aldine Atherton, 1971) pp. 36–42. For further discussion of the attributes of bureaucracy, see Eva Etzioni-Halevy, *Bureaucracy and Democracy: A Political Dilemma* (London: Routledge & Kegan Paul, 1983); Eugene Kamenka, *Bureaucracy* (Oxford: Basil Blackwell, 1989). Bureaucratic self-interest can sometimes reach Gilbertian

heights. In February 2016, the President of the Australian Medical Association, discussing immigration bureaucrats, pointedly asked 'When are these people going to grow up and stop putting on military uniforms and giving themselves medals?' See Deborah Snow, 'AMA President Brian Owler lashes Department of Immigration over health services to asylum seekers', *The Sydney Morning Herald*, 21 February 2016. The reference to medals arose from the revelation that the Department had contracted to spend more than A\$1.3 million on medals for its staff: see Adam Gartrell, 'Immigration spends more than Defence on medals for its staff', *The Sydney Morning Herald*, 16 January 2016.

30. Charles E. Lindblom, *The Policy-Making Process* (Englewood Cliffs: Prentice-Hall, 1980) pp. 65–68.

31. Tom Burns and G.M. Stalker, *The Management of Innovation* (New York: Oxford University Press, 1994).

32. Quoted in Sarah A. Ogilvie and Scott Miller, *Refuge Denied: The St. Louis Passengers and the Holocaust* (Madison: University of Wisconsin Press, 2006) p. 25.

33. Jay Winik, *1944: FDR and the Year that Changed History* (New York: Simon & Schuster, 2015) p. 218.

34. William Russell, *Berlin Embassy* (London: Thin Red Line Books, 2010) pp. 17–18.

35. Tony Stephens, 'Menadue slams Coalition for demonising asylum seekers', *The Sydney Morning Herald*, 8 February 2002.

36. Gary Troeller, 'UNHCR Resettlement: Evolution and Future Direction', *International Journal of Refugee Law*, vol. 14, no. 1, January 2002, pp. 85–95 at p. 92.

37. See Hannah Arendt, *Eichmann in Jerusalem: A Report on the Banality of Evil* (Harmondsworth: Penguin, 1992).

38. John Menadue, 'Taking Advantage of the Earth's Most Vulnerable', *The Canberra Times*, 22 July 2002.

39. Meeting with senior UNHCR official, Amsterdam, The Netherlands, 23 March 2001.

40. Felicia Schwartz and Anton Troianovski, 'U.S. to Boost Refugee Intake by 30,000 Over Two Years', *The Wall Street Journal*, 20 September 2015.

41. See *Summary of Refugee Admissions as of 31-March–2016* (Washington DC: Office of Admissions—Refugee Processing Center, Bureau of Population, Refugees and Migration, Department of State, 2016).

42. 'Statement by Dr. Auguste R. Lindt, United Nations High Commissioner for Refugees, to the Third Committee of the United Nations General Assembly, 3 November 1958'.

43. See Joint Standing Committee on Migration, *Enabling Australia: Inquiry into the Migration Treatment of Disability* (Canberra: Parliament of the Commonwealth of Australia, 2010) pp. 129–138.

44. Ibid., p. 136. For an earlier example of the blocking of resettlement on the grounds of disability, see William Maley, 'Refugees, Multiculturalism, and Duties Beyond Borders', in Chandran Kukathas (ed.), *Multicultural Citizens: The Philosophy and Politics of Identity* (Sydney: Centre for Independent Studies, 1993) pp. 175–190 at p. 185.

45. Chandran Kukathas, 'Are Refugees Special?', in Sarah Fine and Lea Ypi (eds), *Migration in Political Theory: The Ethics of Movement and Membership* (Oxford: Oxford University Press, 2016) pp. 249–268 at p. 266.

46. See Thomas Keneally, *Schindler's Ark* (London: Hodder & Stoughton, 1982).

47. Steven K. Baum, *The Psychology of Genocide: Perpetrators, Bystanders, and Rescuers* (Cambridge: Cambridge University Press, 2008) p. 191. See also Kristen R. Monroe, Michael C. Barton and Ute Klingemann, 'Altruism and the Theory of Rational Action: Rescuers of Jews in Nazi Europe', *Ethics*, vol. 101, no. 1, October 1990, pp. 103–122.

48. See Christian Bjørnskov, 'Social Trust Fosters an Ability to Help Those in Need: Jewish Refugees in the Nazi Era', *Political Studies*, vol. 63, no. 4, October 2015, pp. 951–974.

49. See Daniel J. Steinbock, 'Refuge and Resistance: *Casablanca's* Lessons for Refugee Law', *Georgetown Immigration Law Journal*, vol. 7, no. 4, 1993, pp. 649–705.

50. See Aljean Harmetz, *The Making of Casablanca: Bogart, Bergman, and World War II* (New York: Hyperion, 2002) pp. 208–225.

51. Howard Koch, *Casablanca: Script and Legend* (New York: The Overlook Press, 1992) p. 46.

52. See Folke Bernadotte, *Das Ende: Meine Verhandlungen in Deutschland im Frühjahr 1945 und ihre politischen Folgen* (Zürich: Europa Verlag, 1945). For further discussion of these negotiations, see William Maley, 'Humanitarians and Diplomats: What Connections?', in Michele Acuto (ed.), *Negotiating Relief: The Dialectics of Humanitarian Space* (London: Hurst & Co., 2014) pp. 201–209.

53. See Martin Gilbert, *The Holocaust: The Jewish Tragedy* (London: Fontana-Collins, 1986) p. 701.

54. Ibid., p. 753.

55. This was also an issue that haunted the International Committee of the Red Cross: see Jean-Claude Favez, *Une mission impossible? Le CICR, les déportations et les camps de concentration nazis* (Lausanne: Éditions Payot, 1988).

56. Hillel Levine, *In Search of Sugihara: The Elusive Japanese Diplomat Who Risked His Life to Rescue 10,000 Jews from the Holocaust* (New York: The Free Press, 1996) p. 259.

57. Ibid., p. 9.

58. See Aaron Levenstein, *Escape to Freedom: The Story of the International Rescue Committee* (Westport: Greenwood Press, 1983) pp. 14–25.

59. See Sheila Isenberg, *A Hero of Our Own: The Story of Varian Fry* (New York: Random House, 2001).

60. Carla Killough McClafferty, *In Defiance of Hitler: The Secret Mission of Varian Fry* (New York: Farrar Straus Giroux, 2008) p. 41.

61. See Jeremy Adelman, *Worldly Philosopher: The Odyssey of Albert O. Hirschman* (Princeton: Princeton University Press, 2013) pp. 171–180. One of Hirschman's most influential works was *Exit, Voice and Loyalty: Responses to Decline in Firms, Organizations, and States* (Cambridge: Harvard University Press, 1970), which is directly relevant to forced migration.

62. Varian Fry, *Assignment: Rescue. An Autobiography* (New York: Scholastic Inc., 1992) p. 82.

63. See 'Albert O. Hirschman 1915–2012' (Princeton: Press Release, Institute for Advanced Study, 12 December 2012).

64. For more detail on those rescued, see Alan Riding, *And the Show Went On: Cultural Life in Nazi-occupied Paris* (New York: Alfred A. Knopf, 2010) pp. 73–89.

65. See Robin De Crespigny, *The People Smuggler: The True Story of Ali Al Jenabi, the 'Oskar Schindler of Asia'* (Camberwell: Viking, 2012) pp. 332–338.

66. *SZLDG v. Minister for Immigration and Citizenship* [2008] FCA 11 (17 January 2008) paras. 3, 6.

67. See J. David Riva (ed.), *A Woman at War: Marlene Dietrich Remembered* (Detroit: Wayne State University Press, 2006).

68. For testimony that captures this, see Caroline Moorehead, *Human Cargo: A Journey Among Refugees* (London: Chatto & Windus, 2005).

69. For the classic statement of this point, see F.A. Hayek, *Individualism and Economic Order* (Chicago: University of Chicago Press, 1948) pp. 77–91. See also Peter Andreas, *Blue Helmets and Black Markets: The Business of Survival in the Siege of Sarajevo* (Ithaca: Cornell University Press, 2008).

70. See, for example, Aron Katsenelinboigen, 'Coloured Markets in the Soviet Union', *Soviet Studies*, vol. 29, no. 1, January 1977, pp. 62–85.

71. John Morrison, *The trafficking and smuggling of refugees: the end game in European asylum policy?* (Geneva: Evaluation and Policy Analysis Unit, UNHCR, 2000) para. 3.2.1. See also Michael Dummett, *On Immigration and Refugees* (London: Routledge, 2001) p. 44; Khalid Koser, 'Reconciling control and compassion? Human smuggling and the right to asylum', in Edward Newman and Joanne van Selm (eds), *Refugees and Forced Displacement: International Security, Human Vulnerability, and the State* (New York & Tokyo: United Nations University Press, 2003) pp. 181–194 at pp. 192–193.

72. *United Nations Convention Against Transnational Organized Crime and the Protocols Thereto* (New York: United Nations, 2004) p. 42.

73. For a detailed discussion of relevant law, see Anne T. Gallagher and Fiona David, *The International Law of Migrant Smuggling* (Cambridge: Cambridge University Press, 2014).

74. *United Nations Convention Against Transnational Organized Crime and the Protocols Thereto*, pp. 54–55

75. *Projected Global Resettlement Needs 2016* (Geneva: United Nations High Commissioner for Refugees, 2015) pp. 10, 48.

76. Susan Banki, 'Resettlement of the Bhutanese from Nepal: The Durable

Solution Discourse', in Howard Adelman (ed.) *Protracted Displacement in Asia: No Place to call Home* (Aldershot: Ashgate, 2008) pp. 29–55 at p. 31.

77. Ibid., p. 49.

78. *Projected Global Resettlement Needs 2016*, p. 51.

79. See Khalid Koser, 'The Smuggling of Asylum Seekers into Western Europe: Contradictions, Conundrums, and Dilemmas', in David Kyle and Rey Koslowski (eds), *Global Human Smuggling: Comparative Perspectives* (Baltimore: The Johns Hopkins University Press, 2001) pp. 58–73. See also Michael Birnbaum, 'Smuggling refugees into Europe is a new growth industry', *The Washington Post*, 3 September 2015.

80. Adam Smith, *An Inquiry into the Nature and Causes of the Wealth of Nations* (London: Nelson & Sons, 1873) pp. 6–7.

81. See Amnesty International, *By Hook or by Crook: Australia's Abuse of Asylum-Seekers at Sea* (London: Amnesty International, ASA 12/2576/2015).

82. Hilary Charlesworth, Emma Larking and Jacinta Mulders, 'Submission to the Senate Legal and Constitutional Affairs References Committee Inquiry into Payment of Cash or Other Inducements by the Commonwealth of Australia in Exchange for the Turn Back of Asylum Seeker Boats' 24 July 2015, pp. 1, 2.

83. See Alan Travis, 'UK taskforce will "smash" Mediterranean people-smuggling operations', *The Guardian*, 24 June 2015.

84. For a parallel argument, see Ralph Seccombe, 'Squeezing the balloon: international drugs policy', *Drug and Alcohol Review*, vol. 14, 1995, pp. 311–316.

85. *Global Status Report on Road Safety 2015* (Geneva: World Health Organization, 2015) p. 2.

86. See Peter Gale, 'The refugee crisis and fear: Populist politics and media discourses', *Journal of Sociology*, vol. 40, no. 4, December 2004, pp. 321–340.

87. 'Australia Searches for Asylum Seeker Solution', Cable Reference ID 09CANBERRA1006, U.S Embassy, Canberra, 13 November 2009.

5. ROOTS OF REFUGEE 'CRISES' IN A GLOBALISED WORLD

1. See George Bush and Brent Scowcroft, *A World Transformed* (New York: Alfred A. Knopf, 1998); Jon Meacham, *Destiny and Power: The American Odyssey of George Herbert Walker Bush* (New York: Random House, 2015).

2. For an example of this pessimism, see James N. Rosenau, *Turbulence in World Politics: A Theory of Change and Continuity* (Princeton: Princeton University Press, 1990).

3. David Kilcullen, *Blood Year: The Unraveling of Western Counterterrorism* (New York: Oxford University Press, 2016).

4. See, for example, I. William Zartman (ed.), *Collapsed States: The Disintegration and Restoration of Legitimate Authority* (Boulder: Lynne Rienner, 1995); William Maley, Charles Sampford and Ramesh Thakur (eds), *From Civil Strife to Civil Society: Civil and Military Responsibilities in Disrupted States* (Tokyo: United Nations University Press, 2003); Simon Chesterman, Michael Ignatieff and Ramesh Thakur (eds), *Making States Work: State Failure and the Crisis of Governance* (Tokyo: United Nations University Press, 2005); Ashraf Ghani and Clare Lockhart, *Fixing Failed States: A Framework for Rebuilding a Fractured World* (New York: Oxford University Press, 2008).

5. Thomas Hobbes, *Leviathan* (Cambridge: Cambridge University Press, 1996) p. 89.

6. See Barnett R. Rubin, *The Fragmentation of Afghanistan: State Formation and Collapse in the International System* (New Haven: Yale University Press, 2002) pp. 65, 81–105.

7. Michael Burton, Richard Gunther, and John Higley, 'Introduction: Elite Transformations and Democratic Regimes', in John Higley and Richard Gunther (eds), *Elites and Democratic Consolidation in Latin America and Southern Europe* (Cambridge: Cambridge University Press, 1992) pp. 1–37 at p. 10.

8. For detailed discussion, see Terrence Lyons and Ahmed I. Samatar, *Somalia: State Collapse, Multilateral Intervention, and Strategies for Political Reconstruction* (Washington DC: The Brookings Institution, 1995) pp. 19–24.

9. See Mohamed Sahnoun, *Somalia: The Missed Opportunities* (Washington DC: United States Institute of Peace, 1994); Ramesh Thakur, 'From Peacekeeping to Peace Enforcement: The UN Operation in Somalia', *Journal of Modern African Studies*, vol. 32, no. 3, September 1994, pp. 387–410.

10. See William Maley, 'Confronting Creeping Invasions: Afghanistan, the UN and the World Community', in K. Warikoo (ed.), *The Afghanistan Crisis: Issues and Perspectives* (New Delhi: Bhavana Books, 2002) pp. 256–274.

11. Ahmed Rashid, 'The Taliban: Exporting Extremism', *Foreign Affairs*, vol. 78, no. 6, November–December 1999, pp. 22–35 at p. 27.

12. Rizwan Hussain, *Pakistan and the Emergence of Islamic Militancy in Afghanistan* (Aldershot: Ashgate, 2005) p. 204.

13. See Ahmed Rashid, *Descent into Chaos: The United States and the Failure of Nation Building in Pakistan, Afghanistan, and Central Asia* (New York: Viking Press, 2008) pp. 90–93. As recently as 1 March 2016, the Pakistani Adviser to the Prime Minister on Foreign Affairs, Sartaj Aziz, admitted in a presentation to the Council on Foreign Relations in Washington DC that the 'leadership' of the Afghan Taliban 'is in Pakistan': http://www.cfr.org/pakistan/conversation-sartaj-aziz/p37592 (accessed 28 March 2016).

14. See Declan Walsh, 'Taliban Besiege Pakistan School, Leaving 145 Dead', *The New York Times*, 17 December 2014.

15. For a detailed discussion, see Barnett R. Rubin, *Blood on the Doorstep: The Politics of Preventive Action* (New York: The Century Foundation, 2002).

16. For the most exhaustive account of this attack, see Joost R. Hiltermann, *A Poisonous Affair: America, Iraq, and the Gassing of Halabja* (Cambridge: Cambridge University Press, 2007).

17. See Michael Barnett, *Eyewitness to a Genocide: The United Nations and Rwanda* (Ithaca: Cornell University Press, 2002) pp. 153–181. For further detail on the Rwandan genocide, see Samantha Power, *"A Problem from Hell": America and the Age of Genocide* (New York: Basic Books, 2002) pp. 329–389; Roméo Dallaire, *Shake Hands with the Devil: The Failure of Humanity in Rwanda* (Toronto: Vintage Canada, 2004).

18. See Laurence Binet, *Rwandan Refugee Camps in Zaire and Tanzania 1994–1995* (Paris: MSF Speaking Out Case Studies, 2014).

19. See, for example, Azeem Ibrahim, *The Rohingyas: Inside Myanmar's Hidden Genocide* (London: Hurst & Co., 2016).

20. See Stephen John Stedman, 'Spoiler Problems in Peace Processes', *International Security*, vol. 22, no. 2, Fall 1997, pp. 5–53.

21. For some US perspectives on the US failure in Iraq, see George Packer, *The Assassins' Gate: America in Iraq* (New York: Farrar, Straus and Giroux, 2005); David L. Phillips, *Losing Iraq: Inside the Postwar Reconstruction Fiasco* (Boulder: Westview Press, 2005); and Ahmed S. Hashim, *Insurgency and Counter-Insurgency in Iraq* (Ithaca: Cornell University Press, 2006).

22. *Hard Lessons: The Iraq Reconstruction Experience* (Washington DC: Special Inspector General for Iraq Reconstruction, 2009) p. 326.

23. Larry Diamond, *Squandered Victory: The American Occupation and the Bungled Effort to Bring Democracy to Iraq* (New York: Times Books, 2005) p. 311.

24. For some illustrations of this point, see William Maley, 'Democratic Governance and Post-Conflict Transitions', *Chicago Journal of International Law*, vol. 6, no. 2, Winter 2006, pp. 683–701.

25. See Kate Jenkins and William Plowden, *Governance and Nationbuilding: The Failure of International Intervention* (Cheltenham: Edward Elgar, 2006); Oliver P. Richmond and Jason Franks, *Liberal Peace Transitions: Between Statebuilding and Peacebuilding* (Edinburgh: Edinburgh University Press, 2009); Shahrbanou Tadjbakhsh (ed.), *Rethinking the Liberal Peace: External models and local alternatives* (London: Routledge, 2011); Paul D. Miller, *Armed State Building: Confronting State Failure, 1898–2012* (Ithaca: Cornell University Press, 2013); Oliver P. Richmond, *Failed Statebuilding: Intervention, the State, and the Dynamics of Peace Formation* (New Haven: Yale University Press, 2014).

26. See Barry R. Weingast, 'The Political Foundations of Democracy and the Rule of Law', *American Political Science Review*, vol. 91, no. 2, June 1997, pp. 245–263; Francis Fukuyama, 'Transitions to the Rule of Law', *Journal of Democracy*, vol. 21, no. 1, January 2010, pp. 33–44; Lisa Hilbink, 'The Origins of Positive Judicial Independence', *World Politics*, vol. 64, no. 4, October 2012, pp. 587–621.

27. For a more detailed statement of this case, see Roland Paris, *At War's End: Building Peace after Civil Conflict* (Cambridge: Cambridge University Press, 2004). See also Jack L. Snyder, *From Voting to Violence: Democratization and Nationalist Conflict* (New York: W.W. Norton, 2000).

28. See William Maley, 'Peacekeeping and Peacemaking', in Ramesh Thakur and Carlyle A. Thayer (eds.), *A Crisis of Expectations: UN Peacekeeping in the 1990s* (Boulder: Westview Press, 1995) pp. 237–250.

29. See Lionel Cliffe, Ray Bush, Jenny Lindsay and Brian Mokopakgosi, *The Transition to Independence in Namibia* (Boulder: Lynner Rienner, 1994).

30. See Michael W. Doyle, *UN Peacekeeping in Cambodia: UNTAC's Civil Mandate* (Boulder: Lynne Rienner, 1995) pp. 49–51.

31. Barry N. Stein and Frederick C. Cuny, 'Refugee repatriation during conflict: Protection and post-return assistance', *Development in Practice*, vol. 4, no. 3, 1994, pp. 173–187.

32. For an overview of the roots of the Syrian civil war, see *Syria's Metastasising Conflicts* (Brussels: Middle East Report no. 143, International Crisis Group, 27 June 2013).

33. Susan Harris Rimmer, 'Is the Responsibility to Protect doctrine gender-neutral?', in Ramesh Thakur and William Maley (eds), *Theorising the Responsibility to Protect* (Cambridge: Cambridge University Press, 2015) pp. 266–284 at p. 271.

34. See R. Charli Carpenter, *'Innocent Women and Children': Gender, Norms and the Protection of Civilians* (Aldershot: Ashgate, 2006) pp. 131–162.

35. Leonard W. Labaree (ed.), *The Papers of Benjamin Franklin, Vol. 6* (New Haven: Yale University Press, 1963) p. 242.

36. Raymond Aron, *Paix et Guerre Entre les Nations* (Paris: Calmann-Lévy, 1984) p. 176. See also Anthony Richards, *Conceptualizing Terrorism* (Oxford: Oxford University Press, 2015) p. 18.

37. For an example of this kind of argument, see Tamar Meisels, *The Trouble with Terror: Liberty, Security and the Response to Terrorism* (Cambridge: Cambridge University Press, 2008) pp. 20–29.

38. See Matt Apuzzo, Michael S. Schmidt and Julia Preston, 'Visa Screening Missed an Attacker's Zealotry on Social Media', *The New York Times*,

13 December 2015, p. A1. See also Alex P. Schmid, *Links between Terrorism and Migration: An Exploration* (The Hague: ICCT Research Paper, International Centre for Counter-Terrorism, May 2016).

39. William Maley, 'The Open Front Door: Tourism, Border Control and National Security', *Issue Analysis* No. 42 (Sydney: Centre for Independent Studies, 14 January 2004).

40. The importance of measured responses is a theme running through Matthew Carr, *The Infernal Machine: An Alternative History of Terrorism* (London: Hurst & Co., 2011); Walter Enders and Todd Sandler, *The Political Economy of Terrorism* (Cambridge: Cambridge University Press, 2012); John Mueller and Mark G. Stewart, *Chasing Ghosts: The Policing of Terrorism* (New York: Oxford University Press, 2016); and Benoît Gomis, *Counterterrorism: Reassessing the Policy Response* (Boco Raton: CRC Press, 2016).

41. Michael Planty and Jennifer N. Truman, *Firearm Violence, 1993–2011* (Washington DC: Bureau of Justice Statistics, Office of Justice Programs, U.S. Department of Justice, May 2013) p. 2.

42. See *The 9/11 Commission Report: Final Report of the National Commission on Terrorist Attacks Upon the United States* (New York: W.W. Norton, 2004) p. 311.

43. As a tribute to their memory they should be named: Professor Sayed Bahauddin Majrooh (philosopher); Dr Abdul Rahim Tarshi (medical practitioner), Dr Arthur C. Helton (lawyer and refugee advocate), Mr Hakim Taniwal (Afghan provincial governor), and Mr Tom Little (optometrist and aid worker).

44. Anne Aly, *Terrorism and Global Security: Historical and contemporary perspectives* (Melbourne: Palgrave Macmillan, 2011) pp. 88–92.

45. See Georges Sorel, *Reflections on Violence* (Cambridge: Cambridge University Press, 1999).

46. Fathali M. Moghaddam, *From the Terrorists' Point of View: What They Experience and Why They Come to Destroy* (Westport: Praeger, 2006) p. 111.

47. See, for example, Muhammad Qasim Zaman, 'Sectarianism in Pakistan: The Radicalization of Shi'i and Sunni Identities', *Modern Asian Studies*, vol. 32, no. 3, July 1998, pp. 689–716; S. V. R. Nasr, 'The Rise of Sunni Militancy in Pakistan: The Changing Role of Islamism and the Ulama in Society and Politics', *Modern Asian Studies*, vol. 34, no. 1,

January 2000, pp. 139–180; S.V.R. Nasr, 'International Politics, Domestic Imperatives, and Identity Mobilization: Sectarianism in Pakistan, 1979–1998', *Comparative Politics*, vol. 32, no. 2, January 2000, pp. 171–190

48. See William Maley, 'Hazaras', in John L. Esposito (ed.), *The Oxford Encyclopedia of the Islamic World* (New York: Oxford University Press, 2009) Vol.II, pp. 385–386.

49. Rupert Colville, 'One Massacre That Didn't Grab the World's Attention', *International Herald Tribune*, 7 August 1999.

50. See *Afghanistan: The Massacre in Mazar-i Sharif* (New York: Human Rights Watch, 1998).

51. *Associated Press*, 7 January 2004.

52. 'Police find 11 beheaded bodies in Afghan south', *Reuters*, 25 June 2010.

53. See Hashmat Baktash and Alex Rodrigues, 'Two Afghanistan bombings aimed at Shiites kill at least 59 people', *Los Angeles Times*, 7 December 2011. On 23 July 2016, protestors from a largely-Hazara movement were killed in Kabul in a suicide bombing for which ISIS claimed responsibility: see Mujib Mashal and Zahra Nader, 'ISIS Claims Suicide Bombing of Protest in Kabul, Killing at least 80', *The New York Times*, 24 July 2016.

54. *Afghanistan: Annual Report 2015—Protection of Civilians in Armed Conflict* (Kabul: United Nations Assistance Mission in Afghanistan, 2016) p. 49.

55. See T.W. Arnold, *The Caliphate* (Oxford: Oxford University Press, 1924).

56. Shaykh Muhammad al-Yaqoubi, *Refuting ISIS: A Rebuttal of its Religious and Ideological Foundations* (Marston Gate: Sacred Knowledge, 2015) p. 26.

57. For more detailed discussion, see James P. Piscatori, *Islam in a World of Nation-States* (Cambridge: Cambridge University Press, 1986) pp. 40–75.

58. See, for example, *Escape from Hell: Torture and Sexual Slavery in Islamic State Captivity in Iraq* (London: Amnesty International, MDE 14/21/2014, 23 December 2014).

59. See Anne Barnard and Tim Arango, 'ISIS Making Political Gains', *The New York Times*, 4 June 2015.

60. See David J. Bederman, *International Law in Antiquity* (Cambridge: Cambridge University Press, 2001).

61. For what is still the most evocative account of this disaster, see Walter Lord, *A Night to Remember* (New York: Henry Holt, 1955).

62. Rigas Doganis, *Flying off Course: The Economics of International Airlines* (London: Routledge, 2002) p. 1.

63. See *GNI per capita, PPP (current international $)* (Washington DC: The World Bank Group, 2016) http://data.worldbank.org/indicator/NY.GNP.PCAP.PP.CD (accessed 28 March 2016).

64. See Ian Clark, *Globalization and Fragmentation: International Relations in the Twentieth Century* (Oxford: Oxford University Press, 1997); Ian Clark, *Globalization and International Relations Theory* (Oxford: Oxford University Press, 1999).

65. See W. Max Corden, *Economic Policy, Exchange Rates and the International System* (Oxford: Oxford University Press, 1994); Jagdish Bhagwati, *Free Trade Today* (Princeton: Princeton University Press, 2002); Jagdish Bhagwati, *In Defense of Globalization* (New York: Oxford University Press, 2007).

66. See Anne-Marie Slaughter, *A New World Order* (Princeton: Princeton University Press, 2004); Andrew F. Cooper, Brian Hocking and William Maley (eds), *Global Governance and Diplomacy: Worlds Apart?* (London: Palgrave Macmillan, 2008).

67. See Robert O. Keohane, Stephen Macedo, and Andrew Moravcsik, 'Democracy-Enhancing Multilateralism', *International Organization*, vol. 63, no. 1, Winter 2009, pp. 1–31.

68. For a detailed overview of developments in this area, see Nik Gowing, *'Skyful of Lies' and Black Swans: The new tyranny of shifting information power in crises* (Oxford: Reuters Institute for the Study of Journalism, Department of Politics and International Relations, University of Oxford, 2009).

69. Nigel Nicolson (ed.), *Harold Nicolson: Diaries and Letters 1930–1939* (New York: Atheneum, 1966) p. 390.

70. *A Survey of the Afghan People: Afghanistan in 2015* (Kabul: The Asia Foundation, 2015) p. 12.

71. David Jolly and Jawad Sukhanyar, 'Following Up on Threat, Taliban

Strike at Bus Carrying TV Employees', *The New York Times*, 21 January 2016.

72. See Haroro J. Ingram, 'The strategic logic of Islamic State information operations', *Australian Journal of International Affairs*, vol. 69, no. 6, 2015, pp. 729–752.

73. See http://www.news.com.au/national/the-federal-government-uses-a-comic-book-to-stop-the-boats/story-fncynjr2–1226824447746 (accessed 28 March 2016).

74. Roslyn Richardson, 'Sending a Message? Refugees and Australia's Deterrence Campaign', *Media International Australia*, no. 135, May 2010, pp. 7–18 at p. 16.

75. For the most detailed case study so far of the impact of cellphones on a major power, see Robin Jeffrey and Assa Doron, *The Great Indian Phone Book: How Cheap Mobile Phones Change Business, Politics and Daily Life* (London: Hurst & Co., 2013).

76. See Saskia Sassen, 'Beyond sovereignty: Immigration policy making today', *Social Justice*, vol. 23, no. 3, Fall 1996, pp. 9–20.

6. DIPLOMACY AND REFUGEES

1. For some discussion of the wider context of such engagements, see William Maley, 'Refugee Diplomacy', in Andrew F. Cooper, Jorge Heine and Ramesh Thakur (eds), *The Oxford Handbook of Modern Diplomacy* (Oxford: Oxford University Press), 2013, pp. 675–690.

2. For background on the evolution of diplomacy, see Ivor Roberts (ed.), *Satow's Diplomatic Practice* (Oxford: Oxford University Press, 2009); Jean-Robert Leguey-Feilleux, *The Dynamics of Diplomacy* (Boulder: Lynne Rienner, 2009); Jeremy Black, *A History of Diplomacy* (London: Reaktion Books, 2010); Pauline Kerr and Geoffrey Wiseman (eds), *Diplomacy in a Globalizing World: Theories and Practices* (New York: Oxford University Press, 2013); G.R. Berridge, *Diplomacy in Theory and Practice* (London: Palgrave Macmillan, 2015); and Ole Jacob Sending, Vincent Pouliot and Iver B. Neumann (eds), *Diplomacy and the Making of World Politics* (Cambridge: Cambridge University Press, 2015).

3. High Commissioners are exchanged between Commonwealth countries: see Lorna Lloyd, *Diplomacy with a Difference: the Commonwealth Office*

233

of High Commissioner, 1880–2006 (Leiden: Brill, 2007). High Commissioners in this sense should not be confused with international officials such as the United Nations High Commissioner for Refugees.

4. For overviews of the mechanics of such engagement, see Michael Barnett and Martha Finnemore, *Rules for the World: International Organizations in Global Politics* (Ithaca: Cornell University Press, 2004); Ronald A. Walker, *Multilateral Conferences: Purposeful International Negotiation* (London: Palgrave Macmillan, 2004); Fen Osler Hampson and Paul Heinbecker, 'The "New" Multilateralism of the Twenty-First Century', *Global Governance*, vol. 17, no. 3, July–September 2011, pp. 299–309.

5. See Eileen Denza, *Diplomatic Law: Commentary on the Vienna Convention on Diplomatic Relations* (Oxford: Oxford University Press, 2016).

6. See Christer Jönsson and Martin Hall, *Essence of Diplomacy* (Basingstoke: Palgrave Macmillan, 2005) pp. 119–135.

7. See Pauline Kerr, 'Diplomatic Persuasion: An Under-investigated Process', *The Hague Journal of Diplomacy*, vol. 5, no. 3, 2010, pp. 235–261.

8. See Shaun Riordan, *The New Diplomacy* (Cambridge: Polity Press, 2003); Jorge Heine, 'On the Manner of Practising the New Diplomacy', in Andrew F. Cooper, Brian Hocking and William Maley (eds), *Global Governance and Diplomacy: Worlds Apart?* (Basingstoke: Palgrave Macmillan, 2008) pp. 271–287; Daryl Copeland, *Guerrilla Diplomacy: Rethinking International Relations* (Boulder: Lynne Rienner, 2009).

9. For discussion of the features of crises, see Coral Bell, *The Conventions of Crisis: A Study in Diplomatic Management* (Oxford: Oxford University Press, 1971); Richard Ned Lebow, *Between Peace and War: The Nature of International Crisis* (Baltimore: The Johns Hopkins University Press, 1981); Michele Acuto, 'Diplomats in Crisis', *Diplomacy and Statecraft*, vol. 22, no. 3, September 2011, pp. 521–539.

10. For detailed discussion, see Joseph H. Douglas and Andreas Schloenhardt, *Combating Migrant Smuggling with Regional Diplomacy: An Examination of the Bali Process* (St Lucia: Research Paper, Migrant Smuggling Working Group, Faculty of Law, University of Queensland, February 2012).

11. On the Tampa Affair, see David Marr and Marian Wilkinson, *Dark Victory* (Sydney: Allen & Unwin, 2003).

12. For background to this episode, see Thomas Fuller and Joe Cochrane, 'Turned Away From Land and Abandoned at Sea', *The New York Times*, 15 May 2015; *Deadly Journeys: The Refugee and Trafficking Crisis in Southeast Asia* (London: Amnesty International, ASA 21/2574/2015, October 2015).

13. See Lisa Cox, '"Nope, nope, nope": Tony Abbott says Australia will not resettle refugees in migrant crisis', *The Sydney Morning Herald*, 21 May 2015.

14. Quoted in Michael Gordon, 'People smuggling: "Step up or step aside," Australia and Indonesia warned', *The Age*, 1 February 2016.

15. See *Statement of the EU Heads of State or Government* (Brussels: European Council and The Council of the European Union, 7 March 2016).

16. See Matthew Carr, *Fortress Europe: Inside the War Against Immigration* (London: Hurst & Co., 2015).

17. *EU Turkey Summit: EU and Turkish leaders deal death blow to the right to seek asylum* (London: Amnesty International, 9 March 2016).

18. See *UNHCR's reaction to Statement of the EU Heads of State and Government of Turkey, 7 March* (Geneva: Briefing Notes, UNHCR, 8 March 2016).

19. *UNHCR expresses concern over EU-Turkey plan* (Geneva: News Stories, UNHCR, 11 March 2016).

20. See *EU-Turkey Statement* (Brussels: European Council and The Council of the European Union, 18 March 2016).

21. *EU-Turkey refugee deal a historic blow to rights* (London: Amnesty International, 18 March 2016).

22. For the text of the MoU, see 'Memorandum of Understanding between the Government of the Kingdom of Cambodia and the Government of Australia, relating to the Settlement of Refugees in Cambodia', 26 September 2014, http://www.refworld.org/docid/5436588e4.html (accessed 28 March 2016).

23. ABC 'AM' Programme, 25 September 2014.

24. See Lindsay Murdoch, 'First Failure of Australia's $55 million Cambodia refugee plan', *The Sydney Morning Herald*, 16 October 2015.

25. See Lauren Crothers and Ben Doherty, 'Fifth refugee secretly moved from Nauru to Cambodia under $55m deal', *The Guardian*, 26 November 2015. As of March 2016, only two 'resettled' refugees, Daniel Eskandari and Mohammed Roshid, remained in Cambodia; the other three had returned to their countries of origin, although it is not clear that they intended to remain in those countries.

26. See Heath Aston, 'Safe and inexpensive: Government spruiks relocation from Nauru to Cambodia in fact sheet to asylum seekers', *The Sydney Morning Herald*, 16 April 2015.

27. See http://smartraveller.gov.au/countries/cambodia (accessed 12 March 2016).

28. Duncan McCargo, 'Cambodia in 2014: Confrontation and Compromise', *Asian Survey*, vol. 55, no. 1, January–February 2015, pp. 207–213 at p. 212.

29. Quoted in Lindsay Murdoch, '"I fear that I will die here": Cambodian hell for asylum pair', *The Sun-Herald*, 13 March 2016.

30. For an overview of this problem, see Martin Gottwald, 'Burden Sharing and Refugee Protection', in Elena Fiddian-Qasmiyeh, Gil Loescher, Katy Long and Nando Sigona (eds), *The Oxford Handbook of Refugee and Forced Migration Studies* (Oxford: Oxford University Press, 2014) pp. 525–537.

31. See William Maley, 'Refugees and Forced Migration as a Security Problem', in William T. Tow, Ramesh Thakur and In Taek Hyun (eds.), *Asia's Emerging Regional Order: Reconciling 'Traditional' and 'Human' Security* (Tokyo: United Nations University Press, 2000) pp. 142–156.

32. Gregor Noll, 'Risky Games? A Theoretical Approach to Burden-Sharing in the Asylum Field', *Journal of Refugee Studies*, vol. 16, no. 3, September 2003, pp. 236–252 at p. 251.

33. See Robert D. Putnam, 'Diplomacy and Domestic Politics: The Logic of Two-Level Games', *International Organization*, vol. 42, no. 3, Summer 1988, pp. 427–460.

34. For an overview, see Alexander Betts, *Forced Migration and Global Politics* (Oxford: Wiley-Blackwell, 2009) pp. 80–98.

35. Astri Suhrke, 'Burden-sharing during Refugee Emergencies: The Logic of Collective versus National Action', *Journal of Refugee Studies*, vol. 11,

no. 4, 1998, pp. 396–415 at p. 400. The classic account of the free rider problem is supplied in Mancur Olson, *The Logic of Collective Action: Public Goods and the Theory of Groups* (Cambridge: Harvard University Press, 1965).

36. Suhrke, 'Burden-sharing during Refugee Emergencies', p. 413.

37. On norm creation, see Edna Ullmann–Margalit, *The Emergence of Norms* (Oxford: Oxford University Press, 1977); Robert Axelrod, 'An Evolutionary Approach to Norms', *American Political Science Review*, vol. 80, no. 4, December 1986, pp. 1095–1111; Martha Finnemore and Kathryn Sikkink, 'International Norm Dynamics and Political Change', *International Organization*, vol. 52, no. 4 Autumn 1998, pp. 887–917.

38. See Phil Orchard, *A Right to Flee: Refugees, States, and the Construction of International Cooperation* (Cambridge: Cambridge University Press, 2014) pp. 189–200.

39. Alexander Betts, *Protection by Persuasion: International Cooperation in the Refugee Regime* (Ithaca: Cornell University Press, 2009) p. 32.

40. Alexander Betts, 'International Cooperation in the Refugee Regime', in Alexander Betts and Gil Loescher (eds), *Refugees in International Relations* (Oxford: Oxford University Press, 2011) pp. 53–84 at p. 53.

41. Francis Bacon, 'Of Negotiating', in Francis Bacon, *The Essays* (Harmondsworth: Penguin, 1985) pp. 203–204 at p. 203.

42. Greg Fry, 'The "Pacific solution"?', in William Maley, Alan Dupont, Jean-Pierre Fonteyne, Greg Fry, James Jupp, and Thuy Do, *Refugees and the Myth of the Borderless World* (Canberra: Keynotes no. 2, Department of International Relations, Research School of Pacific and Asian Studies, Australian National University, 2002) pp. 23–31 at p. 22.

43. See 'Tiny Pacific Island Is Facing Money-Laundering Sanctions', *The New York Times*, 6 December 2001. For an earlier account of Nauru's suspect financial activities, see David S. Hilzrenrath, 'Tiny Island Shelters Huge Cash Flows', *The Washington Post*, 28 October 1999.

44. See Commonwealth of Australia, *House of Representatives Hansard*, 12 March 2002, p. 1104.

45. To the best of this writer's knowledge, no document has ever been put in the public domain to establish that the Government of Nauru had any contractual obligation to pay the outstanding accounts. Prima facie it remained the responsibility of individual Nauruans to do so.

46. See Tom Allard, 'Nauru stays on laundry black list', *The Sydney Morning Herald*, 25 June 2002. For details of the decision to apply 'countermeasures' to Nauru, see *Financial Action Task Force on Money Laundering: Annual Report 2001–2002* (Paris: Organisation for Economic Co-operation and Development, 2002) p. 15.

47. See Ben Saul, 'Constitutional crisis: Australia's dirty fingerprints are all over Nauru's system', *The Guardian*, 21 January 2014; George Williams, 'Australia must defend the rule of law in Nauru', *The Age*, 28 January 2014.

48. See *War Crimes in Sri Lanka* (Brussels: Asia Report no. 191, International Crisis Group, 17 May 2010); Gordon Weiss, *The Cage: The Fight for Sri Lanka and the Last Days of the Tamil Tigers* (London: The Bodley Head, 2011); *Report of the Secretary-General's Panel of Experts on Accountability in Sri Lanka* (New York: United Nations, 31 March 2011).

49. For example, US Ambassador Patricia Butenis cabled the State Department on 15 January 2010 that 'responsibility for many of the alleged crimes rests with the country's senior civilian and military leadership, including President Rajapaksa and his brothers ...': 'Sri Lankan War-Crimes Accountability: The Tamil Perspective', Cable Reference ID 10COLOMBO32, U.S. Embassy, Colombo, 15 January 2010.

50. See *"We Will Teach You a Lesson": Sexual Violence against Tamils by Sri Lankan Security Forces* (New York: Human Rights Watch, 2013).

51. Quoted in Ben Doherty, 'Tony Abbott's stance on Sri Lanka's human rights craven and irresponsible', *The Sydney Morning Herald*, 18 November 2013. Writing for a right-wing magazine in March 2016, Mr Abbott, by then no longer Prime Minister, referred to 'the tough but probably unavoidable actions taken to end one of the world's most vicious civil wars': see Michael Slezak, 'Tony Abbott: I was right to put national security before moral posturing', *The Guardian*, 27 March 2016. He did not explain in what sense rape and other forms of sexual abuse might be considered 'probably unavoidable'.

52. See 'Visit to Australia by Mr. Gotabaya Rajapaksa, Secretary, Ministry of Defence and Urban Development to Co-Chair at the Second Joint Working Group on Human Smuggling and other Trans-national Crime

21st to 23rd April 2014, Canberra, Australia' (Canberra: The High Commission of the Democratic Socialist Republic of Sri Lanka, 30 April 2014).

53. John Maynard Keynes, *A Tract on Monetary Reform* (London: Macmillan & Co., 1923) p. 80.

54. See Tony Paterson, 'Revealed: the neo-Nazi manifesto targeting single mothers and mentally ill that AfD doesn't want you to see', *The Independent*, 19 March 2016.

55. See Stefan Kuzmany, 'Deutschland nach dem Wahlsonntag: Rechtsruck ohne Alternative', *Der Spiegel*, 14 March 2016.

56. Telford Taylor, *Munich: The Price of Peace* (New York: Doubleday, 1979) p. 1004.

57. Thucydides, *History of the Peloponnesian War* (Harmondsworth: Penguin, 1972) p. 404.

58. See *Foreign travel advice: Afghanistan* (London: Foreign and Commonwealth Office, 2016) https://www.gov.uk/foreign-travel-advice/afghanistan (accessed 14 March 2016).

59. See, for example, *R (on the application of HN and SA) (Afghanistan) (Lead Cases associated Non-Lead Cases)* v. *Secretary of State for the Home Department* [2016] EWCA Civ 123, 3 March 2016.

60. See Will Horner, 'Refugee crisis: Could Afghans who fled to Greece to escape the Taliban now be forced to return home?', *The Independent*, 24 March 2016.

61. See *Joint Commission-EEAS non-paper on enhancing cooperation on migration, mobility and readmission with Afghanistan* (Brussels: European Commission and European External Action Service, 6738/16, 2 March 2016) p. 3.

62. See William Maley, 'Civil-military interaction in Afghanistan: The case of Germany', in William Maley and Susanne Schmeidl (eds), *Reconstructing Afghanistan: Civil-military experiences in comparative perspective* (London: Routledge, 2015) pp. 98–109.

63. *UNHCR Mission to Manus Island, Papua New Guinea 15–17 January 2013* (Canberra: UNHCR, 4 February 2013) paras.51, 54, 75. See also Madeline Gleeson, *Offshore: Behind the wire on Manus and Nauru* (Sydney: NewSouth, 2016).

64. Senate Legal and Constitutional Affairs References Committee, *Incident at the Manus Island Detention Centre from 16 February to 18 February 2014* (Canberra: Commonwealth of Australia, December 2014) paras 8.6, 8.15.

65. For a scathing discussion of the handling of this case, see Brian Owler, 'Speech to AMA Forum on Health of Asylum Seekers', Sydney, 21 February 2016.

66. David Marr and Oliver Laughland, 'Australia's detention regime sets out to make asylum seekers suffer, says chief immigration psychiatrist', *The Guardian*, 5 August 2014.

67. *Namah* v. *Pato* [2016] PGSC 13, para.74, per Kandakasi J.

68. See Janna Weßels, *Sexual orientation in Refugee Status Determination* (Oxford: Working Paper no. 73, Refugee Studies Centre, University of Oxford, April 2011).

69. See Alexander Betts, 'Dependency on Turkey is dangerous: countries have an obligation to allow access to asylum' (Oxford: Refugee Studies Centre, University of Oxford, 9 March 2016) http://www.rsc.ox.ac.uk/news/dependency-on-turkey-is-dangerous-countries-have-an-obligation-to-allow-access-to-asylum (accessed 28 March 2016).

70. See Jim Yardley, 'Italy is Bracing to Regain its Role as Major Entry Point for Migrants', *The New York Times*, 15 April 2016.

71. *EU/Turkey: Mass, Fast-Track Returns Threaten Rights: Outline Deal Reveals Contradictory Positions on Refugee Protection* (New York: Human Rights Watch, 8 March 2016).

72. Melanie Hall, 'Russia "trying to destabilise" Germany by stoking unrest over migrants, warn spy chiefs', *The Telegraph*, 10 March 2016.

73. See 'Hearing to Receive Testimony on United States Europe Command', U.S. Senate Armed Services Committee, Washington D.C., 1 March 2016. http://www.armed-services.senate.gov/imo/media/doc/16–20_03–01–16.pdf (accessed 28 March 2016).

74. See Bobo Lo, *Russia and the New World Disorder* (Washington DC: Brookings Institution Press, 2015); Graeme Gill, *Building an Authoritarian Polity: Russia in Post-Soviet Times* (Cambridge: Cambridge University Press, 2015).

75. On the agency of groups, see Christian List and Philip Pettit, *Group*

Agency: The Possibility, Design and Status of Corporate Agents (Oxford: Oxford University Press, 2011).

76. Helena Smith and Patrick Kingsley, 'Hundreds of refugees make defiant journey on foot into Macedonia', *The Guardian*, 15 March 2016.

77. Jon Stone, 'Syrian refugees should be trained into an army to fight Isis, Poland's foreign minister says', *The Independent*, 17 November 2015.

78. For a detailed case study, see Jeff Crisp, 'A State of Insecurity: The Political Economy of Violence in Kenya's Refugee Camps', *African Affairs*, vol. 99, no. 397, October 2000, pp. 601–632.

79. See Benny Morris, *The birth of the Palestinian refugee problem, 1947–1949* (Cambridge: Cambridge University Press, 1988).

80. For more detail on UNRWA's history and operations, see Benjamin N. Schiff, *Refugees unto the Third Generation: UN Aid to Palestinians* (Syracuse: Syracuse University Press, 1995); D. Sena Wijewardane, 'Protecting Palestinian Refugees: The UNRWA Experience', in Larry Minear and Hazel Smith, *Humanitarian Diplomacy: Practitioners and their Craft* (Tokyo: United Nations University Press, 2007) pp. 65–83.

81. Robert Bowker, *Palestinian Refugees: Mythology, Identity, and the Search for Peace* (Boulder: Lynne Rienner, 2003) p. 198.

82. Ibid., p. 192.

83. See, for example, some of the views outlined in James G. Lindsay, *Fixing UNRWA: Repairing the UN's Troubled System of Aid to Palestinian Refugees* (Washington DC: Policy Focus no. 91, Washington Institute for Near East Policy, January 2009).

7. REFUGEES, INTERVENTION AND THE 'RESPONSIBILITY TO PROTECT'

1. See R.J. Vincent, *Nonintervention and International Order* (Princeton: Princeton University Press, 1974).

2. Ian Brownlie, *International Law and the Use of Force by States* (London: Oxford University Press, 1963) p. 66.

3. For an overview of balance of power thinking, see Richard Little, *The Balance of Power in International Relations: Metaphors, Myths and Models* (Cambridge: Cambridge University Press, 2007).

4. For further discussion, see William Maley, 'Norms as Frames for

Institutions: The Pact of Paris, Nuremberg, and the International Rule of Law', in Charles Sampford and Ramesh Thakur (eds), *Institutional Supports for the International Rule of Law* (New York: Routledge, 2015) pp. 116–131.

5. For more detail, see Christine Gray, *International Law and the Use of Force* (Oxford: Oxford University Press, 2008).

6. See Eiko R. Thielemann and Torun Dewan, 'The myth of free-riding: Refugee protection and implicit burden-sharing', *West European Politics*, vol. 29, no. 2, March 2006, pp. 351–369.

7. For studies of classical peacekeeping of this kind, see Arthur Lee Burns and Nina Heathcote, *Peace-keeping by U.N. Forces: From Suez to the Congo* (London: Pall Mall Press, 1963); Rosalyn Higgins, *United Nations Peacekeeping: Documents and Commentary*, Vols I-IV (Oxford: Oxford University Press, 1969–1981); Alan James, *The Politics of Peacekeeping* (London: Chatto & Windus, 1969); Indar Jit Rikhye, *The Theory and Practice of Peacekeeping* (London: Hurst & Co., 1984); Alan James, *Peacekeeping in International Politics* (London: Macmillan, 1990); A.B. Fetherston, *Towards a Theory of United Nations Peacekeeping* (Basingstoke: Macmillan, 1994); Paul F. Diehl, *International Peacekeeping* (Baltimore: The Johns Hopkins University Press, 1994); Ramesh Thakur, *The United Nations, Peace and Security: From Collective Security to the Responsibility to Protect* (Cambridge: Cambridge University Press, 2006); Alex J. Bellamy, Paul Williams and Stuart Griffin, *Understanding Peacekeeping* (Cambridge: Polity Press, 2010).

8. See Paul F. Diehl, *Peace Operations* (Cambridge: Polity Press, 2008).

9. See Steven R. Ratner, *The New UN Peacekeeping: Building Peace in Lands of Conflict after the Cold War* (New York: St Martin's Press, 1995); Carolyn Bull, *No Entry without Strategy: Building the Rule of Law under UN Transitional Administration* (Tokyo: United Nations University Press, 2008). On transitional administrations more generally, see Simon Chesterman, *You, the People: The United Nations, Transitional Administration, and State-Building* (Oxford: Oxford University Press, 2004); Richard Caplan, *International Governance of War-Torn Territories: Rule and Reconstruction* (Oxford: Oxford University Press, 2005).

10. See John F. Burns, 'Bosnian Muslims Criticize U.N. Over Official's Killing', *The New York Times*, 10 January 1993.

11. Rosalyn Higgins, 'The New United Nations and Former Yugoslavia', *International Affairs*, vol. 69, no. 2, July 1993, pp. 465–483 at p. 469.

12. For a vivid memoir dealing with these events, see Inder Jit Rikhye, *The Sinai Blunder* (New Delhi: Oxford & IBH Publishing, 1978).

13. See Abiodun Williams, *Preventing War: The United Nations and Macedonia* (Lanham: Rowman & Littlefield, 2000); Henryk J. Sokalski, *An Ounce of Prevention: Macedonia and the UN Experience in Preventive Diplomacy* (Washington DC: United States Institute of Peace Press, 2003).

14. See Duane Bratt, 'Assessing the Success of UN Peacekeeping Operations', *International Peacekeeping*, vol. 3, no. 4, Winter 1996, pp. 64–81.

15. Paul F. Diehl and Daniel Druckman, *Evaluating Peace Operations* (Boulder: Lynne Rienner, 2010) p. 26. For further discussion, see Daniel Druckman and Paul F. Diehl (eds), *Peace Operation Success: A Comparative Analysis* (Leiden: Martinus Nijhoff, 2013).

16. See Virginia Page Fortna, *Does Peacekeeping Work? Shaping Belligerents' Choices after Civil War* (Princeton: Princeton University Press, 2008).

17. See Michael W. Doyle and Nicholas Sambanis, *Making War and Building Peace: United Nations Peace Operations* (Princeton: Princeton University Press, 2006); Lise Morjé Howard, *UN Peacekeeping in Civil Wars* (Cambridge: Cambridge University Press, 2008).

18. See Barbara F. Walter, *Committing to Peace: The Successful Settlement of Civil Wars* (Princeton: Princeton University Press, 2002).

19. Martha Finnemore, *The Purpose of Intervention: Changing Beliefs about the Use of Force* (Ithaca: Cornell University Press, 2003) p. 53. For further background, see Nicholas J. Wheeler, *Saving Strangers: Humanitarian Intervention in International Society* (Oxford: Oxford University Press, 2000); Jennifer M. Welsh (ed.), *Humanitarian Intervention and International Relations* (Oxford: Oxford University Press, 2004); Thomas G. Weiss, *Humanitarian Intervention: Ideas in Action* (Cambridge: Polity Press, 2007); Gary J. Bass, *Freedom's Battle: The Origins of Humanitarian Intervention* (New York: Alfred A. Knopf, 2008); Michael Newman, *Humanitarian Intervention: Confronting the Contradictions* (London: Hurst & Co., 2009).

20. See Fiona Terry, *Condemned to Repeat? The Paradox of Humanitarian Action* (Ithaca: Cornell University Press, 2002); David Rieff, *A Bed for the Night: Humanitarianism in Crisis* (New York: Simon & Schuster, 2002); David Kennedy, *The Dark Sides of Virtue: Reassessing International Humanitarianism* (Princeton: Princeton University Press, 2004). For broader background, see Michael Barnett, *Empire of Humanity: A History of Humanitarianism* (Ithaca: Cornell University Press, 2011).

21. See Richard Betts, 'The Delusion of Impartial Intervention', *Foreign Affairs*, vol. 73, no. 6, November–December 1994, pp. 20–33; Edward N. Luttwak, 'Give War a Chance', *Foreign Affairs*, vol. 78, no. 4, July–August 1999, pp. 36–44.

22. See Danesh Sarooshi, *The United Nations and the Development of Collective Security: The Delegation by the UN Security Council of its Chapter VII Powers* (Oxford: Oxford University Press, 1999).

23. See David M. Malone, *The International Struggle Over Iraq: Politics in the UN Security Council 1980–2005* (Oxford: Oxford University Press, 2006).

24. Anthony Faiola, 'Europe offers deal to Turkey to take back migrants', *The Washington Post*, 18 March 2016.

25. Jean-Jacques Rousseau, *The Social Contract and Discourses* (London: J.M. Dent, 1973) p. 168.

26. See Christian Reus-Smit, 'International Crises of Legitimacy', *International Politics*, vol. 44, 2007, pp. 157–174. For further discussion, see Ian Clark, *Legitimacy in International Society* (Oxford: Oxford University Press, 2005); Ian Clark, *International Legitimacy and World Society* (Oxford: Oxford University Press, 2007).

27. 'People and Politics', *BBC World Service*, 1 January 2005.

28. See Christian Reus-Smit, *American Power and World Order* (Cambridge: Polity Press, 2004).

29. See Barbara Harff and Ted Robert Gurr, 'Toward Empirical Theory of Genocides and Politicides: Identification and Measurement of Cases since 1945', *International Studies Quarterly*, vol. 32, no. 3, September 1988, pp. 359–371.

30. See Jared Cohen, *One Hundred Days of Silence: America and the Rwandan Genocide* (Lanham: Rowman & Littlefield, 2007).

31. See *Report of the Secretary-General pursuant to General Assembly Resolution 53/35: The fall of Srebrenica* (New York: United Nations, A/54/549, 15 November 1999).

32. See *Application of the Convention on the Prevention and Punishment of the Crime of Genocide (Bosnia and Herzegovina v. Serbia and Montenegro), Judgment*, I.C.J. Reports 2007, p. 43.

33. For more detail on the operation of the Commission, see Alex J. Bellamy, *Responsibility to Protect: The Global Effort to End Mass Atrocities* (Cambridge: Polity Press, 2009) pp. 35–65;

34. Martin Gilbert, 'The Terrible 20th Century', *The Globe and Mail*, 31 January 2007.

35. *The Responsibility to Protect: Report of the International Commission on Intervention and State Sovereignty* (Ottawa: International Development Research Centre, December 2001) p.xi.

36. Ibid., p. 13.

37. Ibid., p. 17.

38. Not all protection issues are covered by the doctrine. See Gareth Evans, *The Responsibility to Protect: Ending Mass Atrocity Crimes Once and For All* (Washington DC: Brookings Institution Press, 2008) pp. 64–69.

39. See Angus Francis, 'The responsibility to protect and the international refugee regime', in Angus Francis, Vesselin Popovski and Charles Sampford (eds), *Norms of Protection: Responsibility to Protect, Protection of Civilians and their Interaction* (Tokyo: United Nations University Press, 2012) pp. 215–233 at pp. 221–226; Susan Martin, 'Forced Migration, the Refugee Regime and the Responsibility to Protect', *Global Responsibility to Protect*, vol. 2, nos. 1–2, 2010, pp. 38–59.

40. See Ramesh Thakur, *The Responsibility to Protect: Norms, Laws and the Use of Force in International Politics* (London: Routledge, 2011) pp. 1–13.

41. Ramesh Thakur, 'The Responsibility to Protect at 15', *International Affairs*, vol. 92, no. 2, March 2016, pp. 415–434 at p. 432.

42. See Gareth Evans, 'The evolution of the Responsibility to Protect: from concept and principle to actionable norm', in Ramesh Thakur and William Maley (eds), *Theorising the Responsibility to Protect* (Cambridge: Cambridge University Press, 2015) pp. 16–37 at pp. 23–28.

43. *World Summit Outcome 2005* (United Nations: General Assembly, Resolution A/RES/60/1, 24 October 2005) paras.138–139.

44. See Alex J. Bellamy, *Global Politics and the Responsibility to Protect: From words to deeds* (New York: Routledge, 2011) pp. 26–50.

45. Amitav Acharya, 'The Responsibility to Protect and a theory of norm circulation', in Ramesh Thakur and William Maley (eds), *Theorising the Responsibility to Protect* (Cambridge: Cambridge University Press, 2015) pp. 50–77 at p. 72. See also Marie-Eve Loiselle, 'The Normative Status of the Responsibility to Protect after Libya', *Global Responsibility to Protect*, vol. 5, no. 3, 2013, pp. 317–341.

46. Michael W. Doyle, *The Question of Intervention: John Stuart Mill and the Responsibility to Protect* (New Haven: Yale University Press, 2015) p. 139.

47. Ibid., p. 140.

48. I elaborate this point in William Maley, 'Humanitarian law, refugee protection, and the Responsibility to Protect', in Ramesh Thakur and William Maley (eds), *Theorising the Responsibility to Protect* (Cambridge: Cambridge University Press, 2015) pp. 249–265.

49. See Audrey Kurth Cronin, *Great Power Politics and the Struggle over Austria, 1945–1955* (Ithaca: Cornell University Press, 1986).

50. See John Blaxland (ed.), *East Timor Intervention: A Retrospective on INTERFET* (Melbourne: Melbourne University Press, 2015). For a comprehensive list of interventions from 1815 to 2003, see Doyle, *The Question of Intervention*, pp. 227–259.

51. David Halberstam, *The Making of a Quagmire* (New York: Random House, 1965).

52. Bernard Brodie, *War and Politics* (New York: Macmillan, 1973) p. 211.

53. For different perspectives, see Astri Suhrke, *When More Is Less: The International Project in Afghanistan* (New York: Columbia University Press, 2011); William Maley, 'Statebuilding in Afghanistan: challenges and pathologies', *Central Asian Survey*, vol. 32, no. 3, 2013, pp. 255–270.

54. Robert M. Gates, *Duty: Memoirs of a Secretary at War* (New York: Alfred A. Knopf, 2014) p. 569.

55. See, for example, Samir al-Khalil, *Republic of Fear: The Politics of*

Modern Iraq (Berkeley & Los Angeles: University of California Press, 1989).

56. See Douglas Jehl and Elizabeth Becker, 'Experts' Pleas to Pentagon Didn't Save Museum', *The New York Times*, 16 April 2003.

57. See Francis Fukuyama, *The Origins of Political Order* (New York: Farrar, Straus & Giroux, 2011).

58. See Seymour M. Hersh, 'U.S. Secretly Gave Aid to Iraq Early in Its War Against Iran', *The New York Times*, 26 January 1992.

59. See Joy Gordon, *Invisible War: The United States and the Iraq Sanctions* (Cambridge: Harvard University Press, 2010).

60. For more detailed discussion, see William Maley, 'Twelve Theses on the Impact of Humanitarian Intervention', *Security Dialogue*, vol. 33, no. 3, September 2002, pp. 265–278.

61. See John Mackinlay, 'Defining Warlords', *International Peacekeeping*, vol. 7, no. 1, Spring 2000; pp. 48–62; also Sasha Lezhnev, *Crafting Peace: Strategies to Deal with Warlords in Collapsing States* (Lanham: Lexington Books, 2005); Kimberly Marten, *Warlords: Strong-arm Brokers in Weak States* (Ithaca: Cornell University Press, 2012); Dipali Mukhopadhyay, *Warlords, Strongman Governors, and the State in Afghanistan* (Cambridge: Cambridge University Press, 2014).

8. 'WHEN ADAM DELVED AND EVE SPAN ...': SOME REFLECTIONS ON CLOSING AND OPENING BORDERS

1. On this distinction, see Adam Ferguson, *An Essay on the History of Civil Society* (Cambridge: Cambridge University Press, 1995) p. 119.

2. Quoted in Barnett R. Rubin, *The Fragmentation of Afghanistan: State Formation and Collapse in the International System* (New Haven: Yale University Press, 2002) p.vi.

3. Stanley Hoffman, *Duties beyond Borders: On the Limits and Possibilities of Ethical International Politics* (Syracuse: Syracuse University Press, 1981) pp. 224–225.

4. Francis Keany and Anna Henderson, 'Malcolm Turnbull linking refugee crisis to bombings "dangerous", Belgian ambassador says', ABC News, 24 March 2016'. See http://www.abc.net.au/news/2016–03–24/turnbull-comments-of-refugee-crisis-dangerous-says-ambassador/7272916 (accessed 28 March 2016).

5. Michael A. Clemens, 'Economics and Emigration: Trillion Dollar Bills on the Sidewalk', *Journal of Economic Perspectives*, vol. 25, no. 3, Summer 2011, pp. 83–106 at p. 84. See also Bob Hamilton and John Whalley, 'Efficiency and Distributional Implications of Global Restrictions on Labour Mobility: Calculations and Policy Implications', *Journal of Development Economics*, vol. 14, nos. 1–2, January–February 1984, pp. 61–75.

6. See Neil Vousden, *The Economics of Trade Protection* (Cambridge: Cambridge University Press, 1990) pp. 48–53.

7. See Robert E. Goodin, 'If People Were Money...', in Brian Barry and Robert E. Goodin (eds), *Free Movement: Ethical Issues in the Transnational Migrations of People and of Money* (University Park: Penn State University Press, 1992) pp. 6–22.

8. *World Population Prospects: The 2015 Revision. Key Findings and Advance Tables* (New York: United Nations, Working Paper no. ESA/P/WP241, Population Division, Department of Economic and Social Affairs, October 2015) p. 4.

9. Lord Hewart, *The New Despotism* (Westport: Greenwood Press, 1975).

10. *Plaintiff S157/2002* v. *The Commonwealth* (2003) 211 CLR 476.

11. Cited in *Gouriet* v. *Union of Post Office Workers* [1977] QB 729, per Lord Denning MR at 761–762.

12. See Joseph Raz, *The Authority of Law: Essays on Law and Morality* (Oxford: Oxford University Press, 1979) pp. 214–218.

13. See F.A. Hayek, *The Constitution of Liberty* (London: Routledge & Kegan Paul, 1960) pp. 205–207; Stephan Haggard, Andrew Macintyre, and Lydia Tiede, 'The Rule of Law and Economic Development', *Annual Review of Political Science*, vol. 11, 2008, pp. 205–234.

14. Chandran Kukathas, 'Why Open Borders?', *Ethical Perspectives*, vol. 19, no. 4, December 2012, pp. 649–675 at 654.

15. See 'ABF joining inter-agency outfit to target crime in Melbourne CBD' (Canberra: Australian Border Force, 28 August 2015).

16. See Shalailah Medhora, 'Border Force officials apologise for botched visa crackdown in Melbourne', *The Guardian*, 19 October 2015.

17. See Martin McKenzie-Murray, 'Inside Border Force's power', *The Saturday Paper*, 5 September 2015.

18. John Emerich Edward Dalberg-Acton, First Baron Acton, *Historical Essays and Studies* (London: Macmillan & Co., 1907) p. 504.

19. See Jack Goldsmith, *The Terror Presidency: Law and Justice inside the Bush Administration* (New York: W.W. Norton, 2007).

20. Quoted in *Entry of the 9/11 Hijackers into the United States* (Washington DC: Staff Statement No. 1, National Commission on Terrorist Attacks Upon the United States, 26 January 2004) p. 9. For a comprehensive analysis, see Thomas R. Eldridge, Susan Ginsburg, Walter T. Hempel II, Janice L. Kephart, Kelly Moore, Joanne M. Accolla and Alice Falk, *9/11 and Terrorist Travel: Staff Report of the National Commission on Terrorist Attacks Upon the United States* (Washington DC: National Commission on Terrorist Attacks Upon the United States, 21 August 2004).

21. See *Martin Place Siege: Joint Commonwealth-New South Wales review* (Canberra: Commonwealth of Australia, January 2015) p. 21.

22. *Shaughnessy v. United States ex rel Mezei* 345 U.S. 206, 218 (1953).

23. See Paul D. Halliday, *Habeas Corpus: From England to Empire* (Cambridge: Harvard University Press, 2010).

24. See Daniel Wilsher, *Immigration Detention: Law, History, Politics* (Cambridge: Cambridge University Press, 2012).

25. For in-depth studies of detention in the United Kingdom, see Alexandra Hall, *Border Watch: Cultures of Immigration, Detention and Control* (London: Pluto Press, 2012); Mary Bosworth, *Inside Immigration Detention* (Oxford: Oxford University Press, 2014).

26. *Report of the Inquiry into the Use of Immigration Detention in the United Kingdom* (London: All Party Parliamentary Group on Refugees and All Party Parliamentary Group on Migration, 3 March 2015) p. 9

27. *Hansard* (House of Lords), 15 March 2016, Column 1789.

28. *Report of the Special Rapporteur on torture and other cruel, inhuman or degrading treatment or punishment, Juan E. Méndez. Addendum: Observations on communications transmitted to Governments and replies received* (Geneva: United Nations Human Rights Council, A/HRC/28/68/Add.1, 6 March 2015) para.19.

29. See Roland Bleiker, David Campbell, Emma Hutchison and Xzarina Nicholson, 'The visual dehumanisation of refugees', *Australian Journal of Political Science*, vol. 48, no. 4, December 2013, pp. 398–416.

249

30. See Mark Forbes and Kerry Taylor, 'Refugees denied human face', *The Age*, 18 April 2002; David Marr and Marian Wilkinson, *Dark Victory* (Sydney: Allen & Unwin, 2003) p. 135.

31. See Mohammad Ali Baqiri, 'As a child on Nauru I was NR03–283, but my name is Mohammad Ali Baqiri', *The Guardian*, 15 March 2016.

32. *Betkhoshabeh* v. *Minister for Immigration and Multicultural Affairs* [1999] FCA 16.

33. See *A last resort? National Inquiry into Children in Immigration Detention* (Sydney: Human Rights and Equal Opportunity Commission, 2004); *The Forgotten Children: National Inquiry into Children in Immigration Detention* (Sydney: Australian Human Rights Commission, 2014).

34. See Derrick M. Silove, Zachary P. Steel, and Charles Watters, 'Policies of deterrence and the mental health of asylum seekers in western countries', *Journal of the American Medical Association*, vol. 284, no. 5, 2 August 2000, pp. 604–611; Zachary P. Steel and Derrick M. Silove, 'The mental health implications of detaining asylum seekers', *Medical Journal of Australia*, vol. 175, 2001, pp. 596–599; Zachary Steel, Derrick Silove, Robert Brooks, Shakeh Momartin, Bushra Alzuhairi and Ina Susljik, 'Impact of immigration detention and temporary protection on the mental health of refugees', *British Journal of Psychiatry*, vol. 188, no. 1, January 2006, pp. 58–64; Katy Robjant, Rita Hassan and Cornelius Katona, 'Mental health implications of detaining asylum seekers: systematic review', *British Journal of Psychiatry*, vol. 194, no. 1, March 2009, pp. 306–312.

35. See David Isaacs, 'Are healthcare professionals working in Australia's immigration detention centres condoning torture?', *Journal of Medical Ethics*, vol. 42, no. 7, 2016, pp. 413–415.

36. Quoted in James Reston, 'The Churches, the Synagogues, and the March on Washington', *Religious Education*, vol. 59, no. 1, January 1964, pp. 5–6 at p. 5.

37. Peter Dunne, 'New Zealand offended at our "frontier approach" to justice', *The Age*, 12 November 2015. In August 2016, Amnesty International and Human Rights Watch, in a devastating joint report based on a covert visit to Nauru by senior researchers of the two organisations, concluded that the 'Australian government's failure to address

serious abuses appears to be a deliberate policy to deter further asylum seekers from arriving in the country by boat': see *Australia: Appalling Abuse, Neglect of Refugees on Nauru: Investigation on Remote Pacific Island Finds Deliberate Abuse Hidden Behind Wall of Secrecy* (New York: Human Rights Watch, and London: Amnesty International, 2 August 2016).

38. Anatole France, 'Le procurateur de Judée', in Anatole France, *Balthasar. Thaïs. L'Étui de Nacre* (Geneva: Editions Edito-Service S.A., 1960) pp. 377–394 at p. 394.

39. Howard Goldenberg, 'The clinician and detention', *Journal of Medical Ethics*, vol. 42, no. 7, 2016, pp. 416–417.

40. Judith Shklar, *Ordinary Vices* (Cambridge: Harvard University Press, 1984) p. 37.

41. Friedrich Nietzsche, *Beyond Good and Evil* (Harmondsworth: Penguin, 1990) p. 102.

42. Dennis Chong and James N. Druckman, 'Framing Theory', *Annual Review of Political Science*, vol. 10, 2007, pp. 103–126 at p. 104. See also Dennis Chong and James N. Druckman, 'Counterframing Effects', *The Journal of Politics*, vol. 75, no. 1, January 2013, pp. 1–16.

43. Ayelet Shachar, *The Birthright Lottery: Citizenship and Global Inequality* (Cambridge: Harvard University Press, 2009) p. 49.

44. See Stuart Elden, *The Birth of Territory* (Chicago: University of Chicago Press, 2013).

45. See, however, Boaz Atzili, *Good Fences, Bad Neighbors: Border Fixity and International Conflict* (Chicago: University of Chicago Press, 2012).

46. Margaret Moore, *A Political Theory of Territory* (Oxford: Oxford University Press, 2015) p. 209.

47. On the genesis and complexities of these emotions, see Corey Robin, *Fear: The History of a Political Idea* (New York: Oxford University Press, 2004); Robert J. Sternberg and Karin Sternberg, *The Nature of Hate* (Cambridge: Cambridge University Press, 2008).

48. See, for example, Arash Abizadeh, 'Democratic Theory and Border Coercion: No Right to Unilaterally Control Your Own Borders', *Political Theory*, vol. 36, no. 1, February 2008, pp. 37–65.

49. Katy Long, 'Rethinking "Durable" Solutions', in Elena Fiddian-Qasmiyeh, Gil Loescher, Katy Long and Nando Sigona (eds), *The*

Oxford Handbook of Refugee and Forced Migration Studies (Oxford: Oxford University Press, 2014) pp. 475–487 at p. 485.

50. For a detailed account on which I draw, see Ben Doherty, 'How Australia's immigration detention regime crushed Fazel Chegeni', *The Guardian*, 21 December 2015.

51. For CCTV footage, see https://www.youtube.com/watch?v=Asmw CAnaBTc

52. See Michael Gordon, '"Fazel is free now. God gave him a visa"', *The Age*, 14 November 2015.

53. See *Le* v. *Magistrate Barbara Lane* [2014] WASC 494, 18 December 2014. The same magistrate's conduct had earlier been found to be inappropriate by the Supreme Court in *Beasley* v. *Lane* [2011] WASC 98, 15 April 2011.

54. The 'character test' might more usefully have been applied to some official guests hosted by the Immigration Department, such as Gotabaya Rajapaksa, mentioned in Chapter Six. Section 501(6)(ba)(iii) of the *Migration Act* 1958 covers situations where the Minister reasonably suspects that an individual has been involved in conduct constituting 'the crime of genocide, a crime against humanity, a war crime, a crime involving torture or slavery or a crime that is otherwise of serious international concern'.

55. 'Background Briefing', *ABC Radio National*, 31 January 2016.

56. Doherty, 'How Australia's immigration detention regime crushed Fazel Chegeni'.

INDEX

INDEX

INDEX

International Court of Justice: personnel of, 160

International Crisis Group: members of, 168

International Journal of Refugee Law: 13

international law: 16–17; humanitarian law, 28; refugee law, 16

International Organization for Migration (IOM): establishment of (1951), 129; personnel of, 129

International Refugee Organization: 62, 152; resettlement efforts of, 18

International Rescue Committee: 92

Iran: 109, 117, 143, 177–8; Afghan refugees in, 68, 70, 73; Kurdish population of, 195

Iran-Iraq War (1980–8): 106, 177

Iraq: 27, 66, 101, 177; Baghdad, 176; Coalition Provisional Authority, 115; De-Baathification in, 107; Gassing of Kurds (1988), 106; Halabja, 106; Kurd population of, 107; Operation Iraqi Freedom (2003–11), 71, 101, 107, 113, 164, 166, 175–7; refugees from, 2, 71; Shiite population of, 107, 116, 178; Sunni population of, 107, 116, 178

Islam: 3, 47, 69, 118; Ashura (festival), 115; Deobandi, 67; migrants, 9; political, 116; Shiite, 4, 105, 107, 113–16, 178; Sunni, 4, 105, 107, 113, 116, 178

Islamic State (Daesh/ISIS): 55–6, 109, 123, 177–8; ideology of, 116; territory held by, 72–3, 109–10, 178

Islamism: 151

Ismail, Sondos: family of, 27

Israel: 160, 164; establishment of (1948), 152; resettlement of refugees in, 18; supporters of, 153

Italy: 152; as Kingdom of Italy (1922–43), 92; Monza, 54; refugees arriving in, 1

Japan: 183; Allied Occupation of (1945–52), 174

Japan, Empire of (1868–1947): 92; Tokyo, 92

Al Jenabi, Ali: efforts to apply for asylum in Australia, 93–4

Jesus Christ: 2, 7

Johnson, Lyndon B.: foreign policy of, 175

Jordan, Hashemite Kingdom of: Black September (1970–1), 66, 149; member of UNHCR Executive Committee, 128; Syrian refugees in, 72–4

Joseph: 7

Journal of Refugee Studies: 13

INDEX

INDEX

Yugoslavia: as Kingdom of Serbs, Croats and Slovenes (1918–29), 70; disintegration of (1992), 70–1; establishment of (1919), 70

Zaire: 106

al-Zalime, Ahmad: family of, 27–8

Zionism: 48

Zolberg, Aristide R.: characterisation of refugees, 44

Zweig, Stefan: 4; suicide of (1942), 3–4